LEAD KINDLY LIGHT

LEAD KINDLY LIGHT

Essays for Fr Ian Ker

edited by

Paul Shrimpton

GRACEWING

First published in England in 2022
by
Gracewing
2 Southern Avenue
Leominster
Herefordshire HR6 0QF
United Kingdom
www.gracewing.co.uk

ISBN 978 085244 987 5

Typeset by Gracewing

Cover design by Bernardita Peña Hurtado

CONTENTS

IV. *MEN OF LETTERS*

V. *CONTRIBUTIONS TO THE ACADEMY*

VI. *THE GREAT BATTLE*

EDITOR'S INTRODUCTION

PAUL SHRIMPTON

I T WAS OVER lunch with Serenhedd James on Saturday, 25th September 2021 in Oxford that the idea of a festschrift for Ian Ker emerged. Serenhedd happened to mention that his doctoral supervisor would reach his four score years the following August, adding that someone really *ought* to organise a festschrift for him. I shared the idea with a friend and with his help drew up an initial list of those who could be invited to contribute. Within a few days Tom Longford, the managing director of Gracewing Publishing, had given me his backing for the project. This was a real leap of faith for Tom: to agree to a project that would span just ten months from conception to publication, with all the uncertainty as to whether enough contributors could be found to make it a worthwhile venture and, indeed, whether they could meet the tight deadlines asked of them. It is a tribute to the esteem in which Fr Ker is held that almost all of those who were approached were able to contribute to this collection of essays in homage of him. My thanks go to every one of them for doing so.

Those invited to contribute were asked to offer something original and appropriate. This volume, therefore, does not claim to be exhaustive in its coverage of the life and work of Ian Turnbull Ker, but it does give a glimpse of the range and fecundity of his scholarly endeavours. My sincere apologies must go out to the many others who were overlooked in the process of compiling this festschrift.

It is quite by chance that the eighteen contributions fall into six relatively homogeneous collections, and it is easiest to introduce them under these six headings.

Along the Way of Life: Reminiscences

As one would expect in a festschrift, the first section is biographical. It gives particular attention to the ways in which Fr Ker's critical skills were nurtured and honed, before describing how they were deployed so successfully in his two substantial biographies. The criticism which has sometimes been made of the Newman biography—that it is too focused on its subject and neglectful of context—is addressed head-on by emphasising the distinct advantages of maintaining a close focus. Biographers such as Sheridan Gilley in *Newman and his Age* (1990) aimed at highly contextualised lives of Newman, but in doing so they were forced to sacrifice a great deal. Fr Ker's biography is rightly regarded as the definitive one and the go-to source for Newman scholars wanting a summary of any episode in his life.

The character of Fr Ker, rather than his scholarship, is the principal focus of the two personal memoirs. In his short piece Professor John Roe, one of Fr Ker's colleagues at York University in the early 1970s, relates anecdotes that capture his mischievous sense of humour and lively conversation. Bishop James Conley identifies a different set of qualities as he dwells on the priestly heart of Fr Ker and his capacity for friendship. Numerous individuals have followed Newman into the Catholic Church through the influence of his writings and life; indeed, he is widely regarded as the most influential figure in the English-speaking world for those taking this step over the last two centuries. Bishop Conley's article is a welcome addition to those conversion stories, not least because Fr Ker is a central figure in it.

Much more could, of course, have been written about Fr Ker. If there is one obvious omission it might be to Fr Ker's tireless energy in accepting invitations to speak about Newman at conferences and seminars around the world; only a personal secretary would have been capable of writing about these trips—but of course Fr Ker never had one. Then there were the symposia and conferences he himself organised in Britain, particularly the

International Newman Conferences he organised in Oxford, along with Terence Merrigan: the last two were at Keble College in 2001 and at Somerville College in 2004. Not only did he front the lectures and organise the dinners and visits around town, but many of the petty administrative chores fell to him, just as administrative tasks fell on a certain Dr Newman when he acted as the founding rector of the Catholic University in Dublin. There, almost single-handedly, Newman oversaw virtually every aspect of setting up and running the university. A friend who visited Newman was shocked to see the rector carving the Sunday joint for the students at the collegiate house of St Mary's which Newman oversaw: there was simply no one else with whom he could share the work.

The patch of Newman studies that I have cultivated as an historian of education has left me with a deep respect for Fr Ker. Nothing I have read or turned up in archives has given me cause to question any of the conclusions that he has reached; quite the contrary, my research has repeatedly led to verifying and filling out in detail his earlier findings. It is extraordinary to see how Fr Ker has worked in all the fields covered by that man of 'imperial intellect': poetry, novels, letters, religious tracts, journal and newspaper articles, philosophy, theology, homilies, and pastoral work first as an Anglican clergyman and then as a priest of the Oratory of St Philip Neri. The select bibliography on pp. 345–6 conveys the range of engagement Fr Ker has had with Newman—as well as with G. K. Chesterton. Fr Ker's work on Chesterton highlights another aspect of his own intellectual energy and versatility. After having achieved so much in Newman studies, it is remarkable that he had the energy to work on another major intellectual biography.

The willingness of friends and other scholars to contribute to this volume has reinforced what I already knew: that Ian Ker is the greatest living Newman scholar. He has done more to raise the profile of John Henry Newman than anyone else. True, the 'hard yards' were made by his early mentor Fr C. Stephen Dessain, who saw through to publication twenty volumes of the _Letters and Diaries of John Henry Newman_; this is why Fr Ker recognises him as 'the founder of modern Newman studies'.[1]

I like to think that Fr Ker's achievements were acknowledged, albeit unofficially, one damp morning at Cofton Park, Birmingham in September 2010 during the Mass celebrated by Pope Benedict XVI when he proclaimed Newman to be Blessed. At the end of the Offertory procession Fr Ker mounted the steps, knelt before Pope Benedict and exchanged words with him. This was surely a fitting recognition for so much sterling work—and from a pope who deeply admires Newman.[2]

A Trinity of Cardinals

It is fitting that three princes of the Church should want to pay their respects to the leading Newman scholar.

Cardinal Müller's 'John Henry Newman: An Ecumenical Conversion' is a revised translation of an article that appeared in the German press. This is not the only occasion that the former Prefect for the Congregation for the Doctrine of the Faith has written on Newman. In addition to articles and lectures,[3] he has published

---

[1] _The Achievement of John Henry Newman_ (London: Collins, 1990), p. ix.

[2] Sadly no one could be found to contribute a piece to this festschrift outlining the influence of Newman on the future Pope Benedict. His contact with Newman dates from his early days at the seminary in Munich in 1946 when he was placed under Alfred Läpple, who was working on a doctorate on Newman and conscience. Later, Josef Ratzinger came under the influence of other Newman scholars such as his fundamental theology teacher Gottlieb Sohngen, who supervised his doctorate and tutored him in the _Grammar of Assent_, and Heinrich Fries, who gave him insights into the _Development of Doctrine_ and Newman's thinking on conscience. In April 1990 Cardinal Ratzinger gave an address at a Newman symposium in Rome; and the following year he gave a lecture on 'Newman and Conscience' in Dallas, Texas.

[3] See, for example, 'Development, or Corruption?', _First Things_ (20 February 2018). Cardinal Müller has also given public lectures such as one on 'Blessed John Henry Newman and an unchangeable deposit of faith' in Brisbane, Australia, on 21 July 2018.

John Henry Newman begegnen (2000), a book-length introduction
to Newman. In treating of Newman's conversion as an ecumenical
one, the cardinal outlines Newman's quest for the visible unity of
the Church of Christ within the plurality of Christian communities,
and he goes on to describe him as an apologist for Christianity as
a revealed religion and as a much-needed model of stability. These
are timely considerations for our own times.

On 12th October 2019, the day before Newman was canonised,
a symposium took place in Rome entitled 'Cardinal Newman: a
Celebration' which considered Newman as theologian, educator
and priest. The longest paper, entitled 'Cardinal Newman's
Significance for Catholic Theology', was given by Cardinal Marc
Ouellet, Prefect of the Congregation of Bishops. The Canadian
cardinal pleaded for the Church to take note of Newman's
teachings and argued forcefully that he should be granted the title
Doctor of the Church. Although the cardinal used a translation
from the French original for the symposium, which was later
made available, the text given here has been revised stylistically
for publication in this volume. It is a powerful piece which calls
the Christian world to learn from the 'prophet of equilibrium' the
delicate and dynamic relationship between faith and reason.

Cardinal Pell's contribution is his recent lecture at the annual
St Thomas More Lecture, organised by the Oxford University
Newman Society. The cardinal, who gained his DPhil from
Oxford in 1971, has been a patron of the Newman Society since
2009 when he gave the first St Thomas More Lecture at the
Divinity School of the Bodleian Library. This time, the former
Archbishop of Sydney was invited to speak on 'The Suffering
Church in a Post-Christian Society' at the Examination Schools
on 13th November 2021, but he changed the title to 'The
Suffering Church in a Suffering World'. The question-and-an-
swer session after the cardinal spoke was just as engaging as the
lecture itself and showed that the students in the audience were
delighted with what they heard.[4]

---

[4]   Cardinal Pell offered his lecture for publication in this festschrift in

Some Devotional Theology

This section on Newman as a theologian, together with the subsequent sections on Newman as a writer and as an educator, represent three key areas of Newman's legacy. In *The Achievement of John Henry Newman* (1990) Fr Ker identifies these three themes, along with those of Newman as a preacher and as a philosopher, as the five 'aspects of Newman's achievement which seem to me to constitute his essential genius'.[5] It is of course Newman as a theologian who has received the greatest scholarly attention: Fr Ker's own contribution in this field includes *Newman the Theologian* (1990) and *Newman on Vatican II* (2014), as well as chapters and passages in his other writings. But Newman was no mere academic theologian, as Fr Ker and the contributors in this section emphasise; he lived his theology, and thus was able to imitate those exemplary men—the Fathers of the Church—whom he had studied so assiduously and who led him to the fullness of Christianity. It is on account of this characteristic (as well as his unsystematic approach to theology) that C. S. Dessain sees Newman in continuity with the Church of the first millennium.

> St Bernard is called the last of the Fathers because in him dogma and piety and literature are one. [...] Newman, who leaves later developments on one side, took over where St Bernard left off, and perhaps should be allowed to succeed his title.[6]

All four articles in 'Some Devotional Theology' have patristical overtones; they develop key facets of Newman's lived theology, and, for their sources, draw heavily on Newman the preacher. Fr

---

advance of giving it. I am grateful to Olivia Owen-Sinclair, organiser of the lecture, and to the Oxford University Newman Society for agreeing to allow me to approach the cardinal for permission to publish it.

[5]   *Achievement of Newman*, p. ix.

[6]   C. S. Dessain, 'Newman's Spirituality: Its Value Today', *English Spiritual Writers*, ed. C. Davis (London: Burns & Oates, 1961), p. 160.

Hermann Geissler FSO explores Newman's cardinalate motto *Cor ad cor loquitur* by drawing on Newman's vision of St Paul, articulated in his sermons and grounded in his pastoral experience. As Fr Geissler remarks, Newman's 'teaching, preaching, and writing were not merely academic, but an expression of his zeal for souls'. (p. 88) Like St Paul, Newman had an apostolic heart owing, in part, to his deep understanding of human nature and his ability to understand the hearts of others and to share their joys and sorrows. There are echoes here of Newman's assertion that truth is preserved and communicated 'not by books, not by argument, nor by temporal power, but by the personal influence of such men [...] who are at once the teachers and patterns of it'; in the Oxford University sermon in which these words appear, 'Personal influence, the means of propagating the truth', Newman speaks of 'God's noiseless work', that is, of the effect of unconscious holiness on others.[7]

The theme of the heart and personal influence is taken up again in the next essay, on Newman and St Philip Neri, the founder of the Oratorian Congregation. Fr Keith Beaumont, of the French Oratory, explains that what particularly attracted Newman was the 'beauty of holiness' of St Philip; this quality drew Newman to the man who became his spiritual father, and inspired him to join his Congregation. The pastoral work of Newman the Oratorian has not always received the attention it merits; many assume that Newman's academic achievements were purchased at the expense of pastoral engagement. Nevertheless, Placid Murray was already combatting this misconception over fifty years ago in his *Newman the Oratorian: His Unpublished Oratory Papers* (1969), as more recently has Fr Zeno in *Newman and his Inner Life* (2010) and Gerard Skinner in *Newman the Priest: Father of Souls* (2010). Fr Beaumont's article adds to their arguments by identifying many parallels between the lives of Neri the Apostle of Rome and Newman the 'Apostle of Oxford and Birmingham'.

---

[7]   *University Sermons*, pp. 91–2, 96.

Sr Kathleen Dietz FSO is not the first to write on 'Newman and the Eucharist', as others have attempted to summarise Newman's Eucharistic teaching and practice; her distinctive contribution is to examine the subject with an eye to its historical development. Adopting Newman's own approach as an historical theologian in his *Essay on the Development of Christian Doctrine*, she shows how Newman's understanding of the Eucharist became more detailed and explicit over time, and how it manifested itself in practices of piety—how it flowed 'from doctrine to devotion'. (p. 136) By showing the close connection between Tractarian thinking on the Eucharist and on the Church, she explains how Newman's own thinking on the Eucharist developed alongside his thinking on the Church itself, and how his leap of faith about the latter enabled him to accept transubstantiation. By placing this progressive understanding within the context of practice, we see that Newman teaches us, not just theological subtleties, but a living theology at the heart of Christianity.

Before the Catholic University opened its doors in 1854 Newman requested that it should be placed under the patronage of the Blessed Virgin, under the title *Sedes Sapientiae*. After Rome gave its approval, Newman asked his friend John Hungerford Pollen to design the University seal, which shows an image of the Blessed Virgin standing and holding an open book, surrounded by the legend *Sedes Sapientiae, ora pro nobis*. That this was not an isolated decision has been amply shown in Bishop Philip Boyce's *Mary: The Virgin Mary in the Writings of John Henry Newman* (2001). Fr Carleton Jones adds to this by focusing on 'Mary, Mother of God, New Eve'. In this theological essay, Fr Carleton provides a detailed analysis of one section of the first part of Newman's lengthy *Letter to Pusey* (1865), which deals with the common Patristic patrimony of Christians. By seeking common ground to disarm Pusey and other like-minded Anglicans, Newman provides, among other things, 'an excellent example of non-reductive ecumenical discourse'. (p. 158)

Men of Letters

Fr Ker's academic and professional background as a student and lecturer in English Literature did much to make him an exceptional scholar in dealing with Newman's literary output *qua* literature. Thirty years ago he wrote that 'Newman's literary achievement is still not only underrated but also to a considerable extent unperceived'.[8] If this observation no longer holds as it did then, it is due largely to his own influence in stimulating the study of Newman as a writer and stylist. He had already begun with *Newman After a Hundred Years* (1990), which he co-edited with Alan Hill; and he continued through lectures, essays and published works such as the *Catholic Revival in English Literature, 1845–1961: Newman, Hopkins, Belloc, Chesterton, Greene, Waugh* (2003)—to say nothing of his doctoral students, two of whom take up the baton in 'Men of Letters'.

In 'Turncoat to Treasure: Newman and *Punch*', Dr Serenhedd James examines the reception of Newman in England through the lens of that leading outlet for nineteenth-century humour and satire. It gives an insight into how Newman would have been seen by those of his fellow Englishmen who were not acquainted with the niceties of Tractarian debates or knowledgeable about the Church of Rome. It is easy to forget the disbelief that met Newman's conversion: most of the influential thinkers of the time were anti-Catholic and regarded the Church as the bastion of superstition and discredited beliefs, and yet here was the greatest intellect of the Anglican Church leaving his beloved Oxford and throwing in his lot with the religious outcasts of the 'old faith'. The later acceptance of Newman after his *Apologia*—and then, even more, the cardinalate—is part of the story of the gradual acceptance of his co-religionists.

In the more ecumenical climate of the twentieth century, Newman's role as a robust controversialist has often been played down in favour of a graver image of him as a sage. Both his first

---

[8]   *Achievement of Newman*, p. ix.

biographer, Wilfrid Ward, and the eminent and sympathetic Anglican scholar Owen Chadwick were embarrassed at or even disdainful of Newman's 1850 *Lectures on the Present Position of Catholics*, which mercilessly satirised the anti-Catholic prejudice of his day. Chadwick saw the newly-Catholic Newman 'descending' into satire from his higher Anglican standard. In his essay 'A "Savaging Pen"?' Dr Andrew Nash demonstrates that Newman had in fact been writing highly effective polemical satire throughout his Anglican years. Far from *Present Position* being a new and intemperate departure, it used techniques which had already appeared in many of Newman's articles in the *British Critic* and elsewhere. Dr Nash, who had been a doctoral student of Fr Ker, develops and extends the insights of Ker's landmark essay 'Newman the Satirist' to examine this Anglican satirical writing. Using close textual analysis, he shows how Newman's earlier satire worked and how effective—and entertaining—it was.

In the last of the literary essays in this volume, 'The Dim Beast in the Bright Jungle', Fr James Reidy makes a link between Newman and one of the major themes in the novels of Henry James: the ambiguity of the idea of the English gentleman, so admirably described in Newman's *Idea of a University*. The lure of the 'religion of civilisation', with its 'glossing of immorality by external graces' (p. 234) and its high cultural ideal, is the dilemma at the heart of *The Ambassadors*, where James shows that high civilization and moral deformity can co-exist—just as Newman argued so cogently in the *Idea*.

Contributions to the Academy

Newman's fame in education is almost entirely due to the *Idea of a University*, a work which Fr Ker describes as the only 'educational classic'. It is generally regarded as the most influential book written on the nature and purpose of university education, and is endlessly cited—not just by popes and men of faith, but also by those who value Newman's arguments as the most persuasive there are for a truly liberal education. It is not an easy book to follow, and Newman's arguments have frequently been misinterpreted or taken out of context. In his magnificent critical edition of the *Idea*, Fr Ker has done a splendid service to the world of education by enabling scholars and others to understand more fully what this seminal text has to offer.

The *Idea* contains a host of celebrated themes, which Newman enshrines in some of his finest prose. In 'A Philosophical Habit of Mind', Dr Andrew Meszaros develops one of the themes that lies at the heart of the *Idea*, and puts it into a fuller philosophical framework in order to tease out some implications for the modern university. By holding two ideas in tension—a creative tension— Newman shows that between the 'viewy' individual and the specialist there lies a golden mean: the 'man of philosophical habit'. The academy of today, stocked full as it is of highly-opinionated students and hyper-specialised academics, should take note.

My own offering to this volume, 'Newman and the Idea of a Tutor', pulls together Newman's thinking and practice on this neglected aspect of university teaching, and suggests how it might be (re-)incorporated at the academy in post-Covid times. On one occasion I had the opportunity to receive an unofficial tutorial from Fr Ker, discussing my draft of *The 'Making of Men'*. At three hours it was certainly the longest tutorial I have ever had, and also the most intense. But all the contributors to this volume have been tutored by Fr Ker in some way or other: through his writings, by listening to his lectures, in conversation with him, or by correspondence. And in the course of being tutored, we have all been challenged.

The Great Battle

The two contributions in the final section of this volume take up the theme of Cardinal Pell's lecture by engaging with 'The Great Battle': the spread of infidelity and error in our times. The historian Christopher Dawson commented that

> Newman was the first Christian thinker in the English-
> speaking world who fully realised the nature of modern
> secularism and the enormous change which was already in
> the process of development, although a century had still to
> pass before it was to produce its full harvest of destruction.[9]

In order to address its shortcomings, Newman sought to get to the root of secularism and understand it. In *Newman and his Family* (2013) Edward Short reveals the extent to which John Henry did battle with heresy and apostasy at home, within his own family, before doing so elsewhere: his brothers Charles and Frank both abandoned Christianity, the first for Owenite Social-ism and the second for Unitarianism. With prophetic insight, Newman saw that dark days lay ahead for Christianity, and expressed his concerns repeatedly in his private correspond-ence—and occasionally also in his preaching, such as in his sermon 'The Infidelity of the Future', where he speaks of 'a darkness different in kind from any that has been seen before it', and of 'a world simply irreligious'.[10]

In 'The Combat of Truth and Error', Prof. Stephen Morgan takes us into the battlefield of the world of heresies with the help of John Henry Newman and Gilbert Keith Chesterton. It is fitting that Chesterton should feature alongside Newman in one of these essays as a way of celebrating Fr Ker's two major biographies. Each of his subjects grappled with heresy in his own way as a highly talented polemicist; each had his own original contributions to make, though they wrote at different times, and each employed his own distinctive tools. Prof. Morgan points out that, for all their differences in approach, both were combative controversialists who were willing to expose the inconsistencies and unrealities of modern secularism. As Fr Ker observed in his Chesterton biography, 'Newman received

---

[9]   'Newman and the Sword of the Spirit', *The Sword of the Spirit* (August 1945, p. 1).

[10] Preached at the opening of St Bernard's Seminary on 2 October 1873, this is the ninth and final sermon in the *Catholic Sermons of John Henry Newman* (London: Burns & Oates, 1957), pp. 117, 124–5.

the highest Chestertonian praise for his satirical masterpiece, *Lectures on the Present Position of Catholics*'.[11] Chesterton was later to remark that the 'ascendancy' of Protestant England became 'intellectually impossible [...] on the day when Newman published the first pages of the *Apologia*' and that henceforward Protestantism was no longer 'self-evidently superior'.[12]

In the final essay 'De-Christianising England', the longest in this volume, Fr Dermot Fenlon examines the part played by J. S. Mill in the demise of Christianity in Britain, using Newman's analysis on what was unfolding around him to frame this demise. Just as the essay *On Liberty* is a crucial text for understanding Mill, so the 'Biglietto Speech' represents Newman's counter-commentary, his indictment of 'the one great mischief' of 'liberalism in religion'[13] and its consequences. This wider-ranging piece makes an apt conclusion to the volume, tracing the collapse of Christianity in England through the writings of one of the most influential thinkers in modern times—and providing a running commentary on the working out of secularism through the mind of another influential thinker: St John Henry Newman.

The quality and range of these eighteen essays is a fitting homage to that versatile scholar and priest, Fr Ian Ker. I thank all who have contributed to this volume, as well as Tom Longford and the rest of the Gracewing team, and I hope the readers enjoy reading the articles as much as I have.

---

[11]   *Chesterton: Biography*, p. 331.
[12]   Quoted from *Irish Impressions* (1919) in *Chesterton: Biography*, p. 404.
[13]   'Biglietto Speech', *Campaign*, p. 513.

ABBREVIATIONS

References to Newman's works are to the uniform edition of 1868–81, 36 vols, which was published by Longmans, Green & Co., London.

Apologia	*Apologia pro Vita Sua* (1865)
Arians	*The Arians of the Fourth Century* (1833; 1871)
AW	*John Henry Newman: Autobiographical Writings*, ed. H. Tristram (London: Sheed & Ward, 1956)
BOA	Birmingham Oratory Archives
Callista	*Callista, a Tale of the Third Century* (1855; 1888)
Campaign	*My Campaign in Ireland, Part I*, ed. W. P. Neville (privately printed, 1896); ed. P. Shrimpton (Leominster: Gracewing, 2021)
Chesterton: Biography	I. T. Ker, *G. K. Chesterton: a Biography* (Oxford: Oxford University Press, 2011)
Development	*An Essay on the Development of Christian Doctrine* (1845; 1878)
Difficulties	*Certain Difficulties felt by Anglicans in Catholic Teaching*, 2 vols (1850)
Discussions	*Discussions and Arguments on Various Subjects* (1872)
Essays	*Essays Critical and Historical*, 2 vols (1871)
Grammar	*An Essay in Aid of a Grammar of Assent* (1870)
HS	*Historical Sketches*, 3 vols (1872–73)
Idea	*The Idea of a University: Defined and Illustrated* (1873)

Justification	*Lectures on the Doctrine of Justification* (1838; 1874)
LD	*Letters and Diaries of John Henry Newman*, 32 vols, ed. C. S. Dessain *et al.* (London: T. Nelson, 1961–72; Oxford: Clarendon Press, 1973–2008)
Loss and Gain	*Loss and Gain: the Story of a Convert* (1848)
Meditations	*Meditations and Devotions of the late Cardinal Newman*, ed. W. P. Neville (London: Longmans. Green & Co., 1893)
Miracles	*Two Essays on Biblical and on Ecclesiastical Miracles* (1870)
Mixed Congregations	*Discourses Addressed to Mixed Congregations* (1849)
Newman: Biography	I. T. Ker, *John Henry Newman: a Biography* (Oxford: Oxford University Press, 1988)
ODNB	*Oxford Dictionary of National Biography*, ed. C. Matthew, B. Harrison, L. Goldman & D. Cannadine (Oxford: Oxford University Press, 2004–)
Oratorian	*Newman the Oratorian: His Unpublished Oratory Papers*, ed. P. Murray (Dublin: Gill & Macmillan, 1969)
Parochial and Plain	*Parochial and Plain Sermons*, 8 vols (1834–43; 1869)
Philosophical Notebook	*The Philosophical Notebook of John Henry Newman*, 2 vols, ed. E. Sillem (Louvain: Nauwelaerts, 1969–70)
Present Position	*Present Position of Catholics* (1851)
Sermon Notes	*Sermon Notes of John Henry Newman, 1849–78* (London: Longmans, Green and Co., 1914)
Subjects	*Sermons Bearing on Subjects of the Day* (1843; 1869)
Tracts	*Tracts for the Times* (1833–41)

University Sermons	*Fifteen Sermons Preached before the University of Oxford* (1826–43; 1871)
Various Occasions	*Sermons Preached on Various Occasions* (1857; 1874)
Via Media	*The Via Media of the Anglican Church*, 2 vols (1837 & 1830–41; 1877)
Verses	*Verses on Various Occasions* (1867)

PART ONE

Along the Way of Life: Reminiscences

1 IAN KER AND THE GIFTS OF SANCTITY

EDWARD SHORT

W HILE ST JOHN Henry Cardinal Newman never lacked for admirers in his own time, he had few critics, though, then, as now, many detractors masquerading as critics. Richard Holt Hutton, the close friend of Walter Bagehot and editor of the *Spectator* wrote sensibly about the redoubtable convert, as did Dean Church, the author of what remains the best history of the Oxford Movement; but nearly everyone else in the nineteenth century wrote either encomia or hatchet jobs—or hatchet jobs posing as encomia, as was the case with the brilliantly devious James Anthony Froude and his well-known piece, 'The Oxford Counter-Reformation'. Like Henry James, who gave the best contemporary critical survey of his work in the prefaces he wrote to his New York Edition, Newman had to be content to be his own critic. The innovative nature of his work—from the *Essay on Development* (1845) to the *Grammar of Assent* (1870)—baffled too many of his contemporaries. This lack of critical understanding of Newman's work, especially as it related to faith and reason, bore out his contention that education must take priority in the evangelization of England, the National Church having left so much of the country ignorant of even the rudiments of Christianity. In the twentieth century, this state of affairs began to change when Wilfrid Ward brought out his considerable two-volume biography, *The Life of Cardinal Newman* (1912), which sought to place Newman accurately between the Scylla and Charybdis of Ultramontane and Liberal Catholicism, though it was marred by the biographer paying too little attention to the Anglican years and too much to what he imagined was Newman's hypersensitivity. In 1962, Meriol Trevor released *Newman: The Pillar of the Cloud* and *Newman: Light in Winter*, both of which, relying on the then well-read and percipient Oratorians in Edgbaston, presented a rounded, if uncritical biography of the cardinal. At the same time, the Oratorian Father Charles Stephen Dessain had inaugurated his great edition of *The Letters and Diaries of John Henry Newman*. Yet it was not until Fr Ian Ker brought out his study of the life and work, *John Henry Newman: A Biography* (1988), that Ward's and Trevor's limitations were redressed and Dessain's edition of the letters, to which Fr Ker contributed, was turned to proper account in a book that remains, more than thirty years after its publication, the definitive biography, distinguished alike by its incomparable knowledge of Newman's work and its splendid critical insights into that work's genius and unity. 'Ian Ker is an acknowledged master of Newman studies', Henry Chadwick wrote in a preface to a collection of Newman's sermons compiled by Fr Ker.[1] In this brief essay, I shall capture some of the elements of that masterliness and share with my readers a few biographical details pertinent to Fr Ker's work.

II

Born in Naini Tal in India on 30 August 1942, Ian Turnbull Ker was the son of Charles Murray Ker of the India Civil Service and his wife Joan May Knox, the daughter of another official in the India Service who was first cousin of Ronald Knox. Naini Tal had been set up in the 1860s and 1870s under the Raj as the summer hill station for the North Western Provinces. In 1947, Ian Ker and his parents and two sisters left India after independence was declared and settled in Wimbledon. As Ker recalled, 'I arrived in a bitterly cold England at the age of 5 where there was still no

---

[1]   Henry Chadwick, Preface, *John Henry Newman: Selected Sermons*, ed. Ian Ker (Mahwah: Paulist Press, 1994), p. 7.

central heating (to the disgust of my Canadian-born paternal grandmother) and where wartime rationing was still in force. Apart from a nanny and maid, there were no servants as contrasted with India where there were servants for every possible task.'[2] In 1882, Henry Beveridge had thirty-nine servants at his house in the Bengal Station of Bankipore, a rather large number for 'an unostentatious judge' who was actually in favor of Indian independence, but the English in India often had to employ more servants than they wished if only 'because religion and caste imposed restrictions on what any given servant could perform.'[3]

As a boy, Ian Ker remembers entering into the Sacred Heart Church in Edge Hill, Wimbledon and finding it at once impressive and welcoming. 'I remember as a small boy wandering into the cathedral-like Jesuit church out of curiosity and being welcomed by an old Irishman at the back. There were an unusual number of Catholics in Wimbledon in South London, where I grew up, no doubt because there were a Jesuit school and an Ursuline convent school. The service—which of course, being the Tridentine Mass, I didn't understand—was utterly unlike the middle-of-the-road Church of England matins we attended as a family.' However intriguing Fr Ker found the Jesuit church, his view of Catholics at the time was conventional enough. 'Thanks to history, not religion, lessons at school about Good Queen Bess as opposed to Bloody Mary and to the threatened Spanish Armada, I thought of Catholics as disloyal quasi-foreigners.'

It was his uncle, a Classics don at Trinity College, Cambridge, who recommended that Fr Ker go to Shrewsbury School, whose brightest pupils in the 1960s went to Balliol or Trinity College, Cambridge. That the most famous of Shrewsbury's Old Boys should have been Charles Darwin gives Fr Ker's time there an apt

---

2   Fr Ker's reminiscences throughout the essay are culled from various interviews conducted by the author over the last year.

3   David Gilmour, *The British in India: Three Centuries of Ambition and Experience* (London: Allen Lane, 2018), p. 345.

twist—the theme of development that would so preoccupy Newman being in the air even when Fr Ker was a schoolboy.

From Shrewsbury, Fr Ker duly went to Balliol, about which he was somewhat ambivalent. 'Balliol was the pre-eminent college at Oxbridge for Classics and I only got there through excellent teaching and hard work', he recalls.

> I read 'Mods and Greats', which in those days oddly encompassed both ancient history and ancient and modern philosophy. I loathed ancient history for the very reason that my Classics school teacher had commended it, the paucity of sources/documents; it seemed to consist of reading endless articles in learned journals of an extremely hypothetical nature (if ..., then ...); exactly the sort of argumentation I was later to encounter in Biblical studies. After completing Mods and Greats in which I was taught by the top scholars in their fields—Gordon Williams (who taught me to think) later occupied the Yale chair in Latin, Russell Meiggs (one of the pre-eminent ancient historians of his time and editor of J. B. Bury's *History of Greece*) and R. M. Hare, then the pre-eminent moral philosopher in the English-speaking world. The theory for which Hare was famous—prescriptivism, or 'preference utilitarianism', as it was called, the contention that one should act in such a way as to maximize people's preferences—seemed to me to be obviously refuted as it made no provision for moral weakness, a fact which taught me how very silly very clever people could be.[4]

Meiggs, in both his indifference to the careerism that often entrammels academics and his generous dedication to his students, was not unlike Fr Ker himself. The *Oxford Dictionary of National Biography* gives a vivid portrait of the classicist: 'He did not aspire to promotion [...] giving his energies without reservation to pupils and college; British universities will see few such

---

[4]   Reminiscence of Fr Ker.

careers hereafter. He went his own way, choosing widely different subjects to work on, without regard to fashion.'

After Balliol, Fr Ker won a scholarship to study English at Corpus Christi, Oxford where he was taught by another notable figure, the English don F. W. Bateson. In 1951, Bateson founded *Essays in Criticism*, which succeeded F. R. Leavis's *Scrutiny* as the pre-eminent scholarly journal in its field after the latter folded in 1953. Advocating for what he called the 'scholar-critic', Bateson once wrote that 'Dr Leavis at his best is a much better literary critic than I am but when it comes to scholarship, I am perhaps the better man of the two …' In a witty piece on Bateson in *Essays in Criticism*, Valentine Cunningham quoted the don's conclusion that 'The scholar-critic must be a scholar, a researcher, *before* he can become a really competent critic. There are therefore almost no reputable scholar-critics', to which Cunningham added: 'And so it was with Freddy Bateson.'[5] Yet Bateson may have been surprised to know that in having Ian Ker as his student he had someone who would go on to become one of the most talented scholar-critics that Oxford has ever produced. His work on Newman, Chesterton, and the authors of the Catholic Revival amply attest to this. Indeed, his essay on Evelyn Waugh in his book on the Catholic Revival is probably the single best thing ever written about Waugh.[6] Fr Ker, however, did not achieve this feat by following Bateson's advice. To explain why this should have been the case, we need a little context. According to Prof. Cunningham, who would go on to replace Bateson at Corpus:

> 'The Sense of Fact' became the title of the first chapter of [Bateson's] *The Scholar-Critic*. And those guilty of 'critical *sottisiers*', whether 'eminent bores and charlatans' like Edmund Gosse, or too nodding academics like I. A. Richards

---

[5]   Bateson quoted in Valentine Cunningham, 'F. W. Bateson, Scholar, Critic, and Scholar Critic', *Essays in Criticism* xxix:2 (April 1979), p. 139.

[6]   See Ian Ker, 'Evelyn Waugh: The Priest as Craftsman', *The Catholic Revival in English Literature 1845–1961* (South Bend: University of Notre Dame Press, 2003), pp. 149–202.

or William Empson or C. S. Lewis or F. R. Leavis, or purveyors
of 'pseudo-learning' like T. S. Eliot, would be smitten with
Bateson's fearsomely wielded ass's jawbone of factuality.
'Desert Island Criticism' as he labelled the bad stuff in his
'The Function of Criticism', that is critical judgements of texts
that ignored their contexts (contexts of all sorts), was simply
an 'irresponsible' kind of criticism. 'The "sense of fact"—
which is made the final *sine qua non* of the critic in "The
Function of Criticism" of 1923—was one', Bateson snarled,
'that Eliot only acquired if at all in middle age.'[7]

What is amusing about this is that while Bateson might have been
convinced that 'context' was 'the final *sine qua non* of the critic',
Fr Ker chose to de-emphasize context in his biographies. Thus,
in the case of Newman we are given necessary background on
how Newman related to various figures of Tractarian Oxford and,
later, the Oratories in Brompton and Edgbaston, but for the most
part he expects the reader to supply the wider context on his own.
He does the same regarding the various Fleet Street figures with
whom Chesterton interacted. It was precisely the economy with
which he treated the background that gave him the space he
needed to focus on the riches of Newman's and Chesterton's
work. Apropos this issue of context, I remember sending him
John Gross's study, *The Rise and Fall of the Man of Letters: English
Literary Life Since 1800* (1992), which is full of biographical
information on the bookmen with whom Chesterton crossed
paths, and his writing me back to say that he had absolutely no
use for the book. Some readers took issue with the tight focus of
Fr Ker's biographical *modus operandi*: but most were grateful for
the dazzlingly critical portraits it produced—portraits of an
almost pointillist intensity. 'That there is never a dull page out of
the seven hundred and forty-five of text is due not only to the
vigour and elegance of Newman's prose and the excitement of
his ideas', one reviewer wrote of Fr Ker's Newman biography, 'but
the skill of a presentation which never obtrudes, nor seeks to vie

---

[7]   Cunningham, *op. cit.*, pp. 140–1

with the subject himself. The book reads with the effortlessness which belies the magnitude of the task so well accomplished.'[8] Had it not been for his making the decision to limit context, Fr Ker's life of Newman would almost certainly have gone into a number of volumes, which would have wrecked its aesthetic integrity—an austere integrity, certainly, but one which does full justice to the majesty of Newman and his work.

From Oxford, Fr Ker went to Trinity College, Cambridge where he undertook doctoral work on George Eliot, which the university did not accept. Ian Jack, the crack editor of Emily Brontë and Browning, was apparently not interested in hearing what Fr Ker had to say of George Eliot's treatment of the Christian faith in her fiction. 'If God is anywhere', the agnostic Jack told his obituarist, 'he is in the mind of man'—a sentiment which might explain something of his lack of interest. The honorary doctorates that Fr Ker has since received from several universities in England and North America more than compensated for his unrewarded labors at Cambridge when he was a young man, though Cambridge did eventually award him a doctorate for his published work.

From Trinity College, Fr Ker went to teach at the University of York, about which he recalled: 'I got the job at York because it was a department of English and Related Literature and I was able to teach Latin as well as English literature. I was very lucky to get a job in one of the best English departments in the country and in such a historic and beautiful city at a time when academic jobs in the humanities were growing increasingly scarce.' Coincidentally enough, it was also at York that he encountered Leavis as a colleague, whom he found dour and unapproachable. The *Oxford Dictionary of National Biography* points out that Leavis's last years at Downing College had not been happy. 'Embittered by early insecurities, he had few intimates in Cambridge, though he enjoyed a brief friendship with Ludwig Wittgenstein.' At York, the famously astringent critic was wary of other faculty, with whom he rarely

---

8   Gordon Wakefield, Review of 'John Henry Newman: A Biography', *Scottish Journal of Theology* 43:3 (August 1990), pp. 427–9.

spoke, though he could often be seen walking about the grounds picking up litter. Once, a visitor to the university, noticing Leavis engaged thus, remarked on the neatness of the grounds, to which the vice chancellor replied that York had a very good grounds staff. All joking aside, the fact that Fr Ker came up with serious literary critics like Leavis still on the scene (all progeny in one way or another of T. S. Eliot) is important because he inherited their critical seriousness. Indeed, Fr Ker has often confided in me that he would have liked to have written a critical biography of Eliot—something the world still lacks.

Regarding his conversion when he was at Oxford, Fr Ker remarks:

> Although my father was a professed atheist, I think his dog-
> matic dismissal of Christianity provoked in me the opposite
> reaction and in my teens, I was greatly influenced by C. S.
> Lewis's *Mere Christianity* (1952). Later his argument from
> Origen that either Christ was who he claimed to be or a
> scoundrel influenced my conversion to Catholicism as exactly
> the same argument seemed to me to apply to the pope.[9]

Between writing his great biographies, Fr Ker would write a brilliant response to Lewis with a work of apologetics of his own, *Mere Catholicism* (2007), which argued that mere Christianity, ineluctably, could not be other than mere Catholicism. Over the years, to Fr Ker's delight, this gem of a book has brought many converts into the Church from around the world.

Once Fr Ker decided to convert, the reaction of his parents was mixed. 'My father was indifferent to my becoming a Catholic, my mother wasn't pleased—although she eventually became a Catholic herself. There were already several Catholics in the English Department at York. I always saw my teaching role, like Newman had seen his, as a pastoral as well as an educational role. One reason why I became a priest was because I thought I would like to teach people about Catholicism as opposed to English

---

9   Reminiscence of Fr Ker.

literature. My colleagues were amazed when they heard I was going to become a priest. Although I went to daily Mass I never advertised the fact, nor did I give the appearance of being pious.'

As for his decision to work on Newman, it was serendipitous in the way that providential choices often are.

> I knew a bit about Newman from reading Victorian litera-
> ture and I had read the *Apologia* (1864) once when I was ill
> in bed—without I am afraid it making much of an impres-
> sion on me. It was a chance encounter that got me writing
> about Newman: a colleague invited me to dinner in London
> where I met an Italian academic who was aiming to publish
> a selection of Newman's works in Italian and who invited
> me to edit *The Idea of a University* (1873), which he later
> suggested I turn into an Oxford critical edition.[10]

Fr Ker's friendship with the brilliant Newman scholar, Fr Dessain, would also inform his work on Newman—proof of the vitality of that personal influence of which Newman was always so appreciative.

After his conversion, Fr Ker, as he recalled, was 'offered an endowed chair not in English but in theology and philosophy at the University of St Thomas in St Paul, Minnesota on the basis of what I had published about Newman, even though I had no degree in theology, having studied privately for ordination (like Pope St Paul VI).' St Thomas suited Fr Ker.

> I had been given to understand that mid-western Americans
> were dull characterless people but I certainly didn't find that
> there: I lived in a residence for priests teaching at the
> university and I found myself in the company of some
> wonderful eccentrics. It was one of the happiest times in my
> life and I made many friends there. I returned to England
> because my parents were growing old and needed care (my
> only surviving sibling had long lived in Canada). I also
> regretted no longer doing pastoral work apart from supplies
> and hearing confessions at the local seminary.[11]

---

[10]   *Ibid.*

[11]   *Ibid.*

Fr Ker's fondness for the many students, scholars, priests and religious he has met over the years in North America, Europe and elsewhere points to another similarity he has with Newman, and that is his talent for friendship. Although not always adept at suffering fools as gladly as he might, especially fools given to distorting Newman or the Catholic Faith, Fr Ker has always inspired fondness in those who revel in his wit, his bonhomie, his learning, and his very real, if inconspicuous *pietas*.

Upon returning to England, he joined the theology faculty of Oxford University and became parish priest of the Church of SS Thomas More and John Fisher at Burford in the Cotswolds, thus, ensuring that in his critical, biographical, theological and apologetical work he would always be grounded, as Newman had been, in pastoral work. For both, the cure of souls always took priority in all they did.

III

In the second half of the twentieth century, biography, especially literary biography, enjoyed something of a renaissance—one thinks of such gifted critical biographers as Peter Brown on Saint Augustine, Leon Edel on Henry James, Michael Holroyd on Bernard Shaw, Richard Holmes on Coleridge, Robert Baldick on J. K. Huysmans, F. P. Lock on Edmund Burke, F. S. L. Lyons on Charles Stewart Parnell, Duff Cooper on Talleyrand and Walter Jackson Bate on Samuel Johnson. As a critical biographer, Fr Ker very much belongs in this distinguished company. In his biography of Newman, he encapsulated his subject's quest for reality by translating Newman's epitaph, *Ex umbris et imaginibus in veritatem*: 'Out of unreality into reality'. In his biography of Chesterton, Fr Ker persuasively argued that GKC was Newman's successor precisely because he shared the convert's passion for reality, a quality which Hilaire Belloc also discerned in his friend. 'Truth had for him', Belloc recalled, 'the immediate attraction of an appetite. He was hungry for reality. But what is much more, he could not conceive of himself except as satisfying that hunger [...] it was not possible for him to hold anything worth holding that was not connected with the truth as a whole.'[12] Here was the hunger that drove the Christian witness of both Newman and Chesterton, and Fr Ker brilliantly recreates it in his magisterial biographies.

Another virtue of the Chesterton biography is its identifying and setting out the major themes that preoccupied GKC in his massive, though uneven *oeuvre,* including not only his well-known philosophy of wonder but the principle of limitation that governs his thinking about art, literature, history and religion and the role of the imagination in enabling us to see familiar matters anew.[13] Distillation is one of the hallmarks of Fr Ker's work as a biographer and it is particularly evident in his biography of Chesterton.

Fr Ker's biography of Newman, in all its amplitude and acuity, is a model life not only because of its critical rigor but its unusual precision. Newman lay great store by what he called 'clearness', which he found preeminently in Cicero. 'I may truly say that I have never been in the practice since I was a boy of attempting to write well, or to form an elegant style', Newman once confessed to a correspondent; 'my one desire and aim has been to do what is so difficult—viz., to express clearly and exactly my meaning'.[14] Fr Ker follows Newman in this most demanding of all stylistic virtues. In his limpid prose, there is an unfailing fidelity to both the complexity and the simplicity of Newman's work.

His prose, moreover, is always attentive to Newman's wit. As *Anglican Difficulties* (1850) and *The Present Position of Catholics* (1851) so richly attest, Newman was a satirist of the first order— his only peer is Swift—and one of the best things about Fr Ker's writings on Newman is how nicely they capture this satirical wit in all of its exquisite fun. In an essay on Newman that he contributed to *The Oxford Handbook of English Literature and Theology* (2009), for example, Fr Ker remarks:

---

[12]   Hilaire Belloc, *Saturday Review* (4 July 1936), p. 4.

[13]   *Chesterton: Biography*, p. xi.

[14]   Newman to John Hayes, 13 April 1869, *LD* xxiv, pp. 241–2.

Newman's first novel, *Loss and Gain*, which was also the first book he published as a Roman Catholic, opens his most creative period as a satirist. Running through the novel is a strong, often comic, sense of the real and the unreal. The issue for the hero Charles Reding becomes not so much which is the true religion, but which is the real religion. The doctrinal comprehensiveness of the Church of England is perceived not as a source of strength but as fatal to its reality, for two contradictory views cannot 'both be real'. In the face of broad or liberal Anglicanism, it is no longer a question of satirizing inconsistencies, but of satirizing inconsistency itself as an ideal.[15]

And then Fr Ker proceeds to quote this brilliant little effusion from the junior don, Mr Vincent, who was 'ever [...] converting pompous nothings into oracles' and 'had a great idea of the *via media* being the truth'.[16]

'Our Church', he said, 'admitted of great liberty of thought within her pale. Even our greatest divines differed from each other in many respects; nay, Bishop Taylor differed from himself. It was a great principle in the English Church. Her true children agree to differ. In truth', he continued, 'there is that robust, masculine, noble independence in the English mind, which refuses to be tied down to artificial shapes, but is like, I will say, some great and beautiful production of nature—a tree, which is rich in foliage and fantastic in limb, no sickly denizen of the hothouse, or helpless dependent of the garden wall, but in careless magnificence sheds its fruits upon the free earth, for the bird of the air and the beast of the field, and all sorts of cattle, to eat thereof and rejoice.'[17]

---

[15]   Ian Ker, 'John Henry Newman', *The Oxford Handbook of English Literature and Theology*, ed. Andrew Hass, David Jasper & Elisabeth Jay (Oxford: Oxford University Press, 2009), p. 633.

[16]   *Loss and Gain*, p. 74.

[17]   *Loss and Gain*, pp. 84–5.

Since Fr Ker has brought out several works supplemental to the biography, including essays on different aspects of the saint's life and work, critical editions of the *Idea of a University*, the *Apologia*, and the *Grammar of Assent*, as well as monographs on his spiritual development, engagement with the full spectrum of Christianity, and what the great convert might have made of Vatican II in a book full of shrewd theological insights, he has given his readers a truly living portrait of Newman. All who delight in Newman owe him an inestimable debt.

Once, when speaking with Fr Ker over lunch in a charming little Italian restaurant in Cheltenham Spa, I asked him which proof for the existence of God he found most persuasive, and, without skipping a beat, he replied, 'the lives of the saints'. Since Fr Ker has spent so much of his long, prolific, admirable life celebrating the gifts of sanctity, which only God bestows, there is an ungainsayable authority in this decided judgement.

2 IAN KER: A PERSONAL MEMOIR

JOHN ROE

6 **I**AN, DOES NO light ever penetrate these rooms?' The words of a friend, visiting Ian in his new lodgings in Cheltenham, and letting the *Daily Telegraph* fall from his hands with a sigh.

Ian was unrepentant as ever, and told the story against himself with his usual twinkle. I doubt whether anything will wean him from the Torygraph.

I first met Ian in 1973 at the University of York where I had taken up a lectureship in the Department of English and Related Literature. He had arrived a year or two before me, and his brief was Victorian Literature and Roman Poetry. For someone just embarking on his new job, it was a relief to encounter such a congenial spirit as Ian's, and I was very grateful for his presence around the place. I recall that he wore mid-grey tweed jackets with darkish corduroy trousers, pretty much the young don's outfit in those days. Though some sported jeans and T-shirts, Ian was resolutely a part of tradition. He was also the possessor of a blue Skoda saloon, which I later inherited when he left for the Birmingham Oratory. Much to my regret, that was only a year after I had first got to know him. The Skoda was an entirely Czech manufacture in those days, and as I later discovered rather given to breaking down at inopportune moments. We would sometimes drive out to a pub. Ian's favourite drink was port, as I recall, but he managed beer well enough. He would declare that when the Campus Revolution finally came the Skoda would be the only car *not* set on fire by rampaging student Reds. When I took the car over, Ian told me that one of his former charges had written to him asking, 'Have you really left? The Skoda still mounts the pavement in my direction.'

My first sighting of Ian was at a meeting of the Department's Board of Studies, where the new lecturers were introduced to the rest of the academic staff. He was rather low-key, quietly reading what were called UCCA forms (Universities Central Council on Admissions), while the general discussion went forward. These were forms that applicants for a university place filled in, with comments by their teachers, and we at the university had to spend considerable time assessing them. Ian would invariably look up from his form with an irreverent quip, which made me feel that, however heavy my load, knowing him would surely lighten it. This was quickly confirmed when I read his UCCA report on a student who had later come my way as a supervisee. Part of the assessment process was to interview the candidates. Ian wrote: 'He demolished all my arguments, and then looked anxiously for signs of wounded amour-propre. No signs at all.' Ian's intellect was of course razor-sharp: woe betide any visiting professor who pompously assumed he could get away with an ill-supported thesis in his lecture.

In those days the English Department at York was pretty strongly Leavisian in temper and approach. The great F. R. Leavis had indeed been awarded an honorary professorship by York (something denied him by Cambridge), and he even gave a number of classes to York students in his twilight years. Although our colleagues were certainly pleasant folk by and large, this Leavisian touch induced a degree of seriousness and solemnity, offset sadly by cases of alcoholism, in which—let me say—Ian had no part. Ian was mischievously adept at sending up his colleagues' earnestness. 'Tell us, Margaret', he asked the Departmental Secretary, 'in which filing cabinet are the Vital Responses kept?'

While Ian was a well-liked young lecturer, this spirit of levity did not endear him to everyone. He told me one very amusing anecdote about a visit to The Gun Room (a restaurant now no more) where he was treating a colleague and wife in return for meals Ian had enjoyed at their table. At one point in the conversation Ian made a no doubt thoughtless but belittling reference to those members in the department who did not publish. His colleague rose on the instant from the table and made for the door remarking, in particularly lugubrious tones, 'I have not come here to be insulted.' The friendship, such as it was, never recovered. Readers will no doubt know P. G. Wodehouse's brilliantly funny novel, *The Code of the Woosters*. Whenever Ian launches on this story, which I have encouraged him to do several times, I experience the same delight when the words 'The Gun Room' are pronounced as I do when Bertie whispers the tell-tale name 'Eulalie' into the ear of the repugnant Roderick Spode.

During this time at York, Ian presented such an amused and wryly witty face to the world that it was not easy to see that he was undergoing a deep spiritual self-examination. I certainly was not aware of it. He never spoke to me of Catholicism or of Newman, and his conversion came as a surprise to me. At the end of only one year of our acquaintance, Ian was on his way to the Birmingham Oratory, where among other things he was to help his mentor, the inspiring Charles Stephen Dessain, with editing Newman's *Letters and Diaries*. I would pay him visits now and then, driving down in the Skoda, and much of the time was spent in bringing him up to date as we indulged in cheerful gossip about his former colleagues in York. By then, I understood perfectly why he had made the move to the Oratory, but he left quite a gap in the English Department.

Thereafter our paths diverged for some time. Phone calls or postcards arrived, with the occasional visit by Ian to York. He was beginning to forge his name as the leading Newman scholar. By this time, I was married. When Ian became the parish priest at Burford, our visits back and forth recovered their earlier frequency. This was maintained when our daughter went up to Oxford, to Ian's old college, indeed. We would all drive out along the Cheltenham road to see him. On one occasion my wife Christine was coming separately from York, and furthermore in a car for which I realised belatedly I had not insured her. This occasioned some frantic phone calls to the insurers to get her on the books, which was finally successful. By the time she arrived at Ian's house all was well. However, Ian was not going to miss his opportunity. 'I am relieved to see you here, Christine. I have been attacking John for his lack of chivalry in allowing you to drive down here *uninsured*.' Then he wagged a finger at me: 'Penny wise, pound foolish, John.' Ian's humour is of a kind that brings back an earlier, more civilised time.

One late December evening, Ian invited me to join him for a Christmas supper organised by his parishioners. I found myself sitting at a table with some of the Oxford luminaries, as, for example, George Holmes, the professor for Italian Renaissance History. Imagine my amazement as people spoke affectionately but reverently of 'Father Ian'. What about the boyish, impish Ian of my acquaintance? However, such respect was infectious, indeed almost mandatory, and as the evening wore on, I found myself referring in hushed tones to 'Father Ian'.

Ian's parish of Burford did not consist exclusively of the eminent and well-to-do but included people who found life hard-going, among them members of the growing Polish immigrant community. I occasionally witnessed Ian engaging with some of them in circumstances that required great compassion, sensitivity, and understanding; he was of course more than equal to the task.

On his mantelpiece at Burford, we first saw the small black-and-white photo of a young girl: Ian's sister who died young and to whose memory he has remained devoted. I believe it is her initials which appear on the dedication page of the esteemed Newman biography.

It is a true pleasure and privilege, as an old friend of Ian Ker's, to contribute in a small, anecdotal way to this volume, which justly celebrates his achievements as a scholar of Catholic theology and the great John Henry Newman.

3 THE DIVINE PROVIDENCE OF A TRULY NEWMANIAN FRIENDSHIP

BISHOP JAMES CONLEY

I FIRST MET FR Ian Ker in 1990, more than 30 years ago. I was a young priest, a graduate student in Rome, and Fr Ker was a scholar of great renown, who had published just two years before, the first edition of his magnificent biography on our heavenly intercessor, St John Henry Cardinal Newman.

Newman was not nearly so well-known then, or so well-appreciated, as he is now; and that is largely because Fr Ker's biography would do a lot over the coming decades to inspire devotion to Newman and attention to his scholarship, his letters, his sermons, and his poetry.

In 1990, Fr Ker was the picture of a brilliant Oxford don: aloof, endearing, utterly engaging, and not entirely concerned with the details or particularities before him. But in the summer of that year, he hosted a two-week summer school on Newman, at Somerville College, Oxford. It was an experience I still think of often, a most extraordinary fortnight for which I remain grateful.

The dreamy spires of Oxford were almost magical that summer. Those of us at Fr Ker's summer school listened to some of the best Newman scholars in the world. At meals and in local pubs we engaged in spirited discussion. And we steeped ourselves in the places Newman frequented, and where he lived. Our liturgies were at the Oxford Oratory. We visited Littlemore, where some of the most important things happened in Newman's life. I am not sure if Newman spent time punting on the Thames, but we did that too;

with a few bottles of Pimm's, it felt nearly like a scene out of *Brideshead Revisited*, even without the strawberries.

We, students and faculty, had in common a great love for Newman. And beginning there, we became friends. Many of my fellow students became lifelong friends, in fact; but the friendship that I most treasured was the one I formed with Fr Ker.

Like Newman, Fr Ker was both scholar and parish priest. He was always a parish priest. And in his parish, it did not quite matter that he was the greatest Newman scholar of our time. It mattered that he baptized, and married, and buried, forgave sins, taught catechism to children and offered the Mass, and pointed to hope in Jesus Christ. I was only five years a priest that summer; Fr Ker had been ordained only eleven. We were both quite young, but still, I looked up to him: as a pastor, as a scholar, as a priest, and as a Christian. And so much of what I learned from him shaped the trajectory of my own priesthood.

Fr Ker taught me a great deal about Newman that summer. But he taught me most through the gift of a Newmanian friendship, which called me closer to the Lord.

II

As some readers may know, John Henry Newman played an instrumental role in my own conversion to Catholicism, years before I met Fr Ker in Oxford. In fact, mine was a distinctly *Newmanian* kind of conversion in three ways.

First, my conversion was influenced by Newman's intellect: the clarity of his thought and the fervency of his faith. His relentless search for the truth, convinced me that truth existed and that it could be known with certitude.

Second, my conversion was influenced by friendships, which were informed by Newman's own beautiful and influential friendships, the powerful gift of 'personal influence'.

And third, my conversion was—and I can see this now more than ever, looking back some four decades—the work of God's

Providence. Newman was through and through a disciple of Divine Providence.

I would like to offer some reflections on Newman and my own conversion. I offer them not to write exclusively from the vantage point of self-reference, but because I want to reflect on what Newman offers believers today, why we need Newman today more than ever. I believe I can do that best, and at least without becoming too dry, in the context of my own story.

I became a Catholic through my experience as an undergraduate at the University of Kansas and as a student of the Pearson Integrated Humanities Program. The IHP, as it came to be known, was not explicitly Catholic; it existed, after all, at a large state university. But it was nonetheless influenced and inspired by the understanding of liberal education articulated by Newman in his *Idea of a University*. In fact, several of Newman's discourses, which formed the first half of the *Idea*, were part of the required reading for the Integrated Humanities Program. In truth, the IHP was a kind of intellectual movement strongly influenced by the thought and writings of Newman.

The IHP began in the fall of 1970 and flourished for fifteen years; it became one of the most popular undergraduate courses of studies at the University of Kansas. It was a four-semester program for freshmen and sophomores, six hours per semester for a total of 24 credit hours.

Because the program was an integration of literature, history, philosophy and speech, it satisfied nearly all of the undergraduate distribution requirements for general education courses: English literature and composition, speech and western civilization. As you can imagine, that particular 'perk' drew in a lot of students. And ironically the program was made possible through a substantial grant from the National Endowment for the Humanities. The professors very cleverly sold the program as 'an experiment in tradition'. It was, after all, the 1970s!

Over the course of nearly two decades, there were hundreds of conversions to the Catholic Church. There were so many that a joint lawsuit was filed against the University of Kansas by the American Civil Liberties Union and the Jewish Defense League alleging that the three professors who taught the program, Dennis Quinn, John Senior and Frank Nelick, were proselytizing their students at a state-supported university. These were the days when there were many cults active on college campuses such as the Moonies and the *Hare Krishna.*

There were public hearings held by the dean of the College of Liberal Arts and Sciences at Kansas, which made the program even more popular! But the three professors had impeccable reputations at the university; they were all tenured and had each received the Hope Award, the highest honor given by the university for excellence in teaching. After just a few days of lively hearings, the dean dismissed the case and declared that there was no evidence of any religious proselytizing or indoctrination on the part of the professors.

The IHP experience included scintillating lectures by the three professors who team-taught the course to packed lecture halls of 150 plus students; the memorization of reams of poetry; smaller group discussion classes and rhetoric sessions; evening excursions into the country for star gazing when we would learn the various constellations, as well as how to waltz. It was a program designed not only to expose us to the humanities as an academic discipline, but to our own humanity. The motto of the program was *Nascantur in admiratione* (Let them be born in wonder).

I grew up a nominal Presbyterian in a good family in a suburb of Kansas City. My mother and father were good people. They raised my sister and me through hard work, and with love. We grew up with some exposure to faith. We went to church periodically, and my mother loved to listen to a certain local preacher on the radio. But we did not grow up with any real formation in the Christian faith or with any deep immersion in the Gospel. I did not have the kind of childhood conversion experience that Newman had when he was fifteen, the deep infusion of grace and faith he experienced. Instead, I grew up in a very ordinary way. So it was solely by Divine Providence that I ended up at the University of Kansas in the Integrated Humanities Program.

At the large public high school I attended my education was mediocre at best, in part because I was not a very engaged student. I do not think I read a single book all the way through during my high-school years, but I still gained decent grades. I remember seeing at a college fair during my senior year a brochure for the IHP, which had an illustration of a typical 1970s student on the cover, with long hair, jeans, and a tee shirt. It was night and the young student was looking up at the stars. Across the top of the page was the IHP motto: 'Let them be born in wonder'.

While I was intrigued by the brochure, I must confess that I enrolled in the program because it seemed like an easy way to fulfill my core curriculum requirements. But it was also because my best friend in high school was also interested, and so we signed up together. Really, I joined the program because of the silent hand of Divine Providence working behind the scenes. Such are the ways that Providence brought me into contact with John Henry Newman.

In my sophomore year, in the midst of the IHP and quite by accident, I selected reading by Newman as the topic for a paper I had to write for a separate literature course I was taking on 'Major British authors after 1800'. The text was a selection of discourses from Newman's *Idea* entitled 'The Uses of Knowledge'.

The topic of my paper was 'Knowledge Its Own End'. Newman's point in those discourses was to underscore the unity of truth and the transformative power of a liberal education. While I did not realize this at the time, the point of those selections was to reveal the potential of the intellect, the imagination and the heart, to draw men into a deeper relationship with God himself.

I still remember asking my mother to type that paper for me—she was a secretary by training—and the beauty of Newman's prose. But more than that, I remember the impression his work left on me, and on my mother who also ended up converting years later.

Newman was a clear and honest thinker, and did not shy away from difficulty or controversy. He was confident that men were capable of knowing and loving the truth, and that the whole of their human endeavors could be ordered to knowing, loving, and serving God. Newman wrote with certitude from a Christian worldview, and I was struck as much by his arguments as by his clarity and his confidence.

That Newman paper played a critical role in my 'religious awakening', and in my eventual conversion to Catholicism. In Newman I found a mentor, an ally, a friend, and at times a challenge to my own worldviews. In him I found a lover of truth, beauty, and goodness; a man willing to follow his own conclusions despite having to make difficult choices; and a fervent believer in the Gospel of Jesus Christ.

His intellect formed mine. His love of truth became my own. His love of beauty opened my eyes to beauty. His mind—sharp, creative, clear and compassionate—shaped my own young mind. I needed the intellectual rigor and clarity he offered, because it was so unlike almost anything I had experienced in the relativistic ephemera of the 1970s. It was a time of deep skepticism. It seemed as if all around me there was doubt. Newman alone was able to help me work through this doubt and give me the confidence that I could find certainty. He set me on a path, a trajectory, for a lifelong love of learning.

Newman taught me that it was possible to know things from the inside, from the very essence of the thing itself. He taught me that true education is much more than a system for delivering information; that there is a kind of knowing that puts one in direct contact with the thing itself. It is what Newman would call the difference between notional and real assent to the truth. Speaking about these two kinds of knowledge, Pope Benedict XVI writes that 'one is knowing through instruction, which remains second-hand and does not put the knower in contact with reality itself. The second kind of knowledge, in contrast, is knowing through personal experience, through contact with the things themselves.

As long as we have not tasted an essence, therefore, we don't love the thing to the extent that it is a worthy object of love'.[1]

Newman's style of writing was difficult for me at first. But the clarity of his thought and clarity of faith led me to consider the claims of Christianity, and ultimately contributed to my conversion to Christ and to his Church.

I used to say that I read my way into the Catholic faith. In many ways that is true; the process began with reading Newman. But over the years I have come to realize that it was not only books—even the writings of Newman—that led to my conversion. It was friendship—the special species of friendship between a teacher and his students—and the friendships I enjoyed with my classmates, fellow travelers along the same road.

My friends, many of whom became serious followers of Jesus before I did, made the kind of impression on me that brought me closer to faith. In fact, while checking out churches as a young believer in Kansas, it was a girl who first brought me in contact with the Catholic Church. She was my roommate's girlfriend and interested in taking instruction at the local parish church, but she did not want to go alone. She told her boyfriend, 'I'll go, if Jim goes.' So off we went. And soon after I became a Catholic. But it was all through a series of friendships, and their 'personal influence' on my life.

In one of his Tamworth Reading Room letters, Newman writes that 'the heart is commonly reached, not through the reason, but through the imagination, by means of direct impressions, by the testimony of facts and events, by history, by description. Persons influence us, voices melt us, looks subdue us, deeds inflame us. Many a man will live and die upon a dogma: no man will be a martyr for a conclusion.' Newman continues, 'man is *not* a reasoning animal; he is a seeing, feeling, contemplating, acting animal. He is influenced by what is direct and precise'.[2]

---

[1] Benedict XVI, *On the Way to Jesus Christ* (San Francisco: Ignatius Press, 2005), pp. 35–6.

[2] *Discussions*, pp. 293–4.

My conversion exemplified Newman's sense of the importance of 'direct impressions'—the effect of the personal upon person, the way in which the heart is reached by the imagination, and the way, implicit in his observation about being seeing, feeling, and contemplating creatures, in which beauty has the power to draw us into an encounter with the transcendent God. In part, I came into the Church through what I read. But the effect of what was direct and precise—the effect of the persons who influenced me, the voices, the looks, the deeds of those I admired—cannot be overstated. Newman wrote about persons, voices, looks and deeds because, from the memory of his own experience, he knew the power of friendship. We can learn much from Newman's friendships.

As you may know, Newman faced struggles, difficulties, and discouragements. In the course of those struggles, the support of his friends was often the most immediate source of his consolation. Newman's friends helped him to discern the will of God, and he helped them to do the same. Newman's friends corrected his faults, and he did the same for them. Newman's friends encouraged steadfastness, fidelity, integrity and joy. He said of one long-time friend, 'he subdues me by his many high virtues'.[3] And in the mark of true friendship, Newman did the same.

Newman was a prolific letter writer. He wrote every day to friends in all places, letters of authentic affection and fraternal support. Long after he became a Catholic, he continued to correspond with his Anglican friends, with letters that were personal, candid and from the heart. Newman wrote to friends about his joys and struggles in the Church, letters that challenged their own theological perspectives and practices. He felt that friendship must be honest. He wrote to one friend that 'the greatest of evils in the intercourse of friends is ignorance about each other's feelings'.[4]

Newman enjoyed a long friendship with Ambrose St John, whom he had known since the latter's youth. They became

---

[3]   Newman to Lady A., 15 September 1882, *LD* xxx, p. 127.

[4]   Newman to William Froude, 2 January 1860, *LD* xix, p. 272.

Catholics together, were ordained in Rome together, and were buried in the same grave plot. Ambrose was ten years younger than John Henry but preceded him in death by fifteen years. When he died, Newman wrote, 'I feel it difficult to believe that any bereavement can be greater, or any one's sorrow greater, than mine.'[5]

When Newman became a Catholic, he suffered the loss of many friends. As his friends distanced themselves, he felt that he was 'going [alone] on the open sea'.[6] But, as he was alienated from them, he learned the single most important virtue of friendship: regular, committed, intercessory prayer. He wrote to his friend Henry Wilberforce: 'When I am in [Christ's] presence, you are not forgotten. It is the place for intercession.'[7] He said, of distant friends, 'my one prayer is that they may see God'.[8]

Of course, I offer the same prayer for Fr Ker, that when the Lord calls him—please God, it will not be soon—he will see God. He has certainly shown the Lord to me.

I remember the long walks we took together in his parish in the Cotswolds. I think of cooking meals in his presbytery, and of his generous visit to Wichita State University while I served there as chaplain. I think of his love for his parishioners; for ordinary working people; for the men and women of the Neocatechumenal Way, who have long taken care of him, as he has ministered to them spiritually.

I think of the ways that Fr Ker has revealed to me the will of God for living out a holy priesthood: docility to Providence, openness to the Lord's will, intellectual engagement, commitment to prayer, and love of friends, near and far.

Consider that Newman learned many of the same lessons in friendship. Like Fr Ker, he learned to discern the will of God. He learned to express his faith compellingly. He learned to listen. He learned to admonish, to comfort, and to mourn. And Newman

---

5   Newman to Agnes Wilberforce, 18 June 1875, *LD* xxvii, p. 323

6   Newman to St John, 20 January 1846, *LD* xi, p. 95.

7   Newman to Henry Wilberforce, 26 February 1846, *LD* xi, p. 129.

8   Newman to J. Mozley, 26 February 1880, *LD* xxix, p. 242.

learned to pray for other people in a regular and committed way. In friendships, Newman learned the practice of mercy—because friendship demands the spiritual and corporal works of mercy—from people who expect us to love them.

It is true, Newman mourned deeply for his 'friend of friends' Ambrose St John. But through this loss, he became more merciful to others, because it helped him realise what grieving widows, or parents, or siblings might have experienced. The particular love demanded by his friendship enabled him to universalize the call to mercy. He learned how to mourn, and from that he learned how to comfort.

III

Newman was a disciple of Divine Providence. When he spoke of Providence, he proclaimed of the Lord 'the wonderful truth that He sees and thinks of individuals. [...] He sees what is going on among ourselves at this moment; that this man falls, and that man is exalted, at His silent, invisible appointment.'

> He sees thee, and understands thee, as He made thee. He knows what is in thee, all thy own peculiar feelings and thoughts, thy dispositions and likings, thy strength and thy weakness. He views thee in thy day of rejoicing, and thy day of sorrow. He sympathizes in thy hopes and thy temptations. He interests Himself in all thy anxieties and remembrances, all the risings and fallings of thy spirit.[9]

Newman kept a record of his birthdays in journal entries that recounted the passing years so as to reflect on the ways in which the Lord had moved in his life. He did this because, he says, 'God's presence is not discerned at the time when it is upon us, but afterwards, when we look back upon what is gone and over. [...] Events happen to us pleasant or painful; we do not know at the time the meaning of them, we do not see God's hand in them. If

---

[9]   *Parochial and Plain* iii, pp. 116, 125.

indeed we have faith, we confess what we do not see, and take all that happens as His'.[10]

Newman understood that the Lord is interested in all the moments of our lives; that He sees us as unique, unrepeatable, and lovable individuals; that He guides us because he knows us; that He calls us and speaks to us and works in our lives according to our own particularities; that His providential path is particularized and personalized for each one of us.

Towards the end of his life, he wrote a meditation on the Lord's providential care for him:

> O my God, my whole life has been a course of mercies and blessings shown to one who has been most unworthy of them. I require no faith, for I have had long experience, as to Thy providence towards me. Year after year Thou hast carried me on—removed dangers from my path—recovered me, recruited me, refreshed me, borne with me, directed me, sustained me. O forsake me not when my strength faileth me. And Thou never wilt forsake me. I may securely repose upon Thee.[11]

Things which in the light of hindsight are clearly providential, seem often, as they are happening, to be inconsequential, or even to be tragic. A trust in Providence, Newman knew, challenges us to serenity; to accept the things that are happening to us, whether they are pleasant or painful, because of our trust in the Lord, His love for us, and His goodness.

Looking back over the years at my conversion to Catholicism, I can see that the Lord used small things, but things that He knew would speak directly to me: the cover of a pamphlet about the IHP; the influence of my best friend from high school, Paul (now Archbishop) Coakley, who ended up being my room-mate all four of my college years and to this day is my closest friend; the choice to write a paper on Newman because the selection seemed

---

[10]   *Parochial and Plain* iv, pp. 256, 258.
[11]   'The Providence of God', *Meditations*, p. 421.

manageable—these seemingly small things at the time, He used them all in order to call me into His Church.

Newman trusted the path of Providence and trusted that the Lord would call him through the movements of his heart, through his intuition, through his imagination, his hopes, and his dreams. Before I even knew what Providence was, I can see that the Lord thought of me as his beloved son—calling me to faith, to His Church, and to the holy priesthood through friendship, imagination, intellectual renewal and wonder. In the same way, He has thought of each one of you in particular ways, to call you to take on the work for which He made you, the mission which He has given to you, and to no one else.

IV

Of course, if I have learned to marvel at the unexpected hand of Divine Providence, and learned to be humbled by the way the Lord uses each one of us, I learned that from Fr Ker as well.

In 1991, after the Newman summer school, Michael Barber, SJ—now a bishop—and I decided to invite Fr Ker to give a lecture in Rome. We booked a lecture hall at the North American College, and, as young priests, thought that perhaps a few English-speaking students would come. We designed fliers and distributed them at the universities where North Americans studied, at seminaries, rectories, and residential houses around Rome. We did our best to promote the lecture in the hope that the audience would be sufficiently large that Fr Ker would find the trip had been worth his while.

A few days before the lecture, we received a telephone call informing us that Francesco Cossiga, the President of Italy, wanted to attend, and that there would therefore be a security sweep of the hall before the lecture. Then we received word that Cardinal Joseph Ratzinger wanted to come, too. And once he was coming, other cardinals decided to attend as well. Our little lecture had become a major event.

When the day arrived, we drove with Fr Ker in a taxi up the Janiculum Hill, toward the North American College. We saw the police lights and secret servicemen stationed near the entrance. 'What is all this for?' Fr Ker asked. Fr Barber and I laughed. 'It's for you, of course.'

I was nervous when I introduced Fr Ker, with cardinals and a president sitting in the front row. I had a relic of St Ignatius in my hand, given to me by Fr Barber. I fumbled a bit, but the lecture was a great success. Afterwards, at the reception, we learned that Fr Ker had made an impression on these great men of Church and state, deepening their love for the holy cardinal. Nineteen years later, Joseph Ratzinger, as Pope Benedict XVI, beatified Newman. I marvel at the unexpected joy of the Lord's Divine Providence.

V

My conversion was born of Newman's clear thinking, of a renewal of the mind (as St Paul says), of friendship, and of the Lord's Providence (even before I knew what that was). And I share those things because they are vitally important for the age in which we live, an age of noise, distraction and isolation. It seems clear to me that right now, in the twenty-first century, Newman is uniquely suited to help us address the challenges of our time. This is especially true for young people who are shaped entirely by the culture in which we live and are products of our technocratic times.

We live at a time when technology is flattening our souls, sinking our hearts, lowering our sights, and isolating us from the species of love that is friendship. If we are not careful, our technology can isolate us, cripple our memories and intellects, stifle our imaginations, and make us bored and lonely. Our addiction to a constant stream of new information makes it difficult for us to think clearly and deeply, and makes it more likely that we act without thinking. Newman trains us to do the opposite.

Newman trains us to think through contemporary issues carefully—through history, scripture and experience, and by means of our reason—before we dare to respond. This is an atypical way to go through life, especially for young people today.

Newman trains us to think poetically, to think about the beauty, symbolism and richness of things; and to think prophetically, to think about what the Lord is doing, and what He might be calling us to do. Newman reminds us of the importance of honing the memory, imagination and intellect, so that we might hone our wills and hearts.

Newman, a man with a great mind and large heart, calls us out of the intellectually crippling and utilitarian cycle of a modern technocratic culture. Social media gives us the facsimile of connection, but never the real thing. Studies show that in the social media era, we speak more about being connected, but have fewer friends than ever before. The research of the psychologist Jean Twenge tells us that young people feel more comfortable with their phones than with their peers.[12]

Newman calls us to a different way of living. As the cardinal whose motto was *Cor ad cor loquitur*, he sees the importance of connecting with real persons. In a time when friendship is increasingly a dead or dying art, Newman, and his great love for his friends, offers us a crash course in the school of love that is friendship.

In our technocratic era we can become blind to the hand of Providence because we are averse to silence, reflection, contemplation and prayer. Newman was a prolific journal keeper, who noted the movements of his interior life, knew his own heart and who he was before God; he teaches us how to go before the Lord in silence, how to get to know Jesus Christ, as well as ourselves, and how to cultivate a love with the Lord and his disciples.

---

[12]   Jean Twenge is the author of *iGen: Why Today's Super-Connected Kids Are Growing Up Less Rebellious, More Tolerant, Less Happy—and Completely Unprepared for Adulthood—and What That Means for the Rest of Us* (2017). See her article 'Have Smartphones Destroyed a Generation?', *The Atlantic* (September 2017).

The world needs the lessons of St John Henry Newman. Young people, especially, have much to learn from him.

Seven years ago, in the diocese of Lincoln (in the United States), an idea that had been germinating in my heart for years began to take flesh and become a reality. With the help of the likes of the late Don Briel, John Freeh, and Sr Kathleen Dietz, we launched the Newman Institute for Catholic Thought and Culture at the University of Nebraska in Lincoln. Our program offers integrated courses in history, literature, and philosophy, which UNL students can take in fulfillment of the university's core curriculum requirements. We are blessed to be seeing real success, though we are in the early years of our program.

We are trying to form hearts and minds in a truly liberal Catholic tradition through real intellectual and personal formation. We are trying to live out the principles of the *Idea of a University*. There, Newman says, students 'will be the gainers by living among those and under those who represent the whole circle'.[13] The aim of our program is to help students escape the fracturing and segmentation of contemporary education; to help them to become whole persons, with integrated intellectual lives, rather than to become earners with a specialization, with knowledge but no wisdom, with skills but no freedom. At a university, a student

> apprehends the great outlines of knowledge, the principles on which it rests, the scale of its parts, its lights and its shades, its great points and its little, as he otherwise cannot apprehend them. Hence it is that his education is called 'Liberal'. A habit of mind is formed which lasts through life, of which the attributes are, freedom, equitableness, calmness, moderation, and wisdom; or what in a former Discourse I have ventured to call a philosophical habit.[14]

There is a limit to what such an education can do, as Newman acknowledged:

---

[13]   *Idea*, p. 101.

[14]   *Idea*, pp. 101–2. For more about the 'philosophical habit', see the article by Andrew Meszaros on pp. 245–264.

> Knowledge is one thing, virtue is another; good sense is not conscience, refinement is not humility, nor is largeness and justness of view, faith. Philosophy, however enlightened, however profound, gives no command over the passions, no influential motives, no vivifying principles. Liberal Education makes not the Christian, not the Catholic, but the gentleman. It is well to be a gentlemen, it is well to have a cultivated intellect, a delicate taste, a candid, equitable, dispassionate mind, a noble and courteous bearing in the conduct of life;—these are the connatural qualities of a large knowledge; they are the objects of a University; I am advocating, I shall illustrate and insist upon them; but still, I repeat, they are no guarantee for sanctity or even for conscientiousness [...][15]

Why then, if they are no guarantee for sanctity, are they the object of a program encouraged and supported by the Church. The answer is because our aim, the aim of all Christians, is freedom. All true freedom resides in Christ and points to Christ. And setting minds free, through the power of an authentically liberal education, orients them toward Christ. We are cultivating hearts, and at the same time, we are teaching our students how to form friendships—real friendships—and teaching them how to live examined lives, contemplated lives, considered lives. We are giving them, at the Newman Institute for Catholic Thought and Culture, the foundation and freedom to make sense of what they are experiencing in the lecture hall, in sacred worship, and at Holy Mass. We are helping them to become more human, because experiencing and knowing their humanity will help them to become more Christian—or so we hope. In truth, we are only sowing seeds, and entrusting them to Divine Providence.

But Divine Providence brought me to Christ, to his Church, to the priesthood, and to a deep friendship with Fr Ian Ker, from whom I offer today my gratitude, prayers and enduring friendship. In God's Providence, Fr Ker has been a true friend, an

---

[15] *Idea*, pp. 120–1.

instrumental part of my vocation—and of more vocations than he might realize.

And to honor Fr Ker, the best lesson I can offer is the one that his friendship has taught me so well: Divine Providence has carried you through all of the twists and turns of life along which the Lord has led you. Divine Providence has allowed you to serve the Lord and His purposes, whether or not you know them in this life. We can trust in that Providence and entrust our work to it, just as my friend Fr Ian Ker has done—and just as St John Henry Newman, our patron and intercessor, did.

'Persons influence us, voices melt us, looks subdue us, deeds inflame us',[16] Newman wrote. Fr Ian Ker has certainly influenced me, and for that I am grateful. *Cor ad cor loquitur.*

---

[16]   *Discussions*, p. 293.

PART TWO

A Trinity of Cardinals

JOHN HENRY NEWMAN: AN ECUMENICAL CONVERSION[1]

CARDINAL GERHARD MÜLLER

JOHN HENRY NEWMAN—rightly regarded as one of the most important Christian thinkers of the modern era—was born on 21 February 1801 in the City of London. The span of his life encompasses nearly the entire nineteenth century. The Anglican divine and illustrious leader of the Oxford Movement was admitted into full communion with the Catholic Church in 1845 and died on 11 August 1890 as a cardinal in the Birmingham Oratory, his primary place of work since 1849.

Newman's historical, theological, and spiritual works are equally remarkable. Most of his homilies appear in German editions, many of which boast a profound interpretation of Christianity's central mysteries. His celebrity grew with his *Essay in Aid of a Grammar of Assent*, which answered the question of how we can—with all the finitude of human knowing—arrive at certainty of faith's assent to the historical revelation of God.

His work on the development of dogma is, we can say, nothing short of genius. In it Newman developed principles for the historical continuity and identity of Revelation under the conditions of finite, human knowing within the believing Church

---

[1] This article first appeared as 'John Henry Newman – eine ökumenische Konversion' in *Die Tagespost* in 2000 and was later published in *Mit der Kirche denken. Bausteine und Skizzen zu einer Ekklesiologie der Gegenwart* (Würzburg: J. W. Naumann, 2001), pp. 231–40. It was originally translated into English by Justin Shaun Coyle, who teaches theology and philosophy at Boston College, and appeared in *Public Discourse* (12 October 2019). The translation has been revised stylistically for publication in this volume.

founded by Christ and preserved in, and attended ever more deeply into, truth by the Holy Spirit. Newman's 1852 lectures on the nature of the university, delivered on the occasion of the founding of the Catholic University in Dublin, should be of the highest relevance for contemporary debates on the nature and goal of the university, education, and science, and the legitimacy of revelation-based theology in schools and universities.

Newman's *Apologia pro Vita Sua* is crucial for his spiritual biography. In it he renders the history of his religious convictions and defends himself against accusations that the motives behind his conversion were disingenuous. With this literary masterpiece penned in glittering English (which we could place alongside Augustine's *Confessions* and Blaise Pascal's *Pensées*), Newman restored honor to Catholic clergy in Protestant England, which had been characterized by anti-Catholic polemics since the Reformation. Encouraged by Enlightenment polemics from eighteenth-century France, many people remained firmly convinced that Catholic priests and religious were nothing but evil hypocrites and pitiless agents of the antichrist seated on the Roman pontiff's chair, for whom every means of slaking their hunger for power was justified. Many lived and cultivated the prejudices of the anti-scientific, reactionary Catholic Church and saw in Roman universalism the nemesis of the ideal of the nation state with its imperial, colonial goals. In this context one could suffer the Church only as a national English Church; and the Anglican bishops put themselves at the service of a diluted, national Christianity.

The Plurality of Christian Communities and the Visible Unity of the Catholic Church

By his own account Newman, a respected scholar and celebrated university preacher in Oxford, discovered the biblical and historical instability of the Protestant 'dogma' of the pope as antichrist. After this Newman could no longer shy away from the insight that it was the Catholic Church of the Roman pope (so disdained in England)—and not the Anglican national Church, which had existed since the sixteenth century—which stood in real continuity with the Church of the apostles. With his extraordinary knowledge of the Bible and of the Church fathers he could not escape the conclusion that the Catholic Church is located in full continuity of doctrine and church polity with the Church of the apostles, and that Protestant charges of corrupting the apostolic faith or of supplementing it with unbiblical elements of doctrine rather fall back on themselves. In his *Apologia* Newman wrote: 'And as far as I know myself, my one paramount reason for contemplating a change is my deep, unvarying conviction that our Church is in schism, and that my salvation depends on my joining the Church of Rome.'[2]

This same understanding of the Church as confession of faith finds expression in the Second Vatican Council. The declaration *Dominus Iesus*, published by the Congregation for the Doctrine of the Faith on 6 August 2000, says the same, though it is mostly misinterpreted because largely—by some intentionally—unread. For good reason Newman rejected the theory that the Anglican Church charts a middle way between Catholicism and Protestantism; he also rejected that we could pragmatically settle for the splintering of Christendom with the notion that there are several branches on the Church's one tree. Yet the plurality of communities that exist today cannot count as a partial realization of Christ's Church; the Church of Christ is indivisible. And indivisibility—which expresses itself visibly in the Church's unity of belief, its sacramental life, and its apostolic constitution—belongs inexorably to the essence of the Church. The goal of the ecumenical movement is not, then, a man-made merger of ecclesial confederations. It is rather the restoration of full communion in faith and of the bishops as successors to the apostles, as it has been realized historically and continuously since the

---

[2]   *Apologia*, p. 229.

beginning in the Church, which 'is governed by the successor of Peter and by the bishops in communion with him'.[3]

Why did Newman oppose an ecumenism based on relativism and skepticism? Why did he not settle for the following formula? 'We all believe in the same God, and so the Church's teaching does not matter. Our knowledge of things is not exact. Religion is a matter of feeling, and so the majority of those who share the same sentiments determine which way the Church goes. For ecumenical unity, a mere sense of community and a sentimental relationship to "Jesus" suffices to render unity according to the tastes of the majority. If you feel united, you too can celebrate a Eucharistic feast together—even if the binding doctrine of the Church or the separated Christian communities teach the opposite and recognize these doctrines as relevant to salvation.'

Newman believes in the reality of God, in the fact of a historical self-revelation in Jesus Christ, and in his current presence in the Church which is, in its essential structural elements and apostolic authority of its shepherds, led by the Spirit of God.

Whoever takes seriously the Incarnation must also take seriously the Church as the work of God and beware any manipulation by ideologically stubborn pressure groups. The visible Church is the concretization of the Word of God's incarnate presence in Jesus Christ. Because Israel bears a salvation history, because the Incarnation happened, because Christ has really given up his life on the cross for the salvation of the world and has really risen again—so there is also the concrete obligation faithfully to obey Revelation, which makes present the confession of faith in the promise of salvation, in the sacraments, and in ecclesial authority of the apostles' successors in the episcopate. It is within the context of these confessions that Newman wants to be understood.

The common view that one Christian confession is like another and that true Christianity unfolds only within the interiority of the heart—beyond creed, dogma, sacrament, and magisterial author-

---

[3]   *Dominus Iesus*, 17.

ity—appears indeed quite plausible to a great number of Christians today. But it is untenable in view of holy scriptures' claims about Revelation and the Church. Because the visible, sacramental Church and the invisible community of the faithful belong together indissolubly, Newman had to pose the question: Which among the visible Christian communities now on offer can rightly lay claim to an identity of confession of faith and of historical continuity? He did not understand his conversion as a change from one Christian confession to another. Nor had he determined to take this step because Catholic piety might have appealed more to him emotionally, say, or because a Catholic culture of a romantic style might have suited him more. Quite the opposite! The outer appearance of the Catholic Church would have disgusted him. Newman took the step because he realized in faith and conscience the complete identity of Christ's Church with the visible Catholic Church. This was no slight on the Anglican Church. His conversion is not one person's cause for grief and another's flush of success. Newman belongs to all Christians! He is one of the most impressive witnesses for the visible unity of the Church, which Jesus himself willed and which thus constitutes an unshakeable benchmark of Christian identity (John 17:22ff).

Newman: Apologist for Christianity as Revealed Religion

Newman lived in the nineteenth century, which posed the basic questions which are also decisive for the twentieth century and which will bleed deeply into the twenty-first. These questions concern the fundamental challenge posed by the philosophy of the Enlightenment.

At stake is Christianity's right to exist and the onus of historical revelation as truth and fact before human reason. In the critique of religion by Feuerbach, Marx, Nietzsche, and Freud, the apparent overcoming of revealed faith by modern science and the massive hostility to the Church of Hitler's and Stalin's totalitarian regimes always raise the question: Does God exist, and is his Word allowed to be the measure for our faith and conscience?

In his famous Biglietto Speech at his elevation to the cardinalate in 1879, Newman signals two possible attitudes toward revelation. He calls one the liberal, skeptical posture of agnosticism and atheism. The other he calls the dogmatic posture, that is, the basic willingness faithfully to obey the Word of God, which is represented in the human word of the Church's confession: 'Liberalism in religion is the doctrine that there is no positive truth in religion, but that one creed is as good as another, and this is the teaching which is gaining substance and force daily. It is inconsistent with any recognition of any religion as *true*. It teaches that all are to be tolerated, for all are matters of opinion. Revealed religion is not a truth, but a sentiment and a taste; not an objective fact, not miraculous; and it is the right of each individual to make it say just what strikes his fancy.'[4] Dogmatic thinking opposes this. It acknowledges the fact of the revealed Word of God spoken to humanity in Jesus Christ. In contrast to a merely emotional sense of an impersonal presence of the divine, the Word of God made flesh is rational and clearly expressible. This proves the Church's confession of faith. In the sacramental act given to the Church by Christ, the Word made flesh is again present.

This comparison of both possible attitudes of modern people toward the self-revelation of God in Jesus Christ is not, of course, a question of the concepts of 'liberal' and 'dogmatic', but rather of the thing identified by them.

Newman did not target political liberalism. Indeed, he recognized the humane views of many of its proponents. After the end of the religious wars in Europe and the devastation wrought by the French Revolution and Napoleon's campaigns of expansion over the world, there remained no other choice than to reorganize society on the principles of religious freedom, tolerance, and equality of all before the law. So if religion was entrusted to the individual's consciousness of truth, it was still far from becoming

---

4   'Biglietto Speech', *Campaign*, p. 513.

a private affair or something arbitrary. On the contrary, the challenge to individuals to seek truth and to face up to their obligatory power had increased enormously since the days when European rulers could still determine the religion of their subjects. To be sure, modern freedom of religion includes more than the right of the individual against the state's claims to power and against pressures to conform to society. Decisive for the full realization of this fundamental right is the communal dimension of the question of truth.

Every religious community must be allowed to determine for itself what are and are not the binding or dogmatic elements of its constitution along with the rational, identifiable conditions of their validity.

At this point the modern conflict between belief and unbelief emerges. In opposition to its own principles, liberalism demands its validity totally and exclusively. Its largesse and alleged capaciousness toward all religious orientations often just amount to a militant indifference to the claims of God's Word. Liberalism, as Newman critiques it, is another form of rationalism:

> Liberalism then is the mistake of subjecting to human judgment those revealed doctrines which are in their nature beyond and independent of it, and of claiming to determine on intrinsic grounds which are in their nature beyond and independent of it, and of claiming to determine on intrinsic grounds the truth and value of propositions which rest for their reception simply on the external authority of the Divine Word.[5]

Liberalism claims the sole validity of metaphysical skepticism, even though under the assumptions of liberalism metaphysically valid and indubitable statements are impossible. Liberalism turns against the free right of religious communities to determine the truth content and horizon of their own metaphysical and epistemological principles. In opposition to liberalism of this sort,

---

[5]   *Apologia*, p. 288.

rational justification of the act and content of faith had become a theme of Newman's life.

Here again Newman is impressively relevant. The declaration *Dominus Iesus* rejected the so-called pluralist theory of religion which relativizes Christ and the Church as irreconcilable with the fundamentals and substance of the Catholic faith. This theory about the equality and similarity of several forms of mediation and several mediators is based on epistemological relativism and skepticism. It assumes that every person can, with the help of his ancestral religion and culture, overcome his selfishness in order to engage his fellow human and to open himself to reality, which is always grander than anything we in our finitude can think or do. This is the salvation communicated to every religiously-minded person irrespective of whether, before the ever-vanishing horizon of reality, he imagines God as a personal God or an impersonal *numinosum*, or whether after death he anticipates a personal resurrection or a biological resuscitation of corpses, in unity with the one-and-all of being or else nothing beyond personal consciousness.

For Newman it was clear that the Christian confession of the universal salvific will of the one God and of the uniqueness of Jesus Christ's revelation (cf. 1 Timothy 2:4ff) does not denigrate pre-Christian religions by absolutizing a tradition unique to the Christian West. Whoever debunks as unproven and indemonstrable the fundamental dogma of relativists, metaphysical skeptics, and agnostics for whom a historical self-revelation of God is impossible will also confess that God is already at work in the human pursuit of truth and in desire of all religions for salvation. Thus in Jesus Christ 'all people are saved and come to the knowledge of the truth' (1 Timothy 2:4).

For Newman, then, Christianity is the religion of the future because God, who once and for all has taken up residence in our world in his Word made flesh, is also the future of humanity:

> Revelation begins where Natural Religion fails. The Reli-
> gion of Nature is a mere inchoation, and needs a

compliment,—it can have but one complement, and that very complement is Christianity.

Natural religion is based upon the sense of sin; it recognizes the disease, but it cannot find, it does but look out for the remedy. That remedy, both for guilt and for moral impotence, is found in the central doctrine of Revelation, the Mediation of Christ. [...] Thus it is that Christianity is the fulfillment of the promise made to Abraham, and of the Mosaic revelations; this is how it has been able from the first to occupy the world and gain a hold on every class of human society to which its preachers reached; this is why the Roman power and the multitude of religions which it embraced could not stand against it; this is the secret of its sustained energy, and its never-flagging martyrdoms; this is how at present it is so mysteriously potent, in spite of the new and fearful adversaries which beset its path. It has with it that gift of staunching and healing the one deep wound of human nature, which avails more for its success than a full encyclopedia of scientific knowledge and a whole library of controversy, and therefore it must last while human nature lasts. It is a living truth which never can grow old.

Some persons speak of it as if it were a thing of history, with only indirect bearings upon modern times; I cannot allow that it is a mere historical religion. Certainly it has its foundations in past and glorious memories, but its power is in the present. It is no dreary matter of antiquarianism; we do not contemplate it in conclusions drawn from dumb documents and dead events, but by faith exercised in ever-living objects, and by the appropriation and use of ever-recurring gifts.

Our communion with it is in the unseen, not in the obsolete. At this very day its rites and ordinances are continually eliciting the active interposition of that Omnipotence in which the Religion long ago began. First and above all is the Holy Mass, in which He who once died for us upon the Cross, brings back and perpetuates, by His literal presence in it, that one and the same sacrifice which cannot be repeated. Next, there is the actual entrance of Himself, soul and body, and divinity, into the soul and body of every worshipper who comes to Him for the gift, a privilege more intimate than if we lived with Him during His long-past sojourn upon earth. And then, moreover, there is His personal abidance in our churches, raising earthly service into a foretaste of heaven. Such is the profession of Christianity, and, I repeat, its very divination of our needs is in itself a proof that it is really the supply of them [...]

The promised Deliverer, the Expectation of the nations, has not done his work by halves. [...] He has created a visible hierarchy and a succession of sacraments, to be channels of His mercies [...] In all these ways He brings Himself before us. [...] as human nature itself is still in life and action as much as ever it was, so He too lives, to our imaginations, by His visible symbols, as if He were on earth, with a practical efficacy which even unbelievers cannot deny, so as to be the corrective of that nature, and its strength day by day,—and that this power of perpetuating His Image [...] is a grand evidence how well He fulfils to this day that Sovereign Mission which, from the first beginning of the world's history, has been in prophecy assigned to Him.[6]

Newman: A Model of Stability

Another parallel to the present is the episode of the Achilli affair, which cast a dark cloud over 1851. A vow-breaking, apostatizing Dominican named Achilli had, much to the delight of his smug and Church-critical audience, broadcast the Church's crimes and transgressions, omitting no stereotype or prejudice. When Newman countered this populist approach with historical facts, he was charged with libel. Though all the accusations proved unjustified, he was found guilty and the judge fined him £100,

---

[6]   *Grammar*, pp. 487–9.

though he had to pay costs, and lectured him about his moral degradation since becoming a Catholic.

Even today there is bad blood and eruptions of hatred within the Church. In some countries like Holland, Switzerland, Austria, and Germany there are factions that assume the worst of bishops and the pope. Often theologians and priests who have lost the faith or failed in celibacy or the evangelical counsels lead and agitate for movements that demand Church reform and yet—consciously or not—sow only division and destruction.

Newman is a model of stability amid hostilities that arise from without. But he is also a model for spiritual resistance to the suspicion and distrust that arise within one's own ranks. Today we call this 'bullying'. For years higher personalities within the Church cast a 'cloud of suspicion' over Newman. Newman did not shrink back like a wounded animal; he knew that Christ's Church is more than group dynamics and their surge of sympathy and antipathy on the surface of the Church. The Church penetrates into the mystery of Christ. The Church as sacrament means being taken up into the sonship of Christ, who as head makes the Church his body, uniting individual believers as a community and imparting to it all the charisms and ministries to fulfill its mission of the world's salvation. And so humanity—all too human—cannot destroy the Church; and we cannot yield to despair.

After all the external and internal difficulties he experienced, and the hostility, resistance, and irritation, Pope Leo XIII elevated Newman to the cardinalate. He honored Newman for his belief rooted deeply in the Church and his willingness to serve with all the admirable talents of his spirit, his humanity, and his formation of the Church's heart. 'I was determined to honor the Church', Leo explained, 'by honoring Newman'.

Newman is undoubtedly an impressive Christian thinker who, with his work and life embroiled in conflicts regarding Christianity's legitimacy in modernity, confidently and cogently points to the future of humanity. And this is nothing other than God in Jesus Christ and in his Church. Yet Newman was not only a brilliant theologian and gifted poet but also a great pray-er; he brought the situation of the Church as he perceived and suffered it before God in prayer. It does not take much explanation to show how relevant these words are:

> O God,
> the time is utterly beset.
> The cause of Christ lies as in agony.
> And yet—never did Christ stride more powerfully through the age,
> never was his advent starker,
> never his nearness more sensible,
> never his duty dearer than now.
> So in these flashes of eternity,
> between storm and storm,
> let us here below pray you:
> O God,
> You can illuminate the darkness,
> You and you alone.[7]

---

[7]   Though this poem borrows lines from Newman, it is not his. It derives rather from Johannes Dierkes, *Gedanken und Gebeteim Christuslicht* (Paderborn: Junfermann, 1935), but soon became misattributed to Newman himself. [Justin Shaun Coyle]

THE SIGNIFICANCE OF ST JOHN HENRY NEWMAN FOR CATHOLIC THEOLOGY[1]

CARDINAL MARC OUELLET

THE LONG-AWAITED AND blessed hour of John Henry Newman's canonization has finally come. The course followed by this convert from Anglicanism represents a rich source of teachings for his British fellow-citizens and indeed for the universal Church. On the occasion of Newman's beatification, his biographer Ian Ker observed that 'my reading and re-reading of his writings over the years has only deepened my conviction that John Henry Newman is to be numbered among the Doctors of the Church'.[2]

This expert's appreciation of the illustrious English clergyman presupposed the future declaration of sainthood by the Catholic Church and a new chapter based on the appropriation of the significance of his life and thought. Without wishing to anticipate the Church's judgment on the value of Newman's testimony and teachings, I would nevertheless like to highlight some of the major areas of his contribution to Catholic theology, and its possible implications for the future of modern theology.

If we want to speak accurately of Newman's ideas we must begin by stressing the importance of his life, described as the journey of a believer who encountered faith in adolescence, a

---

[1]   This paper was written in French by Cardinal Ouellet, who read it in translation at the Newman symposium that took place in the Vatican on 12 October 2019. The translation has been revised stylistically for publication in this volume with the help of Dr Marie Daouda and Rev. Dr Peter Damian Grint.

[2]   *Newman: Biography* (rev. ed. 2009), p. 746.

decisive experience that triggered a process of searching for Truth, with many existential and institutional developments. As surprising as it may seem, I consider Newman's first lesson to reside in his celibacy, in his having consecrated his life to God shortly after his first conversion, abiding in an intimate and personal choice. This choice was an echo of his experience of God as Absolute, while also serving the *mission de recherche* (i.e. quest for the truth) that Providence had bestowed upon him for the benefit of his country and of the universal Church.[3]

With all of this as a precondition for any other theological consideration, I now suggest the possibility of Newman's being made a Doctor of the Church on account of three specific areas that he developed extensively and rigorously, drawing from his theological, literary and historical training. His work is filled with circumstantial writings that punctuate his journey and explain his actions and decisions; they are detailed considerations that give his preaching, letters and treatises a clearly apologetic character, but also a pastoral dimension which is novel when compared to his contemporaries. Newman writes to give a rational account of his faith, to explain his faith decisions, but above all to remain faithful to the tribunal of his conscience in God's presence. God

---

[3] See *Apologia*, p. 8: 'I am obliged to mention, though I do it with great reluctance another deep imagination, which at this time, the autumn of 1816, took possession of me [...], viz. that it was the will of God that I should lead a single life. This anticipation [...] was more or less connected, in my mind, with the notion that my calling in life would require such a sacrifice as celibacy involved; as, for instance, missionary work among the heathen, to which I had a great drawing for some years. It also strengthened my feeling of separation from the visible world, of which I have spoken above.' See also Jean Honoré, *Itinéraire spirituel de Newman* (Paris: du Seuil, 1963), pp. 39–40: 'The call to celibacy was not born of an anxious or timid conscience [...]. But it derives from a much broader and *soothing* feeling: that of a vocation that is both a renunciation and a commitment. [...] Sacrifice seems to him to be the pledge of goods that are better and more durable than those of the sensitive world; moreover, it seems to announce the exact path for a promising destiny. Thus the call to celibacy coincides with the premonition of a mission which is burgeoning in Newman.'

never allows him to forget his primordial relationship with Him, assumed once and for all and nurtured through a vital and prayerful dialogue: 'the inward conversion of which I was conscious [...] had some influence on my opinions [...] in making me rest in the thought of two and two only supreme and luminously self-evident beings, myself and my Creator'.[4]

We must ask how Newman confronts the Catholic theology of his time—and of all eras—if we want to consider seriously the possibility of his candidacy as a Doctor of the Church. It seems to me that this English master ranks among such teachers of the Faith as Athanasius and Augustine, whose lives were confessions of faith at the cost of great sacrifice, and who also provided decisive insights into either the content or the act of faith. Now Newman excels in exploring both *fides quae* and *fides qua*, but his most original and innovative contribution consists above all in his describing faith as a personal encounter, an emotional but also a rational adherence which involves a unique certainty, and also a responsibility that cannot be delegated and that imposes a conscious commitment to vital and sometimes dramatic decisions: 'When we pray, we pray, not to an assemblage of notions, or to a creed, but to One Individual Being; and when we speak of Him we speak of a Person, not of a Law or a Manifestation'.[5] The position of nineteenth-century Catholic theology tended to emphasize the noetic dimension of faith at the expense of an emotional and personal dimension, often reducing faith to an intellectual acceptance of abstract proposals. Argumentation had to contend with rationalism, and as a consequence tended to impoverish the vital and nourishing dimension of faith that precedes and sustains all knowledge, and which cannot be reduced to clear and distinct ideas.[6]

---

[4]   *Apologia*, p. 4.

[5]   'The Theory of Developments in Religious Doctrine', *University Sermons*, p. 330.

[6]   See *Grammar*, p. 425: 'If I am asked to use Paley's argument for my own conversion, I say plainly I do not want to be converted by a smart

This tendency has not completely disappeared even today, when the emphasis on knowledge of faith often overrides the relational dimension of faith. You have only to look at the *Catechism of the Catholic Church* to see this.[7] As for academic theology, it is still far from being a Trinitarian deepening of the faith that would highlight the priority of the person over conceptual elements, which are certainly valid and indispensable, but secondary to the personal adherence to the Three Persons, rooted in the Holy Spirit.[8] Newman broadens the understanding of the experience of faith by illustrating all the personal aspects, from the strong but indefinable impression of dogma in the soul,[9] to the awakening of intelligence and imagination, to the mobilization of the powers of will and affections that shape a unique encounter, relationship and communion:

---

syllogism; if I am asked to convert others by it, I say plainly I do not care to overcome their reason without touching their hearts. I wish to deal, not with controversialists, but with inquirers'.

[7]   See the *Catechism of the Catholic Church*, n. 150, where it is stated that 'Faith is first of all a personal adherence of man to God. At the same time, and inseparably, it is a *free assent to the whole truth that God has revealed.*' The reference to the 'personal' appears only once, whereas all developments in chapter 3 concern the 'knowledge of faith' and the interplay of mental faculties in the act of faith, but there is almost nothing on a relational dimension.

[8]   The personal relationship with the Divine Persons is rooted in the structure of Christian initiation which establishes the grace of divine sonship in baptism, the gift of the Holy Spirit in confirmation and the offering of the self to the Father with Christ in the celebration of the Eucharist. This Trinitarian sequence culminating in Eucharistic communion is often absent or reversed in catechesis, which weakens the sense of belonging to the liturgical assembly.

[9]   See *Apologia*, p. 49: 'I have changed in many things: in this I have not. From the age of fifteen, dogma has been the fundamental principle of my religion: I know no other religion; I cannot enter into the idea of any other sort of religion; religion, as a mere sentiment, is to me a dream and a mockery. As well can there be filial love without the fact of a father, as devotion without the fact of a Supreme Being. What I held in 1816, I held in 1833, and I hold in 1864. Please God, I shall hold it to the end'.

The true spirit of faith leads a man to look off from self to God, to think nothing of his own wishes, his present clothes, his importance or dignity, his rights, his opinions, but to say, 'I put myself into Thy hands, O Lord; make Thou me what Thou wilt; I forget myself; I divorce myself from myself; I am dead to myself; I will follow Thee.'[10]

In all the many aspects barely mentioned here, Newman introduces a host of insights and reflections that highlight the primordially personal quality of faith as assent, an eminently subjective and a totalizing synthetic act leading to the strongest conviction, even if it escapes the criteria of the exact sciences or the humanities.[11] In this regard, he builds up a severe criticism of scientism, and he develops great technical concepts set at the border of the psychological and the spiritual, seizing the individual man in his personal deliberations, dissecting the meanderings of his dispositions, motivations and conditionings that belong to life and to actual living in faith.[12]

---

[10] See 'The Testimony of Conscience' in *Parochial and Plain* v, p. 242; J. Honoré, 'Le théologien de la foi', *La pensée de John Henry Newman. Une introduction* (Genève: Ad Solem, 2010), pp. 93–110.

[11] See 'Love the Safeguard of Faith Against Superstition', *University Sermons*, p. 239: 'Right Faith is the faith of a right mind. Faith is an intellectual act; right Faith is an intellectual act, done in a certain moral disposition. Faith is an act of Reason, viz. a reasoning upon presumptions; right Faith is a reasoning upon holy, devout and enlightened presumptions.'

[12] These developments appear in his *Parochial and Plain Sermons*, as well as in his *Oxford University Sermons*, and are systematically quoted in his great work: *Grammar of Assent*. For example, see 'Faith and Reason, Contrasted as Habits of Mind', *University Sermons*, pp. 198–9: 'For is not this the error, the common and fatal error, of the world, to think itself a judge of Religious Truth without a preparation of heart? "I am the good Shepherd, and know My sheep, and am known of Mine." "He goeth before them, and the sheep follow Him, for they know His voice." "The pure in heart shall see God." "To the meek mysteries are revealed." "He that is spiritual judgeth all things." "The darkness comprehendeth it not." Gross eyes see not; heavy ears hear not. But in the schools of the world the ways toward Truth are considered high roads open to all men, however disposed, at all times. Truth is to be approached without homage. Every

Having established the personal and existential dimension of the act of faith and its dynamism of intellect and will, Newman extends his analysis beyond the individual level into the social domain, where he seeks to rationally account for the existence of ordinary believers, especially those who have no theological knowledge and cannot explain their own beliefs, but who are nevertheless animated by a reasonable conviction that guides their lives.[13] This is an entire field that Newman, the man who was seen by his contemporaries as the Apologist of his own life, approaches as a broader rational exercise in order to counter the progressive invasion of scientism, liberalism and fideism.[14] Aware of the progressive decline of belief caused by a scientific mentality that relegates faith to the realm of the irrational or the private,[15]

---

one is considered on a level with his neighbour; or rather the powers of the intellect, acuteness, sagacity, subtlety, and depth, are thought the guides into Truth. Men consider that they have as full a right to discuss religious subjects, as if they were themselves religious. They will enter upon the most sacred points of Faith at the moment, at their pleasure,—if it so happen, in a careless frame of mind, in their hours of recreation, over the wine cup'.

[13]   See 'The Theory of Developments in Religious Doctrine', *University Sermons*, pp. 320–1: 'Now, here I observe, first of all, that, naturally as the inward idea of divine truth, such as has been described, passes into explicit form by the activity of our reflective powers, still such an actual delineation is not essential to its genuineness and perfection. A peasant may have such a true impression, yet be unable to give any intelligible account of it, as will easily be understood.'

[14]   'Liberty of thought is in itself a good; but it gives an opening to false liberty. Now by Liberalism I mean false liberty of thought, or the exercise of thought upon matters, in which, from the constitution of the human mind, thought cannot be brought to any successful issue, and therefore is out of place. Among such matters are first principles of whatever kind; and of these the most sacred and momentous are especially to be reckoned the truths of Revelation. Liberalism then is the mistake of subjecting to human judgment those revealed doctrines which are in their nature beyond and independent of it, and of claiming to determine on intrinsic grounds the truth and value of propositions which rest for their reception simply on the external authority of the Divine Word.' (*Apologia*, p. 493)

[15]   'For thirty, forty, fifty years I have resisted to the best of my powers the

Newman leads a battle of great epistemological and anthropological significance, since it is man himself who is threatened and diminished by the practical atheism resulting from scientism.

In addition to exploring the laws of the existential logic of faith and to defend its rationality, Newman spent a long time studying the development of Christian doctrine, which is the third area meriting consideration for his becoming a Doctor of the Church. From his acquaintance with the Fathers of the Church—especially Athanasius—he discovered that the faith of the Church, in order to keep its integrity, must adapt its language to cultural challenges and the dangers of heresy. It must therefore discern doctrines compatible with the deposit of faith, perhaps adopting a new language, not necessarily scriptural, while remaining faithful to what has been established once and for all by the determining of the canon of the New Testament. Thus, although the deposit does not change, the Church's knowledge of it progresses, deepens and is expressed in a new way, always faithful to the original idea.[16] In his *Essay on the Development of Christian*

---

spirit of liberalism in religion. [...] It is an error overspreading, as a snare, the whole earth. [...] Liberalism in religion is the doctrine that there is no positive truth in religion, but that one creed is as good as another, and this is the teaching which is gaining substance and force daily. It is inconsistent with any recognition of any religion, as true. It teaches that all are to be tolerated, for all are matters of opinion. Revealed religion is not a truth, but a sentiment and a taste; not an objective fact, not miraculous; and it is the right of each individual to make it say just what strikes his fancy. [...] Since, then, religion is so personal a peculiarity and so private a possession, we must of necessity ignore it in the intercourse of man with man. If a man puts on a new religion every morning, what is that to you? [...] Religion is in no sense the bond of society.' ('Biglietto Speech', *Campaign*, pp. 513–14)

16   'The mind which is habituated to the thought of God, of Christ, of the Holy Spirit, naturally turns [...] with a devout curiosity to the contemplation of the Object of its adoration, and begins to form statements concerning Him before it knows whither, or how far, it will be carried. One proposition necessarily leads to another, and a second to a third; then some limitation is required; and the combination of these opposites occasions some fresh evolutions from the original idea, which indeed can

Doctrine, Newman passionately analyses the criteria and conditions for ensuring a doctrinal fidelity not only compatible but also
in harmony with the new dogmas of the Roman Church, since
they express the Church's progressive knowledge of the deposit
of the faith. This observation shook Newman to the core, causing
his criticism of the Church of Rome—formerly accused of
contaminating the deposit with unjustifiable additions—to fall.[17]

In this study of doctrinal development, Newman laid the
foundations for a theology of Tradition according to a broader
and more inclusive vital logic, which reveals the richness of his
ecclesiology. While post-Tridentine theology identifies the
Church with its hierarchy, Newman—in accordance with St
Paul—perceives the Church as the Body of Christ of which we
are members:[18]

> Thus the heart of every Christian ought to represent in
> miniature the Catholic Church, since one Spirit makes
> both the whole Church and every member of it to be His
> Temple.[19]

The dominant conception of Tradition was limited at the time
to the faithful transmission of doctrines by the Magisterium,

---

    never be said to be entirely exhausted' ('The Theory of Developments in
    Religious Doctrine', *University Sermons,* p. 329)

[17]   See *Apologia,* chapters 3 & 4.

[18]   'He [Christ] formed His Apostles into a visible society; but when He came
    again in the person of His Spirit, He made them all in a real sense one, not
    in name only. [...] their separate persons were taken into a mysterious
    union with things unseen, were grafted upon and assimilated to the
    spiritual body of Christ, which is One, even by the Holy Ghost, in whom
    Christ has come again to us. Thus Christ came, not to make us one, but
    to die for us: the Spirit came to make us one in Him who had died and was
    alive, that is, to form the Church. [...] Such is the Christian Church, a
    living body, and *one*; not a mere framework artificially arranged to look
    like one. Its being alive is what makes it one [...] the *Living* Spirit of God
    came down upon it at Pentecost, and made it *one*, by giving it *life*.' ('The
    Communion of Saints', *Parochial and Plain* iv, pp. 169–71)

[19]   'Connexion Between Personal and Public Improvement', *Subjects,* p. 132.

while exaggerating the autonomy of this regulatory body with regard to Holy Scripture. Newman, on the other hand, always takes his starting point in Scripture, which he interprets in an ecclesial way in the spirit of the Fathers, and this leads him to become aware of the problem posed by the principle of individual interpretation, and thus the inconsistency of Protestantism. Gradually, as his discoveries challenged his intellectual assumptions, his search for truth, led by a conscience free of prejudice, brought him to identify the place that guarantees the integrity of the deposit of faith, the authentic way of interpreting it, as well as the legitimacy and necessity of doctrinal developments. This was enough to convince a believer of this caliber, possessed of an exceptional intelligence and governed by an upright conscience, that he should ask to join the Catholic Church. But such a perilous leap was not the result of a syllogism, for this English master had recognized that the Church is essentially not a magisterial authority, but a living body walking in history, the Body of Christ animated by the Holy Spirit—an ecclesiological conviction that anticipated by at least a century the ecclesiology of the Second Vatican Council.[20]

What does Newman's contribution mean today for the future of Catholic theology at the *existential* level of faith, at the *historical* level of doctrinal development, and at the *mystical* level of ecclesiology?

This great witness of the Christian faith says to Catholic theology that, first of all, faith must never be taken for granted and cannot be reduced to formulas. Since it is part of a living and changing relationship in the continuity of a person, it lives as a growing organism within an ecclesial community and a living tradition. The definite adherence that faith requires is total, and a source of peace as well, because it moves beyond the 'notional'

---

[20] See I. Ker, 'John Henry Newman on Vatican II', *Maestri perché testimoni. Pensare il futuro con John Henry Newman e Edith Stein*, ed. Patrizia Manganaro & Michele Marchetto, Acts of the International Conference (Rome: Lateran University Press, 2017), pp. 83–111.

adherence to truths towards the 'real' acceptance of God by the whole person, even when questions and perplexities remain. However, 'ten thousand difficulties do not make one doubt',[21] and theology must help to uncover the rationality of faith, while steering it away from the control of scientific reason that only admits its own canons and criteria. The appropriation of Newman's testimony has only just begun, and it must enter a new phase of systematic study, integration and universal moving towards a broader theological dialogue with the whole of Christianity.

Newman did not classify himself as a 'theologian',[22] especially according to the arid encyclopedic model of his time, but he was more of a theologian than all his contemporaries were, because he thought with God and through his own personal being, as the witness of a living communion able to re-think from scratch vital issues that can never be reduced to formulas. He taught—and he teaches more than ever before—by the example of his life, because

---

[21]   *Apologia*, p. 239.

[22]   'Newman always denied he was a "theologian". Why this refusal? Three explanations can be advanced: firstly, he probably meant that he had never received a formal theological training, which is perfectly correct. The Universities of Oxford and Cambridge at the time were the main training centres for the Anglican clergy. And the curriculum to become a pastor or minister of this Church consisted mainly in the study of classical literature, at times of mathematics, and of how to become a gentleman. In addition, there were some classes on the Bible and—perhaps—some optional theology classes! [...] Secondly, his refusal to be considered as a "theologian" was also, undoubtedly, a self-defence strategy for Newman. He often suffered because of his theological ideas, notably at the time of the publication of the *Essay on Development* in 1845 and especially in 1859 with the *Rambler* affair. His refusal to be considered a theologian was therefore a way of saying: leave me alone! Finally—and this is the most important point here—his refusal of the word theologian bears almost certainly a third meaning. Catholic Newman meant that he was not a "theologian" in the same way as were the theologians of his time, whose theology was purely conceptual or—in Newmanian terms—purely "notional": it was indeed divorced from history, divorced from the study of the Scriptures, and also divorced from spiritual life.' (Keith Beaumont, 'Newman, maître spirituel dans la tradition de l'Église', *Études Newmaniennes* 33 (2017), pp. 11–14)

true masters are essentially witnesses,[23] as St Paul VI said and repeated so well.

It pains me to say nothing about his anthropology, so existential in quality; about his vision of the laity and charisms, which here again anticipated Vatican II; about his ideas on human and Christian education; about his Marian spirituality or about his preaching—not to mention his trials, many of which took place before his conversion, but which were even greater as a Catholic, to the extent that some have talked of the 'martyrdom of Newman'.[24]

But if John Henry Newman's canonization brings us an ineffable joy, filling us with gratitude towards God, it would be totally anachronistic to fall into any kind of triumphalism. The depth of this man of God, and the place he now occupies in the Catholic Church, make us aware of the void his absence would have left if he had not lived—and, consequently, of the theological need for a new ecumenical impetus towards reconciliation and the reconstitution of dislocated elements of Catholic unity. This lack of unity affects the communion of individuals and churches, but it points also to a lack of integration of the doctrinal and spiritual riches that adorn the sister Churches and ecclesial communities still separated from Rome. Newman's contribution, which offers the typical qualities of English culture and the Anglican tradition, can help us assess what was lost due to centuries of separation, polemics and narrowing perspectives, in an attempt to defend confessional identities.

And so the time has come to encourage and multiply initiatives for dialogue and reconciliation in order to accomplish full unity among Christians, despite the difficulties along the way. It is not a question of using Newman's figure to depict the return to the fold. Rather, his life and his theology challenge us to examine carefully the internal difficulties of reconciliation and to take a greater interest in other Christians, in order to move together towards a more perfect attainment of the *Catholica*. This requires

---

23   See *Maestri perché testimoni*, ed. P. Manganaro & M. Marchetto.
24   Denys Gorce, *Le martyre de Newman* (Paris: Alsatia, 1961).

a conversion from all confessions—starting with the Church of Rome—which must be open to possible transformations to clear the path towards the unity so desired by the Lord. On the theological level, what benefit would we not draw from intensifying our exchanges with Slavic, Indian and African traditions, as well as from all the nuances offered by the bilateral dialogues that have been established since the Second Vatican Council? It is enough to mention just a few names among many others (Wladimir Soloviev, Pawel Florenski, Alexander Schmemann, Jean Zizioulas, Karl Barth, Dietrich Bonhoeffer) to realize that Catholic theology needs to open up, with the help of Newman and his vision of doctrinal development, to a pneumatological and Trinitarian enrichment.

The Catholic Church cannot celebrate Newman's canonization without discerning in the event a 'sign of the times' for theology, the *kairos* of his testimony to the Truth, which requires a theological, and even a philosophical, conversion in order to reinvigorate the dialogue between faith and culture. St Paul VI stressed with regret that the divorce between faith and culture marks one of the tragedies of our time, yet we have become indifferent to this divorce. And we note the collapse of the institution of the family, the crisis of education, the fact that the young are being formed or de-formed online by webmasters who transmit superficial emotions and pleasures. The heritage of modern theology has achieved a separation of faith and reason in a way that challenges both faith and reason. Neither of them has yet really recovered from their divorce because their relationship has been reversed: reason has supplanted faith in culture, and faith has become defensive, resorting to fideism or getting bogged down in modernism. Newman was accused of both by his contemporaries, who lacked the conceptual tools to fully appreciate the extent and the value of his position of equilibrium.

The concept of equilibrium, constantly built and maintained, was very much alive among the great medieval Doctors, especially St Thomas, because he rooted the strong philosophical component of his work in Faith, in order to reflect the truths of the Faith. The emancipation of modern reason and its claim to supplant Faith with a universal, consensual, and binding rationality has failed. The appalling manifestations of modern atheism in the tragedies of the twentieth century are there as evidence. Faith needs to save the concrete historical sense of the person and of societies, which cannot survive without hope and love. Newman is a 'prophet of equilibrium', an equilibrium that needs to be found and perfected, a theory he developed from his approach of intellectual Faith. He is therefore in a position to enlighten our contemporaries on the complex—but necessary and vital—relationship between faith, which envelops reason and delimits its field of competence, and reason, which can neither claim to explain everything nor to put away theology in the lumber-room of the irrational. The balance of these relationships in Newman's work is comparable to the intellectual position of St Augustine and St Thomas Aquinas, a position that has unfortunately been lost with scholastic decadence, Lutheran reform and the epistemological shift into anthropocentric and anti-metaphysical modernity. From a philosophical and theological perspective, Newman built a bridge towards the great witnesses of the Patristic and medieval traditions. He thus effectively prepared the ground for the Second Vatican Council and the new arising equilibrium, in conjunction with the renewal of the relationship between nature and grace, along the lines of Henri de Lubac and Hans Urs von Balthasar.[25]

Catholic theology has not yet taken full measure of the conciliar Pentecost, and has not sufficiently renewed its method in the light of the emergence of new charisms, especially with regards to the female half of the human race. These charisms come to the aid of theology by infusing the Holy Spirit, which lends an increased spiritual note to the theological processes, in

---

[25]   See Olivier de Berranger, *Par amour de l'invisible. Itinéraires croisés de John Henry Newman et Henri de Lubac* (Geneva: Ad Solem, 2010), especially 'Newman théologien', pp. 77–85; 'Conscience et dogme chrétien', pp. 133–43.

harmony with an interpretation of Sacred Scripture inspired by
Dei Verbum, and which cannot be reduced to the methods of
historical-critical exegesis. With Newman, theological reason
emanates clearly from the Word of God and provides adequate
rational tools to appreciate scientific truths, while integrating
them according to their epistemological level into the horizon of
faith—a horizon that is broader but cannot be the object of
scientific examination.

Newman gave an important place to theology in the life of the
Church. Indeed, theology is part of the prophetic ministry as the
understanding of the faith that nourishes contemplation, renews
preaching, and provides the cultural tools for a positive, construc-
tive and above all evangelizing dialogue with the world. Newman
himself was a pioneer of an existential and historical theology
with a strong pastoral dimension; he was no less a 'prophet of
ecumenism'[26] before the word was ever used, both because of his
passionate search for truth and because of the dialogue he kept
up with his contemporaries. It was a dialogue that was apologetic
in style and substance without being rationalistic, because he
based it on a personal and meditated adherence to the truth of
God, and to all that implies for an individual who is faithful to his
conscience.

---

[26]   'In the perspective of the nineteenth century, the work of Newman stands
out as a first example of ecumenical theology. Not that he tried to establish
the conditions and paths leading to the reconciliation of the Churches; but
rather because he lays the ground for a reflection on man and God based
on Revelation, in which all emanating confessions can recognize each other
and meet.' (J. Honoré, *La pensée de John Henry Newman*, p. 152)

THE SUFFERING CHURCH IN A SUFFERING WORLD[1]

CARDINAL GEORGE PELL

I N 1868, MATTHEW Arnold wrote the beautiful poem 'Dover Beach' dedicated to two themes, the first of which is the decline of faith.

The Sea of Faith
Was once, too, at the full and round earth's shore
Lay like the folds of a bright girdle furled.
But now I only hear
Its melancholy, long, withdrawing roar,
Retreating, to the breath
Of the night-wind, down the vast edges drear
And naked shingles of the world.
And then he turns, with prophetic insight, to the consequences of this departure:
for the world, which seems
To lie before us like a land of dreams,
So various, so beautiful, so new,
Hath really neither joy, nor love, nor light,
Nor certitude, nor peace, nor help for pain;
And we are here as on a darkling plain
Swept with confused alarms of struggle and flight,
Where ignorant armies clash by night.[2]

What Might a Catholic Say about each of these Themes?

The world has changed mightily since 1868. The British and French Empires are gone, the United States is the only super-

---

[1]   This paper was read at the annual St Thomas More Lecture in Oxford on 13 November 2021. See more details, see p. xi.

[2]   *New Poems* (London: Macmillan & Co., 1867), pp. 113–14.

power, to be joined by a resurgent and aggressive Middle Kingdom, the People's Republic of China. The two major forces hostile to Christianity, and faith of any sort, Communism and Nazism have both been defeated in Europe and the former Soviet world. Living standards, health and education, travel, longevity, and literacy have improved dramatically. We have nuclear bombs and nuclear power. The centre of the world is now found in the Pacific Ocean, not the Atlantic. How has faith coped?

Before describing and analyzing some aspects of faith, speaking as a Catholic leader, I would like to stake my claim, set out our basic position in this ancient, now secular, university, founded from even older monasteries, often by bishops and Catholic princes. We Catholics are here to stay: in England, in my country of Australia, and on every continent. Popes come and go, with different gifts and strengths, but the papacy is still in Rome, the ancient capital of empire, home of the successor of Peter and bishop of that eternal city. The roar that you hear is not the melancholy sound of a once mighty kingdom departing into oblivion. It is the roar of the Lion of Judah, embattled in many parts, humiliated and often reduced in the Western world, but absolutely devoted to its precious tradition, received from Christ and the apostles, and deeply convinced of the lifegiving power of this inheritance in even the most poisonous environments. The gospel Protestants, the Evangelicals, will be with us in these mighty battles. We are here to stay and to struggle. We are not going away.

As a churchman, I have sometimes wondered how appropriate it is to use war stories for gospel purposes because Jesus, unlike Mahomet, was not a warrior and soldier. But I have continued to do so, once in a while.

I was born during the Second World War on the other side of the world and grew up with those stories of heroism and suffering. A favourite story I have used a few times with university students is an incident from the military career of Field Marshall Bernard Montgomery, the United Kingdom's finest solider from the

Second World War, a great man but an unusual personality by any standards. He spent part of his childhood in Tasmania, Australia and I think it did him good. In 1942 the Allies, including some Australian troops, had been pushed eastward across the top of North Africa by Rommel in a succession of defeats. When Montgomery was appointed, he discovered that plans had been drawn up to retreat further south towards the source of the Nile. After a short interval, he called together his headquarters staff, burnt publicly all the plans for withdrawal and announced that they would take their stand where they were and fight there, when they were prepared and ready.

I think my listeners understood the general point I was making, but just to avoid misunderstanding, I want to make clear that our situation will be worsened, numerically as well as religiously, if we abandon our unseemly Christian claims to the importance of worship, prayer, and forgiveness; to the healing power of redemptive suffering; to the stark life-giving truths of Christian teaching on abortion and euthanasia; on sexuality, on monogamous, heterosexual marriage, on heteronormativity, on the importance of children. Those who argue for this often do not appreciate how Christian claims to the importance of serving the poor and standing with the marginalised are also unseemly and can also be abandoned in an attempt to make ourselves more pleasing. On many occasions, I have urged believers to reject all claims to the primacy of conscience (only truth has primacy because while the right of each individual's conscience is important, even sacred, they are often in conflict) and to avoid the excess of inculturation, where, as in some parts of Japan today, this doctrine has been used to prohibit the preaching of the Gospel as something foreign and to be avoided. We stand and struggle under the rule of faith. I will return to this theme, to the elements of Godliness today, later in this paper.

My second initial point is to spell out some basic perspectives on modernity. I believe those of us in the Anglosphere must acknowledge a new development in Catholic history because most of the best commentators on faith and modern life are now writing in English. One might rightly claim that this simply continues the tradition established by our own St John Henry Newman, continued by Chesterton and Belloc, C. S. Lewis and the Oxford chaplain Monsignor Ronald Knox. Tolkien's marvellous contribution stands in parallel to this, but today, in the English-speaking world, we are blessed with writers whose contributions are essential to identifying where the Catholic community is in the marshes and whirlpools of our often frantic prosperity. The Anglophone ascendency is also explained by the fact that the theological giants from continental Europe at the time of the Second Vatican Council, such as Congar, Rahner, von Balthasaar, de Lubac, Danielou and Schillebeeckx, are no longer with us and have not been replaced.

We have George Weigel from the United States, Fr Raymond de Souza from Canada, Ross Douthat at the *New York Times*, Rod Dreher with his 'Benedict option', and perhaps most perceptively of them all, Mary Eberstadt, also from the United States. This short paper is indebted to her teaching. I recommend particularly her marvellously titled book *Adam and Eve after the Pill: Paradoxes of the Sexual Revolution* (2012), which sets out to explain how the invention of the contraceptive pill has produced a revolution in daily life with consequences as important as those which followed the Marxist-Leninist triumph in the Russian Revolution in 1917. This is a large and controversial claim which outlines the challenges we confront.

I wish to recommend an address Eberstadt gave to the Society of Catholic Social Scientists on 18 September this year, entitled 'The Cross amid the Crisis', and I would like to begin by highlighting an insight she used from an interview Evelyn Waugh gave to a newspaper in 1930, giving reasons for his conversion to Catholicism. He said, 'in the present phase of European history, the essential issue is no longer between Catholicism, on one side, and Protestantism, on the other, but between Christianity and chaos'.[3]

---

[3]   'Converted to Rome: Why It Has Happened to Me', *Daily Express* (20

I had long realised, as do nearly all the Protestants, that the issue is no longer between the English and the Irish in the Anglosphere, between the Proddies and the Micks. Indeed, the gospel Protestants will be indispensable allies in the Christian survival and revival when it comes, as is the case in the pro-life battles in the United States. Neither do I anticipate that the millions of Muslims in Western Europe will be a major factor in the immediate future of our religious struggles, although Michel Houellebecq's novel *Submission* (2015) on the first Islamic president of France might be more prescient than myself. I guess that the secular capitalists who needed a labour force had presumed that they could paganize these Muslim immigrants in a generation or so, and benefit, on the way, from their scepticism and occasional hostility to Christianity. Indeed, the movement in the successive generations of immigrants has been in the opposite direction with the development of a widespread radical-ism and of a small core of violent terrorists who also work to intimidate majority Moslem opinion, which is for moderation.

I have long described the confrontation as being between the Judeo-Christians and the secularists. I was well aware of organ-ized and financed secular campaigns, generally using the media in a sophisticated fashion, often highlighting the particular sufferings attendant on the hard cases that make bad laws as they systematically demolished the Christian legal foundations on issues such as divorce, abortion, heterosexual marriage, and now euthanasia and gender. Only in the United States has there been significant progress with public opinion on the pro-life cause, by highlighting the realities of eliminating the unborn human babies. We should not underestimate the long-term significance of the present US Supreme Court which has already begun returning abortion decisions to the individual states where they will legislate as their citizens vote.

October 1930).

What struck me was Waugh seeing chaos as the alternative in 1930 and Eberstadt adopting this term to describe our situation today.

I have come to admire more and more Evelyn Waugh's insight into the hearts of so many different persons. Around ten years ago, I was asked by the library at Sydney University to give a paper on Constantine, the first Christian emperor in the Roman Empire. He is one of my heroes because I believe we should continue to work and to harness whatever sociological forces we can to help carry the semi-religious in the right direction. At this stage, I am not a supporter of the 'Benedict option' for the wider Catholic community, of a flight to small, isolated monastic-type communities of families, much less of a pre-monastic web of tiny family cells as the predominant Christian presence. Here or there, in different countries like Communist China, the Catholic community might be so reduced eventually, but here and now, we should continue to support political and legal initiatives to maintain our religious freedoms, widely understood. In my view, Constantine did a lot of good work for the Kingdom of God through granting religious toleration, favouring Christianity through some tax reforms, and the building of churches such as St John Lateran's and the first St Peter's in Rome, through the public recognition of priests and especially bishops, and cautious legal enactments such as prohibiting fights to the death in the games and the branding of slaves on the face. From his time onwards, for at least fifteen hundred years, he changed the direction of the social currents for the better. I much prefer the religiously indifferent to be lapsing into Christianity than to be lapsing into neo-paganism as 30% of the Australian population has done growing from a base of 12.7% in 1986. To my mind, Constantine is no saint, although he is canonized by the Eastern Christians and saw himself as the thirteenth apostle, but he did much good.

Earlier this year, I was asked to give a paper on Gibbon's *Decline and Fall of the Roman Empire* (6 vols, 1776–88), describing the triumph of barbarism and religion and decided to discover what Waugh and Newman had to say on this genius Gibbon, with his unremitting hostility towards Christianity. In the sermon 'Contest between Faith and Sight' that Newman preached in 1832, across the road at the University Church of St Mary the Virgin,[4] Newman refers to Gibbon, 'who, for [...] his cold heart, impure mind, and scoffing spirit, may justly be accounted as [...] one of the masters of a new school of error, which [...] is framed more exactly after the received type of the author of evil, than the other chief anti-Christs who have, in these last times, occupied the scene of the world.'[5]

Waugh did not let me down either, writing of 'a false historian with the mind of Cicero or Tacitus and the soul of an animal'. For Waugh, Gibbon's style ensured that his version remained in people's minds, like 'the Egyptian secret of the embalmers'.[6] Despite my reverence for Waugh's judgment, I was initially sceptical that the word 'chaos' best fitted today's neo-paganism. I was well aware of the sophistication of our opponents, and I mentioned my hesitation when I met Mary Eberstadt in Rome one month ago. Mary first replied that the phrase was Waugh's, but then went on to explain why the term is accurate.

She acknowledged that the chaos Waugh rejected in the 1930's was different from ours, residing in 'war, dislocation, and stupendous carnage'. However, many social pillars were still firm

---

4   The cardinal was speaking in the Examination Schools, on the south side of The High, whereas St Mary's is on the north side. [Ed.]

5   *University Sermons*, p. 126. In 1854 Newman wrote: 'We may feel great repugnance to Milton or Gibbon as men; we may most seriously protest against the spirit which ever lives, and the tendency which ever operates, in every page of their writings; but there they are, an integral portion of English Literature; we cannot extinguish them; we cannot deny their power; we cannot write a new Milton or a new Gibbon; we cannot expurgate what needs to be exorcised. They are great English authors, each breathing hatred to the Catholic Church in his own way, each a proud and rebellious creature of God, each gifted with incomparable gifts.' ('On the formation of a Catholic Literature in the English tongue II', *Catholic University Gazette* 15 (7 September 1854), p. 114; *Idea*, p. 309.)

6   *Helena* (1950; Harmondsworth: Penguin, 1963), p. 80.

including the battered institution of the family, but outside of Nazism (soon to be defeated at enormous cost) and the longer continuing Communism, she saw that 'a Christian understanding of creation and redemption and meaning still prevailed in the West'. Under Pius XI in the 1930's, and indeed under Pius XII, Catholic teachings remained 'coherent and consistent',[7] the main reason for Waugh's conversion, although chaos had started its work in the Protestant churches.

Eberstadt adopts the term 'chaos' for our situation, recognizing that we are 'ninety light years' removed from 1930. She gives a checklist of six factors.

The first of these is compounding family chaos, dating back decades, which has weakened the family 'on a scale never seen before' through low marriage rates, breakups, abortions, and absentee fathers.

There is compounding psychic chaos, exemplified in the extensively documented rise in mental illness, anxiety, depression, disconnection, and loneliness. She might have mentioned the curse of youth suicide, where prosperous, decent Australia has one of the highest rates in the world.

She then mentions political chaos, the dissolution of clan and community, although I see this as a less virulent example than the others. Democracy still prevails in Australia, Britain, and the United States, despite 'cancel culture' and the removed or damaged statues. Think of Cecil Rhodes.

The anthropological and intellectual forms of chaos she describes are obviously related. For her the thinking about gender is magical and preposterous, whereby 'many people no longer even know what little children know—namely, who they are'. It is extraordinary that young people, sometimes many years before they are entitled to drive a car or cast a vote, can begin to change their sex without their parents' consent; and in the State of

---

[7]   'The Cross amid the Crisis' can be found on Mary Eberstadt's website: www.maryeberstadt.com.

Victoria in Australia, they are denied by law prayers and contrary counselling.

By coincidence, I recently re-read Alexander Solzhenitsyn's 1983 Templeton Address[8] where he warned against the atheist teachers in the Western world teaching their people to hate their own society. Eberstadt is particularly scathing about elite education in the United States, which she sees as 'hiding in a post-modern cuckoo's nest for decades'. Too many who do not believe in truth 'now run institutions charged with discerning it', she claims. She particularly objects to the election of an atheist chief chaplain at Harvard: though 'if there is no truth, there are no contradictions'. In addition to family chaos, psychic chaos, anthropological chaos and intellectual chaos she finds her final example of contemporary chaos in the Catholic Church in the Western world, among those who want to transform Catholic teaching and are often hostile towards those who hold and teach the tradition. This is not a completely new situation, but a re-run and development on a wider range of issues than the confusion after the Second Vatican Council when tens of thousands—even 100,000—of priests left the priesthood. In the terms 'pro-abortion Catholic', she sees as much sense as in the terms 'atheist chaplain' and 'former man'. Here, for her, we have a 'signature irrationalism', a demand that we cancel Aristotle and believe 'A and not-A at one and the same time'.

For a cautious prelate like myself, committed to hoping the glass is half full rather than almost empty, these claims are unpalatable. But while I can point to many places where such extreme alternatives do not flourish, I cannot deny the logic of the claims where such forces are in play. These forces are illogical; they are examples of a radical chaos.

Mary Eberstadt did not mention in her address to the social scientists another spectacular contribution to the chaos, although Ross Douthat in *The Decadent Society: How we Became Victims of our own Success* (2020) devoted space to the topic. Douthat pointed

---

[8]   'Godlessness: the First Step to the Gulag', 10 May 1983.

out that as fertility collapsed because of the 1960's invention of the pill and the consequent renunciation of procreative sex, men and women had more difficulty in 'permanently pairing off'—divorces increased—and cultural alternatives to old-fashioned copulation increased. He quoted a recent study from Japan, probably a path-finder for the West and not a weird exception, which showed that 45% of women and a quarter of men aged 16 to 24 were 'not interested in or desired sexual contact'.

More explicit pornography increased in the 1960's and 1970's, and is now at a whole new level. In the 1980's some feminists and a number of Christians, like myself, believed that a strong link would be revealed between watching pornography and violent, sadistic crimes. This has not happened, although it has certainly influenced a coarsening and a 'pornification' of much of the culture. Constant porn has made arousal more challenging and normal sex less immediately attractive. In the United States surveys show drops in teen sex, teen pregnancy, teen smoking, teen binge drinking, and teen drunk driving. The causes are mixed, but the fantasy world has become a substitute for flesh-and-blood behaviour. An end result like Japan's represents a special problem, and not just for Christians.

Pornography addicts today are like Midas, who was condemned to having everything he touched turned to gold, so he could neither eat not drink nor copulate. Addiction to porn is essentially narcissistic, creating prisoners paralysed by habit. Already it is wrecking marriages. I repeat that it is a spectacular contribution to the chaos—but such habits can be broken, and are broken with perseverance, prayer, and often with group help.

What is to be Done?

Bob Santamaria was an Australian Catholic, a writer, political activist, and strategist, deeply involved in the fight against Communism and in defending the Judeo-Christian foundations of our society. He is the greatest layman the Catholic Church has produced in Australia and I was privileged to preside at his state funeral in Melbourne in 1998. He would regularly state, 'The important question is: what is to be done?', generally leaving unsaid the fact that Lenin is believed to have given prominence to this line in his pamphlet from Switzerland in 1902.[9]

I wish to make two suggestions and the first is a direct appeal to you to understand and support the importance of preserving Catholic identity, the doctrinal unity constructed around the apostolic tradition.

We believe that Jesus is the Son of God, that the basic teachings of the Catholic Church are revealed, not the product simply of human intelligence and experience. We certainly believe in fundamentals, but we are not fundamentalists who reject the use of reason and lament the achievement of theology. Neither do we deny that there is a development of doctrine in many areas within the tradition, starting with issues such as the recognition of the New Testament canon, then the development of Trinitarian doctrines, and moving to doctrines as disparate as the legitimisation of interest, the rejection of slavery, the Immaculate Conception, and the Assumption. The last word does not come from the world, from contemporary understandings, but from within the tradition as authorised by the successor of Peter and the successors of the Apostles.

The second reason for fidelity is found in recent history where the adoption of a radical liberalism in faith, morals, and liturgy provoked the collapse of church life in a generation or two. We have seen examples of this in Catholic Holland, Belgium, and Quebec since the 1960's and in liberal Protestant groups such as the American Episcopalians. Regular prayer, reverent celebrations of traditional liturgy, fidelity to the Ten Commandments do not

---

[9]   Written between the autumn of 1901 and February 1902, 'What is to Done?' was published in March 1902. It can be found in V. I. Lenin, *Collected Works*, vol. v (Moscow: Foreign Languages Publishing, 1961), pp. 347–530.

guarantee religious survival and prosperity, but they are essential prerequisites. A good deal of Catholic decline is self-inflicted.

Some feel that the paedophilia scandal has affected so many countries that a new sort of Catholic Church is required. These crimes have been horrendous and the impact on those who have been abused as children has often been crippling. The figures for the number of abusers and the numbers of those abused are also scandalous, represent a cancer, and the recent statistics from France were another bitter blow.

But sexual abuse comes from sinning, from *not* following the principles of Christian morality, and the historic failures of the Church leadership to deal properly with the problem, especially before the 1990's, are also examples of moral failure, of sin, even though bishops were usually following the responses of the wider society and other institutions at the time.

In Australia, and elsewhere, such as the United States, the Church broke the back of this problem in the 1990's, as the recent Royal Commission acknowledged the collapse in the crime rate, in sexual abuse violations from that decade in Australia.

The scandal of sexual abuse—its profound contradiction of Christian witness—is one expression of weakened faith; it also reflects the moral confusion that increased with the 1960's as the recent revelations of juvenile abuse among the *soixante-huitards*, the revolutionary left after the 1968 uprising in France, have shown. Some changes are necessary and useful, such as the screening of future seminarians and religious, and more emphasis on psycho-sexual development in seminary formation itself, but the whole grim saga, the massive suffering involved, demonstrate that we must practise what we preach, not change our moral teaching. There should not be Australian or German versions of the Ten Commandments.

This crisis has brought consequences for Church membership, but other factors are at play in falling numbers too. As an example of my claims about the destructive consequences of liberalism, in the years between 2011 and 2016 in Australia, the Anglicans lost

579,000 from a community of 3,680,000; the Uniting Church had 195,000 fewer from a base of 1,065,000; and the Catholic Church diminished by 147,000 from a community of 5,439,000 despite bearing the brunt of most of the hostile publicity over abuse. These losses bring no consolation, but the patterns are different.

One might paraphrase my first suggestion by stating that traditional Catholicism, and the Jewish traditions from which it drank, are heading in the right direction. The Catholic story, when centred squarely and courageously on Christ, demonstrates that the message is marketable and improves humanity. The mix works when we work with the Lord.

My second suggestion is that you, my listeners, strive to understand that secular modernity causes multiple forms of suffering that we can often ameliorate when we understand their true origins. We also need to remember that Christ was a healer of the blind, the disabled, the sick and the possessed. We need to bring His healing to others.

Mary Eberstadt is quite explicit that this truth has gone unsaid for too long. Secularism is an inferior culture, small of heart, which defines suffering down, so that victims are not acknowledged as victims but as justified collateral damage. Compare this to the heart of the Lord we see in the Gospels, in his response to the victims of sin and suffering. This is the heart that we must have.

The secularists are wreckers and they are busy at work. Chaos is the end result. Chaos is the main characteristic of the way of life the secularist wreckers are imposing upon us, not liberation. Not health or peace of mind or communities united beneath and beyond their differences, but a tribal, fretful void, anxious, divided and regularly frightened: now by Covid and the spectre of global warming. The forms of misery today are acute and various.

Is the widespread sexual dysfunction caused by pornography in Japan to become the norm in our society, yet another cross for our beleaguered youth? Language is used cleverly to define suffering down. Homosexuals are gays, when all the evidence shows they are often as miserable and sad as the rest of us.

Prostitutes are sex workers sometimes ranked ahead of the churches in the Covid crisis as providing essential social services. Data about the transgender population is often whitewashed, such as data about suicide rates, eating disorders, substance abuse and other forms of mental distress. Similar processes are at work among young people generally, especially those from broken and blended families where love and stability have been missing.

There is a strong correlation between mental distress and the decline of organized religion when social bonds are weakened. Damaged people do not thrive, but Christianity in particular deepens the sense of community and social belonging. Anxiety and depression are connected with disconnection and loneliness. Drugs, such as marijuana, are long-term depressants; drugs damage perceptions and self-understanding—but it is a reassurance even for fevered minds if they are aware that God is in charge, that God is good, and that beyond this vale of tears, all will be well. The damage from drugs—think of the opioid crisis in the United States—now rivals the damage from alcohol.

Children in particular suffer in fractured families, but not just the children; the spouses or partners suffer too from nervous distress, hurt and the subsequent substance abuse from drugs and opioids. In North America at least, and I suspect in Australia and the United Kingdom, the no-religioners, the nones, are the most mentally afflicted. And we have the scourge of youth suicide, so terrible and so sad. So often problems in the home do not stay in the home. We must encourage our teachers to continue their valiant work in our schools to bring help and healing to their student victims of the chaos. There are no substitutes for kindness and long-term support, which is the practical, day-to-day expression of real love.

I believe that today's generation of young Christian intellectuals are presented with an unusual opportunity to speak the truth to the void, to give voice to the voiceless as Eberstadt challenged the social scientists to so act.

Change for the better will only come with two things: when many voices present the facts, figures, arguments, and evidence about the human causes and costs of the secularization push—the chaos should be named and shamed; while Christians continue to show that they will not abandon those who have been abandoned, offering them instead healing and friendship and the Good News of the one true God's great love for us.

Concluding Remarks

Christians are quite rightly warned against rejoicing in the misfortunes of others: the Germans even have a word for this weakness—*schadenfreude*. However, moral culpability is removed when we take consolation from periods of Church history when the situation was quite clearly worse than ours in the Western world today. Neither should we forget the swiftly growing Catholic communities in Africa, and the surprising Christian expansion in China. We still have formidable strengths.

We take consolation in these lessons from history, not because their times were bad, but because the Church threw up reform movements and leaders in these times to mitigate the worst and promote new growth. Even with the paedophilia crisis and a widespread decline in numbers, we have nothing like the corruption and disorder in Rome in the ninth and tenth centuries as the Ottonian and Crescentii families struggled for power. The lurid story of Marozia (890–937), the daughter of the Roman consul Theophylact and Theodora, a 'shameless whore' according to a contemporary source, exemplifies the worst of it.

She became at fifteen the mistress of Pope Sergius II; and Pope John XI was either their son, or the son of Marozia and her husband, Alberic I. On Alberic's death, she married Guy of Tuscany. Together they attacked Rome, imprisoned Pope John X in Castel Sant'Angelo, where he died, perhaps smothered by a pillow. She installed her twenty-one-year-old son as Pope John XI. On the death of Guy of Tuscany, she married his half-brother,

Hugh of Arles, but then her luck ran out. Alberic II, the son of her first husband, imprisoned his mother for five years before her death in 937. Her progeny from the marriage with Guy of Tuscany flourished as the Tusculani family in the next few generations and produced three popes and an anti-pope. Alberic II was also father of John XII, who became pope in 955.

The reform movement that followed this was vigorously encouraged by Pope Gregory VII (1073–85) and its best-known leader was St Peter Damian (1007–72). While he rebuked the Archbishop of Milan for going hunting on Easter Sunday morning, he certainly struggled against worse abuses. His *Book of Gomorrah* (1049), a colourful denunciation of a wide range of clerical infidelity, which raged 'like a cruel beast within the sheepfold of Christ', is a marvellous read—but not for the faint-hearted. He certainly believed in hell.

The fourteenth century saw the coming of the Black Death, killing half the population, and the translation of the papacy from Rome to Avignon for seventy years, from 1305. It also produced Catherine of Siena, who encouraged a return to Rome. Then fifteen cardinals declared the election of Pope Urban VI, a rude and tactless man, to be invalid, launching the Great Western Schism, which lasted forty years, with three rival popes at one stage, and concluded with the election of Pope Martin V in 1417.

This list of corruption, chaos and reform can be easily extended. The German synodal way is unlikely to result in a new split, a new reformation, as in the early sixteenth century when Luther was able to provoke indignation about the level of corruption, especially in continental Europe, but less so in England where the split with Henry VIII was originally more dynastic than theological. More and Fisher died for the papacy when there was not one truly worthy pope during their lifetimes.

We have had some close calls. If Hitler had remained in power, he had decided to set up a pope in every country he had conquered.

The point of this tale of woe is to demonstrate the resilience of the Church, provided we remain faithful, still attached to the vine in these new and treacherous times. Our faith gives us hope and history justifies our confidence. Napoleon famously claimed to an Italian cleric when Pope Pius VI died in French captivity that the Church was finished. 'Sire', replied the Italian, 'we clergy have been unable to destroy the Church in 1800 years. The task will also prove to be beyond your powers.'

Let me leave the last word to an Englishman, probably the best apologist in the twentieth century, although I find some of his writing irritating, much too clever and paradoxical; but at his best, he is magnificent. I speak, of course, of G. K. Chesterton who declared he was a pagan at the age of twelve, an agnostic at sixteen, became an Anglican at marriage, and was received into the Church in 1922 at the age of 48. In his best-known book *Orthodoxy* (1908), he writes of the 'thrilling romance of orthodoxy'. For him, it is easy to be a heretic, easy to let the age have its head. To have fallen into 'any of these open traps of error and exaggeration' would indeed have been simple. 'But to have avoided them all has been one whirling adventure; and in my vision the heavenly chariot flies thundering through the ages, the dull heresies sprawling and prostrate, the wild truth reeling but erect.'[10]

After eighty years of Catholic living, this is my vision also.

---

[10]   *Orthodoxy* (1908; London: Unicorn, 1939), pp. 167–9.

PART THREE

Some Devotional Theology

COR AD COR LOQUITUR: NEWMAN'S VISION OF SAINT PAUL

HERMANN GEISSLER, FSO

REACHING DURING THE Mass of John Henry Newman's beatification in Birmingham on 19 September 2010, Benedict XVI spoke about the relevance of this great English cardinal for the Church in the modern world. Of course, he paid tribute to Newman's 'insights into the relationship between faith and reason, into the vital place of revealed religion in civilized society, and into the need for a broadly-based and wide-ranging approach to education'—issues that 'were not only of profound importance for Victorian England, but continue today to inspire and enlighten many all over the world'. Pope Benedict, however, highlighted in a special way Newman's 'life as a priest, a pastor of souls', mentioning 'the warmth and humanity underlying his appreciation of the pastoral ministry', lived out 'in his devoted care for the people of Birmingham during the years that he spent at the Oratory he founded, visiting the sick and the poor, comforting the bereaved, caring for those in prison'.[1]

When canonizing Newman on 13 October 2019, in Saint Peter's Square in Rome, Pope Francis, continuing the same line of thought, emphasized

---

[1] Benedict XVI, Mass and Beatification of John Henry Newman, Homily, 19 September 2020, *Pilgrim in Britain. Benedict XVI* (London: CTS, 2010), p. 84.

the holiness of daily life, which St John Henry Newman described in these words: 'The Christian has a deep, silent, hidden peace, which the world sees not [...]. The Christian is cheerful, easy, kind, gentle, courteous, candid, unassuming; has no pretence [...] with so little that is unusual or striking in his bearing, that he may easily be taken at first sight for an ordinary man.' Let us ask to be like that, 'kindly lights' amid the encircling gloom. Jesus, 'Stay with me, and then I shall begin to shine as Thou shinest: so to shine as to be a light to others.'[2]

The whole life and work of Newman, both as an Anglican and as a Catholic, was shaped by his fatherly care for souls, beautifully expressed in the words he chose for his motto as a cardinal, *Cor ad cor loquitur* (Heart speaks unto heart). His teaching, preaching, and writing were not merely academic, but an expression of his zeal for souls.

Therefore, it is not surprising that Newman cherished a personal relationship with St Paul, the great missionary of the early Church and spiritual father of many Christian communities. For Newman, St Paul was the 'glorious Apostle', the 'sweetest of inspired writers', the 'most touching and winning of teachers' towards whom he 'ever felt a special devotion'.[3] Newman left us four sermons dedicated entirely to the Apostle of the Gentiles. The theme of these sermons is not so much St Paul's apostolic activity as the interior attitude that shaped his work of evangelization. Newman's reflections on St Paul's apostolic heart have lost none of their relevance, and can be read as an exemplification of the cardinal's motto *Cor ad cor loquitur*.

A Heart Transformed by the Word

No one can truly be an apostle unless he has first been seized by the grace of God and thereby undergone a profound conversion.

---

[2] Pope Francis quotes first from 'Equanimity', *Parochial and Plain* v, pp. 69–71, and then from 'Jesus the Light of the Soul', *Meditations*, p. 279.

[3] 'St Paul's Characteristic Gift', *Various Occasions*, p. 104.

In a sermon from his early Anglican years, 'St Paul's Conversion Viewed in Reference to his Office',[4] Newman argues that Saul's conversion constitutes the beginning of St Paul's ministry.

Saul was perhaps the leading persecutor of the Christians in the early Church. He approved of the stoning of Stephen who, when dying, prayed for his executioners. Shortly thereafter, Saul obtained from the Jewish religious establishment the authorization to imprison the disciples of Christ in Damascus. However, at the gates of this city he was 'struck down by a miracle, and converted to the faith he persecuted'.[5] St Paul's conversion is a demonstration of God's power, of God's triumph over the enemy. 'To show His power, He put forth His hand into the very midst of the persecutors of His Son, and seized upon the most strenuous among them.'[6] At the same time, this conversion is the fruit of Stephen's prayer. 'The prayers of righteous men avail much. The first Martyr had power with God to raise up the greatest Apostle.'[7] Thus, it appears clear: no one can become an apostle unless he is transformed by God's power, a process often sustained by the prayer and suffering of holy Christians.

It is the grace of conversion that makes St Paul the model Apostle whose appeal is undimmed by the passage of time. St Paul experiences the extremes of sin and God's mercy, which so captivates him as to make him the spiritual father of the Gentiles: 'in the history of his sin and its most gracious forgiveness, he exemplifies far more than his brother Apostles his own Gospel; that we are all guilty before God, and can be saved only by His free bounty'.[8] All apostles are called, like St Paul, to testify to God's mercy, first with their lives but also with their words.

---

[4]   'St Paul's Conversion Viewed in Reference to his Office', *Parochial and Plain* ii, pp. 96–106.

[5]   *Ibid.*, p. 96.

[6]   *Ibid.*, p. 97.

[7]   *Ibid.*, p. 96.

[8]   *Ibid.*, p. 99.

St Paul's past life made him a particularly fitting instrument for God's designs for the gentile nations. While the spreading of the Gospel is primarily the work of God's grace, not of men, God nevertheless almost always uses human co-operation to realise his plans. St Paul is, one might say, predestined for his mission to the pagans, not only because of his learning and his spiritual gifts, but also because of the path of faith he followed and his conversion experience. This path had taught him not to be discouraged by the gravity of one's sins; to find the sparks of faith that are hidden in the hearts of men; to identify with those experiencing temptations; to carry humbly God's revelation; and to use wisely his own experiences in bringing others to conversion. Thus, St Paul becomes a 'comforter, help, and guide of his brethren' because he 'know[s] in some good measure the *hearts of men'*.[9] It is consoling to realise that God can use all our life experiences, both good and bad, to spread the Gospel. With these considerations Newman does not imply that to become an apostle or a saint one must first sin. St Paul was not a better Christian on account of his sins, but they 'rendered him *more fitted for a particular purpose* in God's providence, more fitted, when converted, to reclaim others'.[10]

Newman adds that St Paul's past life had not been impious or immoral. He had listened to the voice of his conscience; he had not turned his back on God. However, St Paul's conscience had not been sufficiently illumined by Scripture as, for example, the conscience of Anna and Simeon who, from the Old Testament, had recognised Jesus as the predicted Messiah. St Paul did not recognise Jesus as the Christ and became a persecutor of Christians. Meditating on this fact, Newman draws some conclusions for the believer: he must 'cherish and obey the holy light of conscience within him, as Saul did'; he must also 'carefully study the Scriptures, as Saul did not; and the God who had mercy even on the persecutor of His saints, will assuredly shed His grace upon

---

9   *Ibid.,* p. 101.

10   *Ibid.,* p. 102.

him, and bring him into the truth as it is in Jesus'.[11] The believer who wishes to live as an apostle is called to listen to his conscience and have it illuminated and transformed by the Revealed Word.

A Heart for Human Nature

Profound union with Christ, the fruit of an authentic conversion, leads St Paul to say: 'it is no longer I who live, but Christ who lives in me; and the life I now live in the flesh I live by faith in the Son of God, who loved me and gave himself for me.' (Gal 2:20)[12] A few select saints become so filled with God's life that they seem to lose themselves entirely and no longer appear to possess a human nature. In his sermon 'St Paul's Characteristic Gift',[13] Newman shows that St Paul is numbered among another group of saints 'in whom the supernatural combines with nature, instead of superseding it, invigorating it, elevating it, ennobling it; and who are not the less men, because they are saints'.[14] Newman argues that the characteristic that sets the Apostle apart is that the fullness of the divine gifts does not destroy his humanity but rather elevates and perfects it. For this reason, St Paul understands man with all his strengths, weaknesses, temptations, and aspirations:

> Human nature, the common nature of the whole race of Adam, spoke in him, acted in him, with an energetical presence, with a sort of bodily fullness, always under the sovereign command of divine grace, but losing none of its real freedom and power because of its subordination. And the consequence is, that, having the nature of man so strong within him, he is able to enter into human nature, and to sympathize with it, with a gift peculiarly his own.[15]

---

[11] *Ibid.,* p. 106.
[12] All the references from Sacred Scripture found in this article are taken from the Revised Standard Version, Catholic Edition.
[13] 'St Paul's Characteristic Gift', *Various Occasions*, pp. 91–105.
[14] *Ibid.,* p. 92.
[15] *Ibid.,* pp. 95–6.

If before his conversion the Apostle conducted his life with rigour, now, finding himself among the despised pagans, he speaks as if he were one of them, experiencing solidarity with all those like himself, with all of Adam's descendants. He is conscious of a wounded nature with all its emotions and inclinations towards sin that are typical of man living in a fallen world. In this sense, St Paul, following in the Lord's footsteps, carries the sins of all men and feels himself in full communion with them. He knows human nature intimately because he sees 'in that nature of his which grace had sanctified, what it was in its tendencies and results when deprived of grace'.[16] A faithful missionary is always on the way of conversion and renewal in Christ. Such a missionary is able to enter into the differing circumstances of people's lives, to empathise with their emotions, to understand their struggles and to share their joys and worries.

St Paul also shows his love for human nature by mentioning pagan authorities: at the Areopagus of Athens he refers to an altar with this inscription, 'To an unknown god' (Acts 17:23); in the First Letter to the Corinthians he quotes the poet Menander, 'Bad company ruins good morals' (1 Cor 15:33); in the Letter to Titus he cites the philosopher Epimenides, 'Cretans are always liars, evil beasts, lazy gluttons' (Tit 1:12). The Apostle quotes these authors, because 'he was a true lover of souls. He loved poor human nature with a passionate love, and the literature of the Greeks was only its expression; and he hung over it tenderly and mournfully, wishing for its regeneration and salvation.' God's salvific plan embraces the Greeks and all humanity. Though 'the heathens are in darkness, and in sin, and under the power of the Evil One, He will not allow that they are beyond the eye of Divine Mercy'.[17] St Paul never rejects anything authentically human. With his generous heart he is convinced that God desires all men to be saved (cf. 1 Tim 2:4).

---

[16]   *Ibid.*, p. 97.

[17]   *Ibid.*, p. 98.

St Paul, recognizing that all human beings are descended from Adam, takes 'pleasure in thinking that all men were brethren'. Even more, he 'tenderly contemplates the captivity, and the anguish, and the longing, and the deliverance of poor human nature'.[18] As he puts it: 'the creation waits with eager longing for the revealing of the sons of God' (Rom 8:19). The Apostle emphasises that all men have the same origin and the same goal. They are created by God, and they are called to a life in the glory of God.

A Heart for his People

Newman also speaks of St Paul's love for the people of Israel. If the Apostle felt bound to the whole of the human race, 'what did he feel for his own nation! O what a special mixture, bitter and sweet, of generous pride (if I may so speak), but of piercing, overwhelming anguish, did the thought of the race of Israel inflict upon him!'[19]

Even after his conversion, St Paul will not question God's choice: Israel is God's Chosen People. This theme is particularly evident where he writes: 'They are Israelites, and to them belong the sonship, the glory, the covenants, the giving of the law, the worship, and the promises; to them belong the patriarchs, and of their race, according to the flesh, is the Christ, who is God over all, blessed for ever. Amen.' (Rom 9:4–5) With what gratitude does St Paul look to Israel: 'the highest of nations and the lowest, his own dear people, whose glories were before his imagination and in his affection from his childhood'.[20]

Yet his pride is accompanied by great sorrow and anguish (cf. Rom 9:2). It is precisely this people—a people that has waited centuries for the promised Messiah, that has prepared the way for Him and announced His coming—that has not recognised

---

18 *Ibid.*, p. 99.
19 *Ibid.*
20 *Ibid.*, pp. 99–100.

Him. St Paul could well understand Israel's obstinacy because he himself had shared the same thoughts and feelings about Jesus. Moved by compassion, St Paul, like Moses before him, interceded for his people. He wished 'that I myself were accursed and cut off from Christ for the sake of my brethren, my kinsmen by race' (Rom 9:3). He was ready to give everything for his people and 'pleaded for them, while they were persecuting his Lord and himself'.[21] His heart bleeds on account of his brethren's hardness of heart, so much that he exclaims: 'O dearest ones, O glorious race, O miserably fallen! So great and so abject!'[22]

At the same time, despite everything, St Paul never loses hope for his people. Though the major part of Israel has rejected Christ, he is consoled to think that their obstinacy has become a blessing for the Gentiles, and he hopes in the prophecy of their future recovery. Because of this prophecy, he is convinced: 'a hardening has come upon part of Israel, until the full number of the Gentiles come in, and so all Israel will be saved' (Rom 11:25–6).

Every true apostle may experience similar feelings for his own family and people: gratitude for the good received, sincere readiness to intercede for those who do not know or have forgotten the Lord, and an unbreakable.

A Heart for the Faithful

Newman's sermon 'St Paul's Gift of Sympathy'[23] continues the same line of thought, emphasizing the affection which St Paul nurtures for his brothers and sisters in the faith. In this context, he highlights the Apostle's *humanitas*: 'a virtue which comes of His supernatural grace, and is cultivated for His sake, though its object is human nature viewed in itself, in its intellect, its affections, and its history. And it is this virtue which I consider is so characteristic of St Paul; and he himself often inculcates it

---

[21]   *Ibid.*, p. 101.

[22]   *Ibid.*, p. 100.

[23]   'St Paul's Gift of Sympathy', *Various Occasions*, pp. 106–20.

in his Epistles, as when he enjoins bowels of mercy, benignity, kindness, gentleness, and the like.'[24] This virtue is manifest in St Paul's life and work.

Newman stresses that St Paul is so full of tender love for his fellow Christians that 'in the tenor of his daily thoughts, he almost loses sight of his gifts and privileges, his station and dignity, except he is called by duty to remember them, and he is to himself merely a frail man speaking to frail men, and he is tender towards the weak from a sense of his own weakness.'[25] St Paul knows that not only do others need God's grace, but he himself has need of it above all others. He rejoices in calling himself, and the other Apostles, servants of the people: 'what we preach is not ourselves, but Jesus Christ as Lord, with ourselves as your servants for Jesus' sake' (2 Cor 4:5). Admitting his own weakness, he states: 'we have this treasure in earthen vessels, to show that the transcendent power belongs to God and not to us' (2 Cor 4:7). Precisely this awareness links him all the more intimately with his spiritual sons and daughters.

The Apostle constantly speaks of his weaknesses and hardships. Recalling his arrival in Corinth, he writes: 'I was with you in weakness and in much fear and trembling; and my speech and my message were not in plausible words of wisdom, but in demonstration of the Spirit and power' (1 Cor 2:3–4). With regard to his interior struggles, he openly states: 'we do not want you to be ignorant, brethren, of the affliction we experienced in Asia; for we were so utterly, unbearably crushed that we despaired of life itself' (2 Cor 1:8). Concerning difficulties around him and in him, he discloses: 'when we came into Macedonia, our bodies had no rest but we were afflicted at every turn—fighting without and fear within' (2 Cor 7:5). Mentioning a special revelation granted to him by the Lord, he admits: 'to keep me from being too elated by the abundance of revelations, a thorn was given me in the flesh, a messenger of Satan' (2 Cor 12:7). Sympathising with

---

[24]   *Ibid.*, p. 109.

[25]   *Ibid.*

the elders of Miletus, St Paul said to them: 'You yourselves know how I lived among you all the time from the first day that I set foot in Asia, serving the Lord with all humility and with tears and with trials' (Acts 20:18–19).

Why does St Paul speak so openly of his weaknesses and internal struggles? Newman explains: 'A man who thus divests himself of his own greatness, and puts himself on the level of his brethren, and throws himself upon the sympathies of human nature, and speaks with such simplicity and such spontaneous outpouring of heart, is forthwith in a condition both to conceive great love of them, and to inspire great love towards himself.'[26] Being an apostle should not be confused with worldly heroism or a perfectionist attitude. To fulfil his designs God does not need human heroes, but hearts full of love: hearts seized by the fire of His love and, thus purified and transformed, made capable of drawing others into intimacy and leading them lovingly to Christ.

Repeatedly Newman stresses that the grace in St Paul's heart does not repress his human nature; rather this nature is healed, sanctified, and ennobled. Though he loses what is sinful, the Apostle retains everything authentically human. He lives in communion with his beloved Lord, but at the same time is deeply sensitive to the feelings of those around him. Newman sees this sympathy as the essence of St Paul's humanity:

> Wonderful to say, he who had rest and peace in the love of Christ, was not satisfied without the love of man; he whose supreme reward was the approbation of God, looked out for the approval of his brethren. He who depended solely on the Creator, yet made himself dependent on the creature. Though he had that which was Infinite, he would not dispense with the finite. He loved his brethren, not only 'for Jesus' sake,' to use his own expression, but for their own sake also. He lived in them; he felt with them and for them; he was anxious about them; he gave them help, and in turn he looked for comfort from

---

[26] *Ibid.*, pp. 112–13.

them. His mind was like some instrument of music, harp
or viol, the strings of which vibrate, though untouched, by
the notes which other instruments give forth, and he was
ever, according to his own precept, rejoicing with those
who rejoice, weeping with those who weep; and, thus, he
was the least magisterial of all teachers, and the gentlest
and most amiable of all rulers.[27]

The link between St Paul and his companions in the apostolic
mission is particularly strong. He rejoices 'at the coming of
Stephanas and Fortunatus and Achaicus' (1 Cor 16:17). Elsewhere
he states: 'my mind could not rest because I did not find my
brother Titus' (2 Cor 2:13). Later he adds: 'But God, who comforts
the downcast, comforted us by the coming of Titus' (2 Cor 7:6).
He greets Phoebe, Prisca and Aquila and 'also the church in their
house', Epaenetus, Mary, Andronicus, Junias, and many other
brothers and sisters (cf. Rom 16:1–16). Writing to the Philippians
he says that Epaphroditus 'was ill, near to death. But God had
mercy on him, and not only on him but on me also, lest I should
have sorrow upon sorrow' (Phil 2:27). To Timothy he laments
that 'all who are in Asia turned away from me' (2 Tim 1:15). Later
he explains more clearly: 'At my first defence no one took my
part; all deserted me. May it not be charged against them!' (2 Tim
4:16). With deep sorrow he states that some of his friends
abandoned him: 'For Demas, in love with this present world, has
deserted me and gone to Thessalonica; Crescens has gone to
Galatia, Titus to Dalmatia. Luke alone is with me' (2 Tim
4:10–11). At the end of this letter he writes: 'Greet Prisca and
Aquila, and the household of Onesiphorus. Erastus remained at
Corinth; Trophimus I left ill at Miletus. Do your best to come
before winter. Eubulus sends greetings to you, as do Pudens and
Linus and Claudia and all the brethren.' (2 Tim 4:19–21)

Newman is profoundly touched by the compassion and pain
expressed in these words of St Paul. The Apostle's heart, trans-

---

[27]   *Ibid.*, p. 114.

formed by the Heart of the Lord, is able to touch the heart of Christians because of his tender love towards them.

> He, in a word, who is the special preacher of Divine Grace, is also the special friend and intimate of human nature. He who reveals to us the mystery of God's Sovereign Decrees, manifests at the same time the tenderest interest in the souls of individuals.[28]

The true Christian is big-hearted, has a universal point of view, and prays for everyone. At the same time, however, he turns with love to those around him because he recognises the dignity of the individual and the unique vocation of each person. His concern is the eternal salvation of every single person.

His love for every person is at the root of the Apostle's indignation when he discovers within the Christian community feelings of envy, jealousy, and rivalry. He considers these attitudes shameful and unworthy,

> not only as injurious to his Saviour, but as an offence against that common nature which gives us one and all a right to the title of men. As he loved that common nature, so he took pleasure in viewing all who partake of it as one, scattered though they were all over the earth. He sympathized with them all, wherever and whatever they were; and he felt it to be one special mercy, conveyed to them in the Gospel, that the unity of human nature was henceforth recognized and restored in Jesus Christ The spirit of party, then, was simply antagonistic to the spirit of the Apostle, and a great offence to him, even when it did not go so far as schism.[29]

To the community in Corinth, whose loyalties are divided between himself, Apollos, Cephas, and Christ, he asks: 'Is Christ divided?' (1 Cor 1:13) St Paul has no doubt: 'Here there cannot be Greek and Jew, circumcised and uncircumcised, barbarian, Scythian, slave,

---

[28]   *Ibid.*, p. 116.
[29]   *Ibid.*, p. 117.

free man, but Christ is all, and in all.' (Col 3:11) The believer who possesses an apostolic heart nurtures the same aspirations as Jesus and repeats with him his prayer that 'all (may) be one [...], so that the world may believe' (Jn 17:21). He is a servant of unity, knowing that division contradicts the will of Christ, scandalizes the world, and damages the cause of evangelization.

A Heart Trusting in the Lord

Newman's notes for a sermon, 'On St Paul the Type of the Church as Missionarising',[30] complete his reflections on St Paul's apostolic heart. The sermon opens by stressing that St Paul was above all 'a sower of the Word'. He 'sowed in all places', and he was a champion, not merely as David against Goliath but, rather, 'against the world'.[31] This activity, begun by the Apostle, will be continued in the Church throughout the world, not just in the sowing of the Word, but also in the struggle and fight for the faith.

St Paul is the model *par excellence*. He struggled against Jewish Zealots, for example against the men who 'made a plot and bound themselves by an oath neither to eat nor drink till they had killed Paul' (Acts 23:12). He had to fight against pagan fanatics as well. This battle can be seen, for instance, in the revolt of the silversmiths in Ephesus (cf. Acts 19:21–31). He had to confront the indifferent; for example, Festus the governor who declared him mad (cf. Acts 26:24), or the Greek philosophers who mocked when they heard him speak of the resurrection of the dead (cf. Acts 17:32).

Newman applied these examples to his own day: the Church in England in the nineteenth century had to fight against Evangelical zealots and face the indifference of politicians. The former called Rome the antichrist; the latter were only interested in political expediency. Most certainly this experience is also true

---

[30] 'On St Paul the Type of the Church as Missionarising', *Sermon Notes*, pp. 62–4. As a Catholic, Newman prepared in written form only the most important sermons; the others were preached 'freely', according to Catholic customs, using short notes.

[31] *Ibid.*, p. 62.

of our own day: the hostility and indifference of today's main-
stream culture make it difficult for many to receive the Good
News and to bear witness to it.

But Newman is not a pessimist. On the contrary, he is full of
trust, because in faith he sees the greatness and the unity of the
Church of the ages. 'This awful unity of the Church is our
consolation', because 'the Church comes from God' and 'nothing
comes strange and new to her'. Newman concludes that the
vocation of every generation of Christians is 'to sow and to fight,
and to leave the rest to God'.[32]

Conclusion

It is striking that in his sermons on St Paul, Newman does not
describe a missionary strategy or emphasise the Apostle's extraordinary feats. It is not so much the external activities that Newman
is interested in, but the interior movements of the Apostle's *heart*.
Some pieces which make up the mosaic of an apostolic heart are:
an openness to the transforming power of the Word, which is an
expression of the Lord's loving Heart; a deep knowledge of human
nature, that helps us to understand the hearts of the people, to
empathise with them, and to share their joys and worries; a
sincere love for our own family and people, which shows itself in
gratitude, intercession, and hope; a profound sympathy for the
brothers and sisters in the faith, becoming all things to all men
(cf. 1 Cor 9:22); the courage to commit ourselves in the good fight
for the cause of the Gospel and, above all, in an unbreakable trust
in the power and goodness of the Lord's loving Heart.

Newman did not only preach on the apostolic heart of St Paul,
but through God's grace felt called to follow the example of the
'glorious Apostle', being an authentic witness to the faith and a
true father of souls. From his youth, Newman's heart was touched
and transformed by God's Word. Step by step, he became a lover
of the Truth who, by his humble and courageous witness, his

---

[32]   *Ibid.,* pp. 63–4.

sincere friendship, and his faithful ministry, touched many human hearts and helped them to find peace in the 'One Fold of the Redeemer'.[33] During his entire life, Newman remained a man of prayer, entrusting all his intentions and worries, along with all the faithful and even those who do not believe, to the loving Heart of the Lord and striving, by the power of grace, to live according to the Gospel, so that his heart might beat with the Lord's Heart. Newman therefore became a preacher not only by his word, but also, and even more, by his prayer and his whole life.

Thus, Newman truly realised the motto *Cor ad cor loquitur*, putting into action what the then-Cardinal Joseph Ratzinger described in a conference given during a Newman Symposium in 1990:

> The characteristic of the great doctor of the Church is that he teaches not only through his thought and speech, but also by his life, because within him thought and life are interpenetrated and defined. If this is so, then Newman belongs to the great teachers of the Church, because he both touches our hearts and enlightens our thinking.[34]

Ian Ker is undoubtedly one of the great Newman scholars. His biography on Newman and his numerous studies are indispensable for those who want to understand Newman's thought and legacy. Following the footsteps of the Apostle of the Gentiles and of St John Henry Newman, Ian Ker, however, is not only an outstanding intellectual, writer, and lecturer, but also, and first of all, a happy priest, a true father of souls, a man of God who lives according to Newman's motto *Cor ad cor loquitur*. Indeed, he has followed the 'kindly light' of the Lord's Heart, finding perfect peace in the port of the Church. He has lovingly cared for the faithful, illuminating and strengthening their hearts with the

---

[33]   Newman to his sister Jemima, 8 October 1845, *LD* xi, p. 9.

[34]   Introductory words for the third day of the Newman Symposium in Rome, 'John Henry Newman—Lover of Truth', 26–28 April 1990, *Benedict XVI and Cardinal Newman*, ed. P. Jennings (Oxford: Family Publications, 2005), p. 35.

light of truth and the power of sacramental grace, especially those who find hope in the new communities and ecclesial movements. Our wish for Ian Ker is that he may continue to place his trust in the loving Heart of Jesus, according to St John Henry Newman's prayer:

> O most Sacred, most loving Heart of Jesus, Thou art concealed in the Holy Eucharist, and Thou beatest for us still. [...] O my God, when Thou dost condescend to suffer me to receive Thee, to eat and drink Thee, and Thou for a while takest up Thy abode within me, O make my heart beat with Thy Heart. [...] So fill it with Thee, that neither the events of the day nor the circumstances of the time may have power to ruffle it, but that in Thy love and Thy fear it may have peace.[35]

---

[35] 'The Sacred Heart', *Meditations*, p. 326.

ST PHILIP AND ST JOHN HENRY: MASTER AND DISCIPLE

KEITH BEAUMONT, CO (FRENCH ORATORY)

S T PHILIP NERI is one of the most colourful and attractive figures of the Catholic Reformation of the sixteenth century. It was he whom the Catholic Newman chose as his patron saint, on whom he sought to model himself as a priest, and whose Congregation of the Oratory he established in England. Indeed, after his two 'conversions' of 1816 and 1845, it was Newman's discovery of St Philip which constituted the third most important event in his spiritual life.

Newman's acquaintance with the figure of St Philip goes back to before his conversion of 1845. In the dedication to the future Cardinal Wiseman of his first published work as an Oratorian, his *Discourses Addressed to Mixed Congregations* (1849), he states that the saint's 'bright and beautiful character had won [his] devotion, even when [he] was a Protestant'.[1] It was Wiseman, moreover, then Apostolic Administrator of the Central District in England and as such responsible for both Oxford and Birmingham, who first suggested to him that he should consider founding in England the Oratory of St Philip Neri, which he believed, according to Newman, to be 'specially suited to the state of the country'.[2] Newman's correspondence between 1845 and the canonical erection of the first English Oratory on 1st February 1848 contains many references to St Philip, as do his numerous chapter addresses to the members of the Oratory over the next thirty years.[3] But Philip is present also in a number of other

---

[1] *Mixed Congregations*, pp. v–vi.

[2] Memorandum, 10 May 1878 in *Oratorian*, p. 390.

important works: he figures in the ninth and final discourse of Part I of *The Idea of a University*, in several of Newman's *Sermons Preached on Various Occasions*, and in his posthumously published *Meditations and Devotions*.

From the outset, Newman's choice of the Oratory founded by St Philip was inseparably linked to his deep attraction to the figure of Philip himself. Desirous of serving his new Church as a priest, he was confronted with the question of *which* form of priestly life would best suit his particular talents and those of the disciples who had grouped themselves around him during his years at Littlemore. The issue was complicated by the fact that England was then, and was to remain until the early years of the twentieth century, a 'missionary country' under the direct authority of the Congregation for the Propagation of the Faith (commonly known as 'Propaganda'). Newman was particularly sensitive to this 'missionary' situation: if he rejected the idea of becoming a simple diocesan priest, it was in part because he considered (quoting the views of Dominic Barberi who had received him into the Catholic Church) that such 'priests were for keeping up a system' but that 'an order was the only thing for converting a country'.[4]

In September 1846 he and one of his oldest companions from Littlemore, Ambrose St John, were sent by Wiseman to Rome in order to 'complete' their theological studies at the Collegio Romano, the seminary run by Propaganda for the service of 'missionary' countries. Newman continued during this time, as he had done before, to reflect on the question of his future. He considered several hypotheses in turn. He briefly thought of founding a 'school of theology',[5] and then a new foundation to be called the 'Congregation of the Most Holy Trinity' devoted to an intellectual and apologetic apostolate;[6] both ideas, for various

---

[3]   These are to be found in *Oratorian*.

[4]   Newman to Dalgairns, 9 November 1845, *LD* xi, p. 30.

[5]   Newman to Dalgairns, 9 July 1846, *LD* xi, pp. 195–6.

[6]   A brief memorandum to this effect was drawn up on 15 June 1846 (*Oratorian*, pp. 149–50).

reasons, among them suspicion in Rome and elsewhere regarding the orthodoxy of certain of the ideas in his *Essay on Development*, had to be abandoned. He thought long and hard about joining one of the existing religious orders,[7] notably the Jesuits and the Dominicans, but finally rejected both options.[8] He then returned to Wiseman's suggestion that he and his companions should become Oratorians. In December 1846 he and St John visited the Roman Oratory whose premises he found to be 'the most beautiful thing of the kind we have seen in Rome'; he was particularly impressed by the library and the personal apartments of the Fathers, adding that it was 'like a College with hardly any rule'.[9] In January 1847 he began a novena in order to determine whether his 'vocation' was indeed to the Oratory; shortly afterwards, the decision was taken. Three factors seem to have determined Newman's choice; his own situation as a former fellow of an Oxford college and as the leader of a group of fellow-Oxonians;[10] the 'missionary' situation of England in the mid-nineteenth century; and his attraction to the person of St Philip.

---

[7]   See the 'Memorandum of 1878', *Oratorian*, p. 391.

[8]   It was partly the (then) extremely rigorous discipline of the Society of Jesus which caused this rejection, together with what seemed to Newman their intellectual pusillanimity: he complained to a correspondent that the Jesuits displayed 'a deep suspicion of *change*' and 'a perfect incapacity to create anything *positive* for the wants of the times' (*LD* xii, pp. 103–4). As for the Dominicans, he did not yet know of the renewal of the order in France by Lacordaire and concluded rather hastily that the Order of Preachers was 'a great idea extinct' (*LD* xi, p. 195)! He was later to revise both these judgements.

[9]   Newman to Dalgairns, 31 December 1846, *LD* xi, p. 305.

[10] With typical tongue-in-cheek humour, Newman declared in a chapter address in early 1848 that 'the nearest approximation' to an Oratorian community that he knew was 'one of the Colleges in an Anglican University. Take such a College, destroy the Head's house, annihilate wife and children and restore him to the body of fellows, change the religion from Protestant to Catholic, and give the Head and Fellows missionary and pastoral work, and you have a Congregation of St Philip before your eyes.' (*Oratorian*, p. 191). Traditionally, of course, in the Oxford colleges all the fellows, with the exception of the Head, were obliged to remain celibate.

Newman was ordained a Catholic priest on 30 May 1847. In June he left the College of Propaganda and began an Oratorian noviciate, together with Ambrose St John and several other former members of his Littlemore community who had travelled to join them. The noviciate was remarkable for its brevity—only five months—and for its absence of content. However, Newman profited from his abundant free time to document himself thoroughly on St Philip and on the history of the Oratory, reading everything then available (all in Latin and Italian) on the two subjects.[11] (He also found time to write his first novel, *Loss and Gain*, the story of a journey of conversion and a witty and satirical portrait of Oxford at the time of the Tractarian Movement.) Although he never succeeded, for lack of time, in writing the history of St Philip and of his Oratory of which he dreamed, he did produce a number of lengthy and valuable sketches of both. Major, more recent studies of St Philip confirm the accuracy of his portrayal.[12]

---

[11]   Early biographies are those by Antonio Gallonio, a disciple of Philip for 25 years: *Vita Sancti Philippi Nerii* (Latin ed. 1600; Italian ed. 1601; *The Life of St Philip Neri*, trans. Jerome Bertram, CO, 2005); and Pietro Giacomo Bacci, *Vita di San Filippo Neri, Fiorentino* (1622). Both of these draw heavily on the sworn testimonies collected for the Process of Beatification; these have been published as *Il Primo Processo per San Filippo Neri*, ed. G. Incisa della Rochetta & N. Vian, 4 vols (Rome: Vatican Library, 1957–63).

[12]   Two outstanding studies of Philip Neri are those by Louis Ponnelle & Louis Bordet, *Saint Philippe Neri et la société romaine de son temps (1515–1595)* (1928), and Antonio Cistellini, *San Filippo Neri, l'Oratorio et la Congregazione oratoriana. Storia e spiritualità* (1989). Excellent shorter studies are those of Oratorians Louis Bouyer, *Saint Philippe Neri* (1946; English. trans. *St Philip Neri. A Portrait*, 1958), and Paul Türks, *Philipp Neri oder das Feuer der Freude* (Freiburg-im-Breisgau: Herder, 1986); *Philip Neri. The Fire of Joy* (1995). A collection of all Newman's writings on St Philip, in French translation, preceded by a detailed study of the relationship between the two men, has been published by Keith Beaumont under the title: *John Henry Newman: Saint Philippe Neri* (Paris: Ad Solem, 2010).

It is perhaps useful here to sketch a brief portrait of Philip Neri. He was born in Florence in 1515, the son of a notary. He received a solid Christian education, particularly at the hands of the Dominican Friars of the Convent of San Marco, whose memory he would forever revere. At the age of 18 he was sent to stay with his uncle Romolo, a wealthy but childless merchant living in San Germano, between Rome and Naples, not far from the celebrated Benedictine monastery of Monte Cassino. His family hoped that he might inherit his uncle's fortune; Philip, however, displayed a total lack of interest in commerce, and a growing detachment from things of 'the world' in general. He may well have come under the influence of Benedictine monks from Monte Cassino, and in any case was seized by an intense desire for prayer. Henceforth, God, and the desire to lead others to Him, would be the centre of his life.

In 1534 or 1535 he arrived in Rome, where he was to remain for the rest of his life. There he led for several years the life of an 'urban hermit', living in an extremely simple and frugal manner, wandering around the city, and spending long periods of time praying in its churches and in the catacombs. Such was his frequentation of such places that it was said by some contemporaries, with a degree of exaggeration, that Philip 'lived' in the catacombs for ten years. There was nothing morbid in this: quite simply, alongside a place of solitude and silence, he sought a sense of communion with the Christian men and women of early times.[13] It was there that, shortly before the Feast of Pentecost in 1544, he underwent an experience in which, as Newman describes it, 'the Holy Ghost came down upon him in a ball of

---

[13] According to Newman, it was St Benedict who 'sent him to those ancient basilicas, and cemeteries, and catacombs of the Holy City which spoke of the early monks and the primitive religion [...], with the old martyr Popes, and their saintly court and retinue, their deacons and chamberlains, and chaplains; with St Callistus, and St Sebastian, and St Laurence; with St Mark and St Marcellian, with St Agnes and St Cecilia, with St Nereus and St Achilleus, with St Papias and St Maurus [...].' ('The Mission of St Philip Neri', *Various Occasions*, p. 224)

fire [...] and filled his heart with consolations so overwhelming that, lest he should die of ecstasy, he came up into the world of men, and set about a work to flesh and blood more endurable'.[14]

He then joined a small community of pious people who engaged in a range of charitable activities—visiting the sick, consoling the dying, succouring the poor. He was particularly moved by the state of the many pilgrims who flocked to Rome, frequently in a state of physical exhaustion and spiritual distress. To meet their needs he founded in 1548, with his spiritual director Persiano Rosa, a confraternity named the *Trinità dei Pellegrini*; this expanded to such an extent that in the Jubilee Year of 1550 it was able to give hospitality to five hundred pilgrims a day. During all this time he engaged also, as a layman, in a work of evangelization, first amongst his fellow-Florentines (who formed a large colony within the city), then amongst an increasingly wider circle of people of all classes; later on, people came to him from even further afield as his fame spread throughout Italy and to other countries of Europe.

He was ordained a priest, at the insistence of his spiritual director, at the then extremely advanced age of 36, his humility, it seems, having prevented him from previously seeking ordination. Through preaching, confession and spiritual direction, he inspired many with the fervour which he himself experienced. According to his early biographers, he performed also a great many miracles of healing. He pretended to be uneducated but (as two Dominicans sent by Pope Pius V to verify his orthodoxy discovered to their astonishment) he possessed a very detailed and sound grasp of theology. He sent his many penitents and disciples to work voluntarily in the city's hospitals, bringing to patients both spiritual consolation and food (which in those days was not provided by the hospital).

As a priest, he celebrated Mass daily at a time when the practice was rare among priests; he also encouraged his disciples to communicate regularly, when frequent communion was

---

[14]   *Ibid.*, p. 224.

almost unheard of. He encouraged people to confess regularly at a time when this too was virtually unheard of, some of his disciples coming to confession every day. Hearing confessions became, in fact, for Philip a form of spiritual direction. He saw frequent confession and communion as a means of opening oneself up to the Holy Spirit.

It was shortly after his priestly ordination that the *oratorio* or 'oratory' was born. Every afternoon there gathered around him an informal group of disciples for whom Philip instituted a series of 'spiritual exercises'—the term was and is a generic one. These consisted of a time of silent prayer, Bible-reading, preaching—on the Bible or on the life of a saint—music and singing, finishing once more with silent prayer. Here, according to his first biographer, 'the nobility and the poor came together to pray'.[15] As numbers grew, he asked several of his disciples to preach despite their being laymen (a practice which aroused suspicion on the part of some members of the Curia).

The room in which all this took place was called the *oratorio* (from the Latin *orare*, to pray) and the name quickly became transferred to the exercises themselves. In Philip's own eyes, this *oratorio* was his life's work: he had no other ambition than to serve this prayer group which had formed around his person, and certainly no wish to found a 'congregation' in the conventional sense. It was Pope Gregory XIII—a close friend—who in 1575 obliged him to give to this informal community a canonical (and clerical) status. The papal bull of 1575 founding the Congregation of the Oratory[16] defined it as 'a Congregation of secular priests', an expression which seemed at the time almost a contradiction in terms. Philip in fact categorically *refused* to allow its members to take vows: the Oratorians were to live in community, like the members of a religious order or congregation, but the sole link between them was to be that of fraternal charity; each was able

---

[15]   Gallonio, *Life of St Philip Neri* (San Francisco: Ignatius Press, 2005), p. 60.
[16]   In the language of the Oratory of St Philip Neri the word 'congregation' signifies 'community', each individual Oratory being a 'congregation'.

to keep his own property, and to leave the congregation when he wished. This absence of vows in the context of community life was totally unprecedented in the history of the Church, though it was later to serve as a model for numerous other institutes.

Philip also categorically refused the many requests to found other Oratories,[17] even when emanating from men whom he greatly admired such as (the future) St Charles Borromeo in Milan. Scores of other Oratories sprang up spontaneously, however, in imitation of that of Philip—150 of them in the seventeenth century according to Newman[18]—in Italy and elsewhere. Philip always gave as the reason for this refusal the fact that his own Oratory lacked priests, and that sending members to other towns and cities would fatally weaken it. Newman, however, saw another reason for this stubborn refusal: quite simply, 'the idea of propagation did not enter into the mind of St Philip. In his original idea, propagation was impossible, there was nothing to propagate, because he was introducing a set of Exercises, rather than a Community of men'.[19]

During the last twenty or thirty years of his life, whilst remaining a simple priest, Philip became the most celebrated man in Rome amongst all classes of the population. In Newman's words,

> Nothing was too high for him, nothing too low. He taught poor begging women to use mental prayer; he took out boys to play; he protected orphans; he acted as novice-master to the children of St Dominic. He was the teacher and director of artisans, mechanics, cashiers in banks, merchants, workers in gold, artists, men of science. He was consulted by monks, canons, lawyers, physicians, courtiers; ladies of the highest rank, convicts going to execution, engaged in their turn his solicitude and prayers. Cardinals

---

[17]   An exception being Naples, founded against Philip's will by his disciple Tarugi who presented his master with a *fait accompli*.

[18]   'History of the Rise of the Oratory', *Oratorian*, p. 165.

[19]   *Ibid.*, p. 165.

hung about his room, and Popes asked for his miraculous
aid in disease, and his ministrations in death.[20]

Philip's later years were spent more and more in prayer. He was
increasingly subject also to ecstasies, which he did everything in
his power to avoid, in vain; these were particularly frequent
during his celebration of the Mass, and it is reported that he
sometimes placed his cat on the altar as a means of distraction!
The presence of the Holy Spirit within him became more and
more all-absorbing. He died in 1595, mourned and venerated as
a saint by the population of Rome. (Even today, he is venerated
by most Romans, whether Catholics or not.) He was canonized
in 1622, along with Ignatius Loyola, Francis Xavier, Teresa of
Avila and Isidore the Farm-servant (patron saint of Madrid), the
good people of Rome declaring that the Church had that day
canonized 'four Spaniards and a saint'!

What can Newman possibly have had in common with such
a man? The question is incomprehensible so long as—and this is
true, sadly, of many academic studies of Newman—one considers
him *solely* as an intellectual, ignoring the fact that he is also one
of the great spiritual figures and spiritual masters of modern
times. In reality, many things bring them together. Despite their
differences in historical context, in culture, in temperament
(Newman appears as English as Philip[21] was Italian and Florentine) and in literary output (Philip wrote almost nothing, and
towards the end of his life destroyed almost all of the little he
wrote), one can point to many parallels between the two. And
Newman's writings on St Philip tell us a great deal about the
author himself and his ideas. Philip was, in effect, for Newman
both a model and a source of spiritual strength: in the concluding
paragraph of Part I of *The Idea of a University* he declares that,
as regards himself, 'whether or not I can do any thing at all in St
Philip's way, at least I can do nothing in any other'.[22]

---

[20] 'The Mission of St Philip Neri', *Various Occasions*, p. 239.
[21] Curiously, one tends spontaneously to speak of 'Philip' in the case of Neri,
whereas 'John Henry' hardly seems appropriate in Newman's case!

What are, then, these parallels? The following pages will attempt to answer this question.

Renewal through a 'Return to Origins'

It is scarcely necessary to emphasize Newman's passionate interest in the 'Church of the Apostles' and the 'Church of the Fathers'. Philip shared this attitude. Despite a popular image of Philip as a practical joker or as a performer of miracles, both men were conscious reformers of their respective churches. And both sought to bring about reform and renewal through a return to the origins of Christianity, in the Bible, and in what they believed to be the relatively simpler forms of Christian life, of Christian spirituality, and of Church organisation during the early centuries.

In his *Litanies of St Philip*, Newman invokes the latter as *Vir prisci temporis*, 'Man of primitive times'.[23] He stresses the fact that this 'return to origins' was the result of a conscious design on Philip's part:

> It was then a very bold and original undertaking on the part of St Philip, more original perhaps than any thing in the Rule of St Ignatius. [...] there was a plainness and simplicity in the external laws of the primitive Church, whether as to doctrine, ethics or worship, peculiar to itself. Now in the sixteenth century, after heresies and schisms innumerable, St Philip comes forward to bring back all who [would] listen to him to primitive times [...].[24]

The first and most fundamental of these 'sources' to which it was necessary to return was of course the Bible. Philip placed at the centre of the 'exercises' making up his *oratorio* the reading of and preaching upon what was called *il Libro*. This preaching took the form of short sermons given in simple and plain language which

---

[22] *Idea*, p. 238.

[23] *Meditations*, pp. 119, 121. A similar formula, 'Saint of primitive times', occurs in the third of the 'Four Prayers to St Philip' (*Ibid.*, p. 280).

[24] *Oratorian*, p. 203.

contrasted with the grandiloquence of the period; though this may seem self-evident today, such a procedure struck contemporaries as a novelty. However, for Philip the Bible was not just a source of moral teaching and exhortation, it was also a means and an aid to prayer. Philip thus reconnected with the monastic tradition of *Lectio divina* expressed in the four-part formula *lectio, meditatio, oratio, contemplatio*: the reading of the Bible leads to meditation, which leads in turn to orison (vocal prayer), and finally to contemplation (simply 'being there' in the presence of God).

This reading of and meditation upon Scripture was also, in Philip's view, a principal means of *conversion*, replacing the different forms of asceticism of the monastic tradition. Newman quotes to this effect one of Philip's 'spiritual sons', Agostino Manni, the author of a collection of his sayings, who declared that for him 'the hearing daily the Word of God should be the compensation for fastings, vigils, silence, and psalmody; for the Divine Word heard with attention was equal to any such exercise'.[25]

It was the desire to rediscover, and to return to, primitive Christianity which led Philip also to encourage his disciple Cesare Baronio[26] to embark on a study of the history of the Church; the result was the publication between 1588 and 1607, in twelve massive folio volumes, of his *Annales Ecclesiastici* which covered the first twelve centuries of the history of the Church, and on which Newman himself at times drew upon in his patristic studies. These were intended as a reply to the very Protestant *Historia Ecclesiae Christi* of the Magdeburg theologians which purported to show that the Church of Rome was the Antichrist. Baronius had full access to the Vatican archives, and his erudite and authoritative work did much to alter contemporary under-

---

[25] 'Remarks on the Oratorian Vocation', 1856, *Oratorian*, p. 331.

[26] Baronio (1538–1607), whose name is generally Latinized as Baronius, succeeded Philip as superior of the Oratory in 1593 and was made a cardinal in 1596. He is said to have narrowly missed being elected Pope on two occasions.

standing; Philip may not have been an intellectual, but he fully understood, like Newman, the importance of history.

Finally, this 'return to origins' was exemplified, in Philip's view and in that of his disciples, in the former's conception of the 'exercises' making up the *oratorio*. A celebrated passage in Baronius' *Annals*, quoted by Newman, exemplifies this; the historian's enthusiasm causes him suddenly to leap from the past into the present in a celebration of Philip's Oratory:

> In his exterior worship, [Philip] imitated, as Cardinal Baronius observes, the form furnished by St Paul, in his first Epistle to the Corinthians. 'It is by a divine counsel,' says that glory of the Oratory, speaking in his Annals, in the tone of an historian, 'that there has been in great measure renewed in our age in Rome, after the pattern of the Apostolic assembly, the edifying practice of discoursing in sermons of the things of God. This has been the work of the Reverend Father Philip Neri, a Florentine, who, like a skilful architect, laid the foundation of it. It was arranged, that almost every day those who were desirous of Christian perfection should come to the Oratory. First, there was some length of time spent in mental prayer, then one of the brothers read a spiritual book, and during the reading the aforesaid Father commented on what was read. Sometimes he desired one of the brethren to give his opinion on some subject, and then the discourse proceeded in the form of dialogue. After this, he commanded one of them to mount a seat, and there, in a familiar, plain style, to discourse upon the lives of the Saints. To him succeeded another, on a different subject, but equally plain; lastly, a third discoursed upon ecclesiastical history. When all was finished, they sang some spiritual hymn, prayed again for a short time, and so ended. Things being thus disposed, and approved by the Pope's authority, it seemed as though the beautiful form of the Apostolical assembly had returned, as far as times admitted.'[27]

---

[27] Quoted in 'The Mission of St Philip Neri', *Various Occasions*, pp. 225–6.

The Centrality of Prayer

Prayer was, as Newman rightly noted, at the heart of Philip's life and 'mission' (and the same is true of Newman himself). HHis habit of spending, during his early years in Rome, long hours, and sometimes whole nights, in prayer in churches and in the catacombs has already been noted. This was a habit which he never lost, though the demands of his priestly office later obliged him to desert the catacombs. Indeed, as the years went by the desire for prayer seems to have become even stronger. Towards the end of his life he had built a *loggia* on the roof of his house in which he could pray at night under the stars.[28] Yet he was always ready to break off prayer in order to receive his penitents, by day or by night; and he never failed to be on duty in the church in order to hear confessions when it fell to him to do so.

Mention was made earlier of his probable frequentation of Benedictine monks from Monte Cassino. One finds an almost certain echo of the celebrated injunction of the Rule of St Benedict, *Nihil amori Christi praeponere* ('Prefer nothing to the love of Christ') in Philip's declaration: 'He who desires anything other than Christ does not know what he wants; he who desires anything other than Christ does not know what he asks for'. But Philip was drawn also to the writings of the Desert Fathers, the hermit-monks of the fourth and fifth centuries; when his friend Cardinal Federico Borromeo caught him reading one such work, he declared apologetically: 'I read people who lived like me'.[29] He prayed also in the manner of these monks, using short formulas repeated regularly in order to focus the mind on God. Many of these are strongly Christocentric, for example:

> I seek you and cannot find you: come to me, my Jesus!
>
> Jesus, be Jesus for me.

---

[28]   There is an interesting parallel here with St Ignatius Loyola during the last years of his life.

[29]   Quoted by Paul Türks, *Philip Neri. The Fire of Joy* (Edinburgh: T. & T. Clark, 1995), p. 54.

I will never love you if you do not help me, my Jesus.

What will I do if you do not help me, my Jesus?

Lord, do not hide yourself from me.

Lord, do with me as you know and as you will.[30]

Philip displayed also a deep devotion to the Holy Spirit, a devotion echoed in the prayers of Newman addressed to his patron saint in which he invokes him as, amongst other things, 'Vessel of the Holy Ghost'.[31] And in the third of his 'Four Prayers to St Philip' we find the following petition:

> And I beg of thee to gain for me a true devotion to the Holy
> Ghost, by means of that grace which He Himself, the Third
> Person of the glorious Trinity, bestows. Gain for me a
> portion of that overflowing devotion which thou hadst
> towards Him when thou wast on earth [...]. Gain for me,
> O holy Philip, such a measure of thy devotion towards
> Him, that, as He did deign to come into thy heart miracu-
> lously and set it on fire with love, He may reward us too
> with some special and corresponding gift of grace. O
> Philip, let us not be the cold sons of so fervent a Father.[32]

In his sermons, Newman emphasized the central place of prayer in the life of the early Christians, proposing as a model the practice of the Apostolic era. A passage from an Anglican sermon of 1843, 'The Apostolical Christian', reads almost like a portrait— in anticipation—of St Philip:

> This is the very definition of a Christian,—one who looks
> for Christ; not who looks for gain, or distinction, or power,
> or pleasure, or comfort, but who looks 'for the Saviour, the
> Lord Jesus Christ.' [...] And accordingly, prayer [...] is
> another characteristic of Christians as described in Scrip-

---

[30]   Quoted by L. Ponnelle & L. Bordet, *Saint Philippe Neri et la société romaine de son temps (1515–1595)* (Paris: Éditions du Vieux Colombier, 1928; 1958), pp. 546–8. The authors list 54 such prayer formulas.

[31]   *Meditations*, p. 276.

[32]   *Ibid.*, pp. 279–80.

ture. [...] This habit of prayer then, recurrent prayer, morning, noon, and night, is one discriminating point in Scripture Christianity [...]. In a word, there was no barrier, no cloud, no earthly object, interposed between the soul of the primitive Christian and its Saviour and Redeemer. Christ was in his heart, and therefore all that came from his heart, his thoughts, words, and actions, savoured of Christ. The Lord was his light, and therefore he shone with the illumination.[33]

His prayer life—and the presence within him of the Holy Spirit—was undoubtedly the source of the deep inner joy which Philip radiated, which all who met him sensed, and which caused Cardinal Agostino Valier to publish, four years before his death, a short work entitled *Philip or the Dialogue of Christian Joy*. Newman was fully aware of the divine origin of this joy: Philip, he declared, was 'great simply in the attraction with which a Divine Power had gifted him'.[34]

Philip and Newman did not just content themselves with praying, however; they also sought consistently to deepen the prayer life of their listeners (and, in Newman's case, readers). According to his disciple Gallonio, '[i]n his daily discourse, [Philip's] principal aim was to inspire the hearts of his followers to prayer, to frequent the sacraments, and to do other works of devotion', desiring to 'form Christ' in his disciples.[35] Many of Newman's Anglican sermons contain exhortations to prayer; and in an early, unpublished sermon, preached several times, he goes so far as to state that praying, rather than hearing a sermon, is the chief reason for coming to church.[36]

---

[33] *Subjects*, pp. 279–81.

[34] *Idea*, p. 201.

[35] *The Life of St Philip Neri*, p. 49.

[36] 'On the objects and effects of preaching – (on the anniversary of my entering on my living)', *Sermons 1824–1843*, ed. Placid Murray, vol. i (Oxford: Clarendon Press, 1991), p. 25.

An Emphasis on Greater Interiority

In his writings and discourses on St Philip, Newman deals at
length with the latter's repeated refusal of religious vows. Whilst
Newman did not display the same hostility, he nonetheless shared
Philip's rejection of them in regard to the Oratory, once complaining (admittedly in a somewhat joking vein and in reference
to his huge library) that 'the notion of giving up property' would
'try [his] faith very much'.[37] Yet this refusal of vows in the context
of his Oratory did not prevent Philip from sending scores of new
recruits to the Jesuits (to the extent that he was given the
nick-name of the Society's 'bell of call'[38]) and especially to the
Dominicans. And nor did it prevent Newman from directing a
number of young men and women towards religious orders, all
of which embraced vows.

Newman explains Philip's hostility towards religious vows in
terms of a desire to preserve a spirit of freedom, and above all of
a quest for greater *interiority*. Philip's rejection of 'external' vows
and observances was due, he maintains, to his burning desire to
'inscribe the law' on the hearts of his disciples, in such a way as
to make of them 'living laws':

> St Philip then formed a community, yet without vows and
> almost without rules; and he aimed at doing this [...] by
> forming in his disciples a certain character instead. [...] It
> was St Philip's object therefore, instead of imposing laws
> on his disciples, to mould them, as far as might be, into
> living laws, or, in the words of Scripture, to write the law
> on their hearts.[39]

However, if the Oratory distinguished itself *externally* from
religious orders and congregations, it must, according to

---

[37]   Newman to Dalgairns, 31 December 1846, *LD* xi, p. 306.

[38]   *Idea*, p. 235.

[39]   Address of 9 February 1848, *Oratorian*, p. 206. The Biblical reference is
to Jer. 31:33: 'I will put my law within them, and I will write it upon their
hearts' (RSV trans.).

Newman, aim at and possess their *interior* 'perfection': thus the Oratory must *resemble* a 'religion' (that is to say, a religious institute) without actually *being* one:

> From all this I conclude that St Philip's wish and aim was, that his Congregation should be in one sense a religion, i.e. *taking away* externals, vow, rule, poverty, bodily mortifications and the like; that is, it was to have the internal perfection of a religion, whatever that may be said to consist in. [...] Its characteristic is that it is a *sort* of religion, though not properly a religion [...].[40]

Seeking God in *'the World'*

Both Philip and Newman combined a contemplative temperament with a deep pastoral concern. Philip, as stated above, worked tirelessly among the poor and the sick. As for Newman, there is a deep continuity between the work of the young deacon of St Clement's, one of the poorest parishes in Oxford, visiting *all* his parishioners with particular attention paid to the poor and the sick, and the elderly Oratorian coming to the aid, financially and in other ways, of the poor Irish families living in the vicinity of the Oratory in Edgbaston. Yet both men exercised this charitable activity with such discretion, not to say secretiveness, that it was not until after their deaths that their astonished Oratorian brethren discovered its full extent.

Newman emphasizes the importance accorded by Philip to seeking God *in* 'the world', and therefore to the spiritual life of the laity. He sees a parallel here with St Ignatius Loyola:

> From St Benedict's time there had been a broad line between the world and the Church, and it was very hard to follow sanctity without entering into Religion. St Ignatius and St Philip, on the contrary, carried out the Church into the world, and aimed to bring under her light yoke as

---

[40] 'The Santa Croce Papers', August–September 1847, *Oratorian*, pp. 399, 401.

> many men as they could possibly reach. [...] It was his
> mission to save men, not from, but in the world.[41]

Philip and Newman also shared a deep human sympathy with regard to other men. Philip had about him a simplicity and natural charm which enabled him to enter into contact easily with the simple and ignorant; but at the same time he possessed (whilst pretending to be ignorant) a knowledge and culture which enabled him to converse with the most highly educated.[42] Newman, quoting his biographer Pietro Bacci (who himself quotes St Paul) describes him, in the conclusion to the final Discourse of *The Idea of a University*, in the following terms:

> In the words of his biographer, 'he was all things to all
> men.[43] He suited himself to noble and ignoble, young and
> old, subjects and prelates, learned and ignorant; and
> received those who were strangers to him with singular
> benignity, and embraced them with as much love and
> charity as if he had been a long while expecting them. [...]
> He gave the same welcome to all: caressing the poor
> equally with the rich, and wearying himself to assist all to
> the utmost limits of his power. [...] Nay, people came to
> him, not only from all parts of Italy, but from France,
> Spain, Germany, and all Christendom; and even the
> infidels and Jews, who had ever any communication with
> him, revered him as a holy man.'[44]

A further trait shared by both men was, in Newman's eyes, a positive attitude towards all forms of culture. In 'The Mission of St Philip Neri' his love of typologies causes him to sketch parallel portraits of Philip and his Florentine compatriot, the great

---

41   *Various Occasions*, pp. 228, 239.
42   Philip's personal library, preserved at the Roman Oratory, contains over three hundred volumes of philosophy, spirituality and sermons. See 'La Libreria di san Filippo' in *Messer Filippo Neri, Santo, l'Apostolo di Roma* (Rome: Edizioni de Luca, 1995), pp. 112–13.
43   1 Cor 9:22.
44   *Idea*, pp. 236–7.

Dominican reformer Savonarola, who had attempted between 1494 and 1498 to reform the moral and religious life of his fellow-citizens by violence, both verbal and physical: twice he organized an enormous bonfire in the centre of Florence onto which the population was invited to throw profane works of art, literature, jewellery, fashionable clothes and other secular objects, the whole then being set alight and consumed by the flames.[45] Philip was as passionate a reformer as Savonarola; yet he sought to achieve his aims by diametrically opposite means. He was 'to pursue Savonarola's purposes, but not in Savonarola's way; rather, in the spirit and after the fashion of those early Religious, of which St Benedict is the typical representative'.[46] Elsewhere, Newman declares that Philip 'preferred to yield to the stream, and direct the current, which he could not stop, of science, literature, art, and fashion, and to sweeten and to sanctify what God had made very good and man had spoilt'.[47]

Let there be no mistake, however, about the ultimate *aim* of Philip (as of Newman also): it was, as with Savonarola, to bring about a *conversion* of men's hearts. Philip's gentle and patient pedagogy aimed at precisely the same goal as the Dominican's violence.

The 'Spiritual Humanism' of St Philip

Philip illustrated, in Newman's eyes, the truth of the traditional theological adage *gratia perfecit naturam*, that grace does not replace nature but, by penetrating it and transforming it from within, brings it to perfection. This view is forcefully expressed in his two Dublin sermons devoted to the Apostle Paul, both of which are also in part (the one explicitly, the other implicitly) portraits of St Philip (and doubtless, too, unconscious portraits of the author himself). In 'St Paul's Characteristic Gift', he

---

[45] *Various Occasions*, pp. 210–17.
[46] *Various Occasions*, pp. 224–5.
[47] *Idea*, p. 235.

declares that men such as Paul (and implicitly also Philip) are outstanding examples of a category of saints, 'of the highest order of sanctity',

> in whom the supernatural combines with nature, instead of superseding it,– invigorating it, elevating it, ennobling it; and who are not the less men, because they are saints. They do not put away their natural endowments, but use them to the glory of the Giver; they do not act beside them, but through them; they do not eclipse them by the brightness of divine grace, but only transfigure them. They are versed in human knowledge; they are busy in human society; they understand the human heart; they can throw themselves into the minds of other men; and all this in consequence of natural gifts and secular education. While they themselves stand secure in the blessedness of purity and peace, they can follow in imagination the ten thousand aberrations of pride, passion, and remorse. [...] Thus they have the thoughts, feelings, frames of mind, attractions, sympathies, antipathies of other men, so far as these are not sinful, only they have these properties of human nature purified, sanctified, and exalted; and they are only made more eloquent, more poetical, more profound, more intellectual, by reason of their being more holy.[48]

In similar vein, Newman exhorts his fellow-Oratorians, in a chapter address, to aim 'at being something more'—more, and not just other—'than mere University men, such as we all have been. Let grace perfect nature, and let us, as Catholics, not indeed cease to be what we were, but exalt what we were into something which we were not'.[49]

Humour and Humility

The popular image of Philip as a practical joker is not wholly misplaced. He regularly employed humour, irony, and even

---

[48]   *Various Occasions*, pp. 92–3.
[49]   *Oratorian*, p. 221.

mockery in order to jolt people into greater self-awareness and to teach them humility, that most fundamental (but today least understood) of Christian virtues. One can quote many anecdotes to this effect. For example, a lady who held a high opinion of herself, insisting on always having *her* place in church, systematically arrived late so that others would notice her, until the day when Philip had two ushers wait for her and escort her in full view of the congregation to her place, after which she was never late again. When his gifted but somewhat ostentatious disciple Tarugi asked if he might wear a hairshirt, Philip replied: 'certainly, so long as you wear it *over* your doublet'. He insisted on the utmost simplicity in the manner of preaching, and one disciple who failed to respect this rule was compelled to repeat his excessively elaborate sermon seven times. When a vain young noblemen came to see him so that he could boast to his friends that he had met 'the saint', Philip acted the clown, with the result that the young man went away in a fit of pique and told his friends that he had met not a saint but an idiot; this being reported back to Philip, he declared: 'Tell him that if he comes back tomorrow it will be even worse'!

Newman desired his fellow-Oratorians to share this spirit. He wished to have in his own institute 'companions who have a good deal of fun in them—for that will be especially wanted in an Oratory', adding that '[i]f we do not have spirit, it will be like bottled beer with the cork out'[50] and writing to Dominic Barberi that 'we must manage to be cheerful in order to convert young persons'.[51]

Philip's humour was directed not only against others, however, but also against himself, taking a self-deprecatory form. He placed himself in situations of incongruity and even ridicule in order himself to practice the virtue of humility. Several of his prayer formulas also reveal this trait of character, for example: 'Lord, mistrust Philip'. (Newman, too, particularly in his letters, displays

---

[50] Newman to Dalgairns, 2 March 1847, *LD* xii, pp. 54–5.
[51] 14 March 1847, *LD* xii, p. 62.

this same—very English, but totally un-French—self-deprecatory humour.)

Newman emphasizes many times over the humility of Philip, which he held up as an example to others and which he himself strove to emulate. Though men came from all over Christendom to see him, though 'the first families of Rome' were 'his friends and penitents', though 'Cardinals, Archbishops and Bishops were his intimates', 'who was he', asks Newman, 'but an humble priest, a stranger in Rome, with no distinction of family or letters, no claim of station or of office, great simply in the attraction with which a Divine Power had gifted him?'[52] The conclusion to 'The Mission of St Philip Neri' declares him to be his followers' 'true model,—the humble priest, shrinking from every kind of dignity, or post, or office, and living the greater part of day and night in prayer, in his room or upon the housetop'.[53] And Newman addresses this exhortation to his Oratorian brethren:

> May this spirit ever rule us more and more! For me, my
> dear Fathers of the Oratory, did you ask me, and were I
> able, to gain some boon for you from St Philip [...] I would
> beg for you this privilege, that the public world might never
> know you for praise or for blame, that you should do a
> good deal of hard work in your generation, and prosecute
> many useful labours, and effect a number of religious
> purposes, and send many souls to heaven [...]; but that by
> the world you should be overlooked, that you should not
> be known out of your place, that you should work for God
> alone with a pure heart and single eye, without the distrac-
> tions of human applause, and should make Him your sole
> hope, and His eternal heaven your sole aim, and have your
> reward, not partly here, but fully and entirely hereafter.[54]

---

[52]   *Idea*, pp. 237–8.
[53]   *Various Occasions*, p. 240.
[54]   *Various Occasions*, pp. 241–2.

A Spirituality of 'Surrender' to God

Lastly, the spirituality of the two men led ultimately to an attitude which Newman, following the tradition of English spiritual authors, calls 'surrender' to God. According to one of Philip's many maxims, the aim of every Christian must be to 'give himself up to God in love [...], that is to love God and to surrender himself lovingly to Him'.[55] As for Newman, here is but one among many passages which one could quote from his sermons and prayers:

> But when a man comes to God to be saved, then, I say, the essence of true conversion is a *surrender* of himself, an unreserved, unconditional surrender; and this is a saying which most men who come to God cannot receive. They wish to be saved, but in their own way; they wish (as it were) to capitulate upon terms, to carry off their goods with them; whereas the true spirit of faith leads a man to look off from self to God, to think nothing of his own wishes, his present habits, his importance or dignity, his rights, his opinions, but to say, 'I put myself into Thy hands, O Lord; make Thou me what Thou wilt; I forget myself; I divorce myself from myself; I am dead to myself; I will follow Thee.'[56]

Conclusion

Philip sought, as do all true reformers, to bring men and women back to God. But his *manner* of achieving this differed from that of his most famous contemporaries. He created no new organisation to further the cause of the Church, as did St Ignatius; indeed, by temperament he was totally incapable of such a work. Nor did he produce any new doctrinal synthesis, as did the sons of St Dominic, the second of Newman's three great 'patriarchs'; of that too he was quite incapable. But he drew people to himself, as was said at the time, 'as iron is drawn to a magnet'. And what

---

[55] Quoted in San Filippo Neri, *Gli scritti e le massime*, ed. A Cistellini (Brescia: La Scuola, 1984), p. 12.

[56] 'The Testimony of Conscience', *Parochial and Plain* v, pp. 241–2.

above all else drew them to him was his personal holiness—more specifically the presence, of which all who met him were aware, of the Holy Spirit working within him.

Philip corresponds to, and illustrates, Newman's conception of 'personal influence', which lies not in the force of argument but in what he likes to call—in a formula borrowed from the King James Bible and the translation of the Psalms in the Anglican *Book of Common Prayer* (but absent from most of our modern translations)—'the beauty of holiness'. Dostoevsky is reported to have said that beauty would save the world; for Newman—as also, we may suppose, for Philip—it is rather personal holiness, and the 'beauty of holiness', which would achieve that aim. Two passages from sermons, one Anglican, the other Catholic, illustrate admirably this theme:

> [Christianity] has been upheld in the world not as a system, not by books, not by argument, nor by temporal power, but by the personal influence of [its saints]. [...] Men persuade themselves, with little difficulty, to scoff at principles, to ridicule books, to make sport of the names of good men; but they cannot bear their presence: it is *holiness embodied in personal form*, which they cannot steadily confront and bear down. [...] *A few highly-endowed men will rescue the world for centuries to come.*[57]

> St Philip was an obscure priest, with only the jurisdiction of a confessor; yet the highest and the lowest agreed in this, that, putting aside forms as far as it was right to do so, and letting influence take the place of rule, and charity stand instead of authority, they drew souls to them by their *interior beauty*, and held them captive by the regenerate affections of human nature.[58]

---

[57]   'Personal Influence, the Means of Propagating the Truth', *University Sermons*, pp. 91–7. Italics mine.

[58]   'St Paul's Gift of Sympathy', *Various Occasions*, pp. 119–20. Italics mine.

NEWMAN AND THE EUCHARIST: A NARRATIVE

SISTER KATHLEEN DIETZ, FSO

HEN I WAS approached to write a contribution for this book in honor of Fr Ian Ker, I was taken back in memory to a talk of his in which he spoke about Newman's devotion to the Eucharist. I do not remember where the talk was held or what year it was, but the talk made a deep impression on me—perhaps not so much an impression of Newman as an impression of Fr Ker. Through that talk I understood that Fr Ker knows Newman not only intellectually but also, and more importantly, personally—and that he loves him. In the academic world of Newman studies where many scholars have only a *notional* knowledge of Newman and his works, Ian Ker stands out not only as the greatest Newman scholar, but as one who has a *real* knowledge of Newman leading to, as well as motivated by, love.

I have styled this paper a 'narrative' because it will trace Newman's understanding of and devotion to the Eucharist in his life. Given its scope, it will do no more than touch upon various aspects of the Eucharist in Newman's life and writings. It is impossible to separate Newman's understanding of the Eucharist from his understanding of the Church, that is, from his ecclesiology. Related to it are questions of apostolic succession, ordination, and liturgy, as well as faith and devotion. It is obvious that these subjects cannot be exhaustively dealt with in an article of this size, but they must be looked at if we are to come to a correct appreciation for Newman's understanding of the Eucharist.

The Formative Years

Newman tells us in his *Apologia pro Vita Sua*, 'I was brought up from a child to take great delight in reading the Bible; but I had no formed religious convictions till I was fifteen.'[1] Then, he informs us, 'a great change of thought took place in me. I fell under the influences of a definite Creed, and received into my intellect impressions of dogma, which, through God's mercy, have never been effaced or obscured.'[2] This dogmatic principle, that is, the principle that there is objective truth, was to inform Newman's entire life from then on.

During that decisive autumn of 1816, Newman was accompanied by the Rev. Walter Mayers, who gave Newman several works to read, all of the school of Calvin. Thus Newman accepted and imbibed Calvinistic teaching and held such doctrines until he came under the influence of the Fellows of Oriel College, into whose company he was elected in 1822.

At the age of sixteen, Newman began to study at Trinity College, Oxford. Many years later, in musing upon a photograph of Trinity Chapel which hung in his room, he recalled 'with what feelings' he went up to the communion table in November 1817 for his first Communion. He was in mourning for Princess Charlotte and 'had silk black gloves—the glove would not come off when I had to receive the Bread, and I had to tear it off and spoil it in my flurry'.[3]

It was the custom at Trinity that the whole college would take part in the Communion Service on Trinity Sunday. The next day was the traditional Trinity Gaudy which consisted mainly in a wine party at which many got drunk. To Newman, who was not given to excess drinking and whose tenor of mind would not permit him to enjoy such conviviality, the Gaudy did 'more harm to the College than the whole year [could] compensate' precisely

---

[1]   *Apologia*, p. 1.

[2]   *Ibid.*, p. 4.

[3]   *Philosophical Notebook* ii, pp. 195, 197.

because those who got drunk threw 'off the allegiance and service of their Maker, which they [had] pledged the day before at His Table' and in so doing, showed 'themselves true sons of Belial'.[4]

Newman's devotion to Holy Communion is evident in his journal entries of the next few years. Indeed, he saw 'communicating' as one of the means to growth in holiness. This devotion to Communion was not by any means incompatible with Evangelicalism.[5] Newman prepared for each participation in the Communion Service with a strict self-examination in the manner of Evangelicals. Thus we find him writing on 4 August 1821, 'I have this week been preparing myself for the Sacrament, which, God willing, I hope to take with my brother Francis once a fortnight during the Long Vacation.'[6] This is followed by a self-examination based on questions posed in Doddridge's *Rise and Progress of Religion in the Soul*.[7] We find Newman's journal at this time is filled with self-examinations interspersed with notes that he 'took the Sacrament'.[8]

After being elected Fellow of Oriel College in 1822, Newman began to be acquainted with the members of the Oriel Common Room whose influence, in part, brought about 'a great change in his religious opinions' between 1824 and 1826.[9] This influence,

---

[4]   Newman to Walter Mayers, 6 June (Trinity Sunday) 1819, *LD* i, p. 66.

[5]   'It is a not too well-known fact that the practice of Holy Communion began to be restored to the place of honor which it once held, but which it had for a long time ceased to enjoy in the English Church, not by the High Church party, but by the Evangelicals. [...] The churches of the early Evangelicals were distinguished by the large number of communicants at the Communion service' (Thomas L. Sheridan, SJ, *Newman on Justification: A Theological Biography* (Staten Island: Alba House, 1967), pp. 48–9.

[6]   *AW*, p. 174.

[7]   See Philip Doddridge, *The Rise and Progress of Religion in the Soul* (London: J. Waugh, 1745), pp. 172–3.

[8]   See for example *AW*, pp. 181, 183, 185, 188, 189.

[9]   Newman described the members of the Oriel Common Room as 'being as remarkable for the complexion of their theology and their union among themselves in it, as for their literary eminence. [...] In religion they were neither high Church nor low Church, but had become a new school [...]

coupled with his practical experiences of working among the people of St Clement's parish,[10] brought him gradually to leave his evangelical views behind and to embrace more catholic principles. In the throes of the internal conflict which this caused, Newman noted in his diary that principle which would eventually lead him to the Roman Catholic Church. 'I think', he wrote, 'I really desire the truth, and would embrace it, wherever I found it.'[11]

Among the doctrines which Newman learned at this time, two especially have a bearing on the subject at hand. He learned the doctrine of Apostolic Succession from one of the Oriel Fellows while taking a walk in Oxford,[12] and from his close friend, Hurrell Froude, also an Oriel Fellow, Newman was led gradually to a belief in the Real Presence of Christ in the Eucharist.[13]

The Oxford Movement

In June 1833 Parliament passed the Irish Church Reform Bill, a manifest encroaching of the state in Church matters. In reaction,

---

which was characterized by its spirit of moderation and comprehension' (*AW*, p. 73).

[10] Newman accepted the curacy of St Clements in May 1824 and was ordained deacon on 13 June. 'He began an intensive visitation of the parish, throwing himself into ordinary pastoral work as energetically and unsparingly as he had applied himself to academic study' (*Biography: Newman*, p. 21).

[11] *AW*, p. 78.

[12] This doctrine became the rallying cry of the Oxford Movement, which Newman spearheaded.

[13] It should be mentioned that from the time of his first (Anglican) Communion, Newman had an awe and reverence for the Sacrament. As an Evangelical he assiduously prepared for receiving the Sacrament through rigorous self-examination, as we have seen. As he moved away from Evangelicalism and came to believe in the Real Presence, so did he move away from that type of preparation. He felt that fasting or some form self-denial around the reception of Holy Communion would be 'very desirable' lest one 'should grow familiar with so awful a mystery' (Newman to Miss Holmes, 31 December 1840, *LD* vii, p. 473). See also *Biography: Newman*, p. 203.

a movement began which became known as the Oxford or Tractarian Movement, with Newman as one of its leaders.

The Irish Reform Bill had been simply a symptom and result of a deep-rooted and fundamental illness in the Church of England at the time. This illness, which was growing ever more serious at an alarming rate, had long been felt by Newman and the others who began the Oxford Movement, but the Irish Bill brought forth their battle cry and they began combatting not only the symptoms, but the illness itself. What was this illness? It was the wrong understanding of the Church and of those things intimately or even essentially associated with her, that is, the lack of a correct and full ecclesiology. For this reason the *Tracts for the Times* and the other publications of members of the Movement, while covering a wide variety of topics, all have to do with the Church in one way or another, and hence with the Eucharist, which is intimately bound up with a correct understanding of the Church.

In his *Apologia pro Vita Sua*, Newman lists three principles which he promoted in the Movement and which he saw as fundamental to it: 1. The principle of dogma; 2. 'the truth of a certain definite religious teaching, based upon this foundation of dogma; viz. that there was a visible Church, with sacraments and rites which are the channels of invisible grace';[14] and 3. 'my then view of the Church of Rome', i.e. anti-Romanism.[15] The first two are principles which are foundational to his understanding of the Eucharist.

Apostolic Succession

The main weapon of the Oxford Movement was the written word, and on the front-lines of the battle were the *Tracts for the Times*. Tract 1, entitled *Thoughts on the Ministerial Commission, Respectfully Addressed to the Clergy*, was written by Newman and published in September 1833. This Tract brought out one of the main principles of the Movement: apostolic succession. This

---

[14]   *Apologia*, p. 49.
[15]   *Apologia*, p. 52.

principle is intimately connected with the sacramental principle and forms the main argument of the Movement against the suppression of the Irish Sees by means of the Irish Reform Bill. Newman's question in the *Tract* was, 'on *what* are we to rest our authority, when the State deserts us?' He then remarks that he fears the English clergy have 'neglected the real ground on which our authority is built,—our apostolical descent'.[16] He then goes on to give a definition of that descent:

> The Lord Jesus Christ gave His Spirit to His Apostles; they in turn laid their hands on those who should succeed them; and these again on others; and so the sacred gift has been handed down to our present Bishops, who have appointed us as their assistants, and in some sense representatives. [...]

> Thus we have confessed before God our belief, that through the Bishop who ordained us, we received the Holy Ghost, the power to bind and to loose, to administer the Sacraments, and to preach.[17]

Newman maintains, therefore, that no-one is truly ordained who is not thus ordained, and that this ordination is necessary in order to administer the sacraments and to preach because it is a divine ordinance, 'for when God appoints means of grace, they are *the* means.'[18]

On the first day of 1834, Newman wrote to a friend: 'We have got into trouble (as you know) on the doctrine of the Lord's Supper. I hold most entirely to every word that has been said—but doubtless it might have been said better [...] It is not a minor matter to be passed over—it is intimately connected with the doctrine of the Apostolical Succession—If *consecration* be necessary for the Sacrament, can we suppose *any one* may consecrate?'[19]

---

[16] Tract 1, p. 2, *Tracts*.

[17] Tract 1, pp. 2–3, *Tracts*.

[18] Tract 1, p. 3, *Tracts*.

[19] Newman to Hugh James Rose, 1 January 1834, *LD* iv, p. 158. The trouble to which Newman referred was the accusation that the Tractarians held the same teaching on Transubstantiation as the Roman Church—just

Newman addressed himself again and again to the subject of apostolic succession in the Tracts, especially in three of them.[20] His arguments remain the same: that the Apostles left successors, that the bishops are plainly those successors, that there has been a perpetual succession, that no one has the right to preach or administer the sacraments unless he has been called by God.

The Visible Church

Already in his second Tract Newman begins to express the principle of a visible Church, on which he will later elaborate in Tracts 11, 20 and 47. He notes that the Creed has from earliest times expressed belief in the One, Catholic and Apostolic Church. This is a fact to be believed and is therefore practical. The Divines of the English Church have always seen it as meaning 'that there is on earth an existing Society, Apostolic as founded by the Apostles, Catholic because it spreads its branches in every place; i.e. the Church Visible with its Bishops, Priests and Deacons'.[21]

The first two Tracts, it can be said, form the basis for the other Tracts written by Newman. We see in them above all the second principle which Newman enumerated as being the basis of the Movement, namely, the principle of the existence of a visible Church with sacraments which are a means of grace.[22] It is

---

months into the Movement, and the cry of Popery is heard. Thus began what would become an important aspect of the Oxford Movement: the problem of Rome. To offset this, they published Tracts 27 and 28, Bishop Cosin's *The History of Popish Transubstantiation,* in February and March 1834. But the problem remained, and soon afterwards Newman wrote to his sister about a mutual friend, saying that his 'great ground against us, is, that language about the Eucharist which was allowable in the Fathers, is dangerous since the Popish corruptions' (Newman to his sister Jemima, 18 May 1834, *LD* iv, p. 253).

[20]   Tracts 15, 19, 74.

[21]   Tract 2, pp. 2–3, *Tracts.*

[22]   Newman elaborated on his understanding of a visible Church in subsequent Tracts. These Tracts form a series called 'The Visible Church. Letters to a Friend' (Tracts 11, 20 and 47).

important to note, however, that bound together with this second principle and, in fact, presupposed by it, is the first principle, the principle of dogma. Without the principle of dogma, that is, without an objective, revealed truth, the visible Church would have no meaning and no basis for existence. Necessary to the visible Church are the bishops in apostolic succession as those responsible for the purity of doctrine, for the unity of the Church and for the sacraments.

Newman's Sermons

One of Newman's contemporaries, R. W. Church, puts the Tracts in context:

> The Tracts were not the most powerful instrument in drawing sympathy to the movement. None but those who remember them can adequately estimate the effect of Mr Newman's four o'clock sermons at St Mary's. The world knows them, has heard a great deal about them, has passed its various judgments on them. But it hardly realises that without these sermons the movement might never have gone on, certainly would never have been what it was. [...] While men were reading and talking about the Tracts, they were hearing the sermons; and in the sermons they heard the living meaning, and reason, and bearing of the Tracts [...] The sermons created a moral atmosphere in which men judged the questions in debate.[23]

---

[23]   R. W. Church, *The Oxford Movement: Twelve Years, 1833–1845* (London: MacMillan & Co., 1891), pp. 113–14. Many a man could remember years later the effect of the sermons on himself and could describe the atmosphere and the delivery. They served to form the whole man, not leaving him to be only intellectually convinced by the arguments in the Tracts, but pointing him to a continual personal conversion as being the essence of a genuine religiosity. Nor was it the sermons alone in and of themselves which served this purpose. It was the sermons as delivered by Newman, not because he was a great preacher in terms of rhetoric or animation or any special effect in delivery, but because he was what he preached.

It is impossible to do justice to Newman's sermons in this short essay, but a sampling of their content on the Eucharist may give an understanding of that richness, simplicity and moral beauty which so attracted the Oxford students at the time. It is astounding how many sermons Newman preached on the Eucharist, or at least with reference to the Eucharist, while he was an Anglican.[24] The overarching themes are those of faith in that which cannot be seen[25] and awe and reverence for so great a gift of the Lord.

In a sermon which he did not publish we find this interesting comparison and call to faith:

> Did you see His very cross, it w[ou]ld look only like what it was, a beam of wood—& you w[ou]ld have to believe what you did not see, that Xt was once laid upon it. Use but the same faith now in another way, & you have a like privilege to feed upon. You do not see any thing but bread and wine in His holy supper—but believe what you do not, cannot see. Doubt not that in some unknown way He is present, [...] and, if so, is there not something very over-powering in the thought?[26]

Newman preached on Luke 24:5–6, 'Why seek ye the living among the dead? He is not here, but is risen' in his sermon for Easter entitled 'Christ, A Quickening Spirit'. He notes that Christ did not conclude his work of mercy among us when He ascended into Heaven. He exclaims, 'Blessed for ever be His Holy Name!' And goes on to explain that before Christ's ascension, 'He remembered our necessity, and completed His work, bequeathing to us a special mode of approaching Him, a Holy Mystery, in which we receive (we know not how) the virtue of that Heavenly

---

[24] See Alf Härdelin, *The Tractarian Understanding of the Eucharist* (Stockholm: Uppsala, 1965), pp. 354–5.

[25] 'On this point of faith as it related to the Eucharist, Newman was insistent, maintaining that the eucharistic Presence was a presence to faith and not to sight' (John Tracy Ellis, 'The Eucharist in the Life of Cardinal Newman', *Communio* 4:4 (1977), p. 323).

[26] Härdelin, *op. cit.*, p. 187, n. 21.

Body, which is the life of all that believe. This is the blessed Sacrament of the Eucharist'. Newman then takes the opportunity to bring home to his congregation the 'unspeakable sacredness' of that 'great gift'.[27]

In his remarkable sermon, The Eucharistic Presence', Newman shows himself a gifted exegete, first is remarking on the Gospel of John as a theological explanation of the synoptic Gospels, and then in explaining the Bread of Life discourse in chapter six.[28] It is not difficult to imagine that the members of his congregation would never read the Gospel of John again without hearing his sermon echo in their minds. He concludes with these words: 'Let us pray Him then to give us such a real and living insight into the blessed doctrine of the Incarnation of the Son of God, of His birth of a Virgin, His atoning death, and resurrection, that we may desire that the Holy Communion may be the effectual type of that gracious Economy. No one realizes the Mystery of the Incarnation but must feel disposed towards that of Holy Communion.'[29] What is remarkable here is the flow of Newman's sermon from doctrine to devotion; the obvious congruence of the Incarnation with the Eucharist.

The 'Problem' of Transubstantiation

Almost from the beginning of the Oxford Movement the Eucharist loomed large—in the Tracts and in Newman's sermons. Insofar as the Movement was an ecclesial movement, it had to address the sacramental nature of the Church, which meant that, of necessity, the Eucharist came to the fore. Nonetheless, it was very important to Newman that 'the controversy about the Holy Eucharist' be put in the background of the controversy with

---

[27]   *Parochial and Plain* ii, pp. 144, 145.

[28]   Newman uses another passage of chapter six of John's Gospel in his sermon, 'The Gospel Feast', again showing his accomplishment as a biblical exegete, and understanding the reference again to be to the Eucharist. See *Parochial and Plain* vii, pp. 160ff.

[29]   *Parochial and Plain* vi, p. 151.

Rome, because it is 'almost certain to lead to profane and rationalistic thoughts in the minds of the many, and cannot well be discussed in words at all, without the sacrifice of "godly fear"'[30] He proceeds to note that transubstantiation, should it be discussed at all, should be opposed on the grounds of it being an innovation at a certain time, not being found in the teaching of the early Church.

The subject of transubstantiation arose inevitably. How else could the Tractarians oppose Rome on the subject of the Eucharist when they, too, believed in the Real Presence? In a letter written in 1834, Newman calls it 'unnecessary and irreverent' for the Roman Church to insist that 'the bread and wine are *changed* into that same flesh and blood which were on the Cross', but he acknowledges that it 'seems safe and according to Scripture to say He is present *in* the bread and wine'.[31]

In Tract 90, Newman addresses the question of transubstantiation in his comments on Article 28 of the Thirty-Nine Articles. 'What is here opposed as "Transubstantiation", is the shocking doctrine that "the body of Christ", as the Article goes on to express it, is *not* "given, taken, and eaten, after an heavenly and spiritual manner, but is carnally pressed with the teeth"; that It is a body or substance of a certain extension and bulk in space, and a certain figure and due disposition of parts, whereas we hold that the only substance such, is the bread which we see.'[32]

Newman testifies in his *Apologia* that before his conversion he did not believe in transubstantiation but afterwards did.[33]

---

[30]   Tract 71, p. 9, *Tracts*.

[31]   Newman to Mrs William Wilberforce, 17 November 1834, *LD* iv, p. 368. See *Biography: Newman*, p. 112, where Ian Ker comments that Newman interpreted transubstantiation to mean that Christ's Body and Blood were literally present on the altar. See also Härdelin, *op. cit.*, p. 187.

[32]   *Via Media* ii, p. 315.

[33]   'People say that the doctrine of Transubstantiation is difficult to believe; I did not believe the doctrine till I was a Catholic. I had no difficulty in believing it, as soon as I believed that the Catholic Roman Church was the oracle of God, and that she had declared this doctrine to be part of the

What changed was not his view of the Eucharist, but his view of
the Church. Conversion to the Catholic Church is not a conversion to individual doctrines, but a conversion to the Church as
such, a belief in the Church.[34] It is not believing more but
believing something different.

Newman's problem with transubstantiation was a problem of
imagination, first of all. This is why he called the doctrine
'shocking'.[35] Dr Charles Russell, who taught St Patrick's College,
Maynooth, started to correspond with Newman in 1843; he
understood instinctively that Newman's problems with the
Church of Rome were not in the first place theological, but
imaginative.[36] When he wrote to Newman, he did not know him
personally, but felt drawn to Newman with a 'strangely powerful
impulse' for which he could scarcely account, even to himself.
Grieved to find in Newman's writings many misunderstandings
of Roman Catholic teaching, he began his letter on that which
was closest to their hearts: the Eucharist.

> I trust that the date of this letter [Maundy Thursday] will
> sufficiently explain why I take the liberty of calling your
> attention to one precious doctrine in particular—that the
> Blessed Sacrament—a doctrine, I doubt not, as dear to you
> as it is to myself. I beg, then, with the most respectful
> earnestness, to assure you that you have utterly miscon-
> ceived our belief upon this point, raising up to yourself in
> it horrors, which every member of our Church discards as
> impious and revolting.[37]

Russell goes on to reiterate the understanding of the Eucharist
attributed to the Roman Catholic Church in Newman's exposi-

---

     original revelation. It is difficult, impossible, to imagine, I grant;—but how
     is it difficult to believe?' (*Apologia*, p. 239)

[34]   This is the meaning of Charles's cry from the heart, 'O Mighty Mother!'
     in *Loss and Gain* (p. 333).

[35]   *Via Media* ii, p. 315.

[36]   See *Apologia*, p. 194.

[37]   Russell to Newman, 8 April 1841, *LD* viii, p. 172

tion of Article 28 in Tract 90. He once again repudiates in the strongest language the notion that Catholics could believe such things:

> It is to this I beg to call your attention in the spirit of most respectful, but, I must add, of most earnest remonstrance. Far from entering in any way into our belief of the Eucharist, the gross imaginations ascribed to us are rejected with horror by every Catholic.[38]

Russell was the first to write to Newman about these points of Catholic doctrine with which Newman struggled. Whereas others argued theologically, Fr Russell simply presented the devotional practices of the Church of Rome in action, which was exactly those aspects which Newman found the most difficult to accept. His manner was never obtrusive, but he did not hesitate to express the conviction that if Newman became acquainted with the real Roman Catholicism, he would find no stumbling block in it.

Russell could and did present the teachings of Catholicism theologically when it was necessary, as when he wrote to Newman about the teachings on the Eucharist, but he knew it was necessary first to overcome his prejudices before approaching the one theological hurdle which remained to be cleared: the conviction in Newman's mind that devotions to the saints, especially to Mary, and the teaching on transubstantiation were not 'primitive', that is, were not taught by the early or primitive Church.

Russell's efforts did pay off, as acknowledged by Newman when he wrote of Russell that he had 'perhaps, more to do with my conversion than any one else'. The remaining hurdle to be overcome was the question of certain doctrines of Rome, includ-

---

[38] 'Your whole exposition of the Article proceeds on the supposition that our conception of "Transubstantiation" is of the most gross and repulsive nature, that we think of the adorable Body of Our Lord in the Eucharist as *of an earthly and fleshly thing*; of the eating and drinking as animal and corporeal actions, a carnal eating—it is painful to write it in this sense— "tearing with the teeth", of the Blessed Body—a natural and bloody drinking of the adorable Blood' (*ibid.*).

ing transubstantiation, not being primitive. To overcome this
obstacle, Newman began writing his *Essay on the Development
of Christian Doctrine*; as he proceeded, he found that, 'my view
so cleared that instead of speaking any more of "the Roman
Catholics", I boldy called them Catholics. Before I got to the end,
I resolved to be received'.[39]

After Newman's Conversion

As is evident from his correspondence and writings, Newman
believed in the Real Presence of Christ in the Eucharist long
before his conversion to the Roman Catholic Church. The
difference in his belief after his conversion was, as we have seen,
that he believed the doctrine of transubstantiation—of the
substantial presence of Christ in the Eucharist. The practical
consequence was that he became very devoted to Our Lord
present in the tabernacle. How often we find him writing about
the 'incomprehensible blessing to have Christ in bodily presence
in one's house, within one's walls'.[40]

> It has been sometimes objected that some of us have gone
> over for the privileges we hoped to gain in the Catholic
> Church. [...] We went over not realizing those privileges
> which we have found by going. I never allowed my mind
> to dwell on what I might gain of blessedness—but cer-
> tainly, if I had thought much upon it, I could not have
> fancied the extreme, ineffable comfort of being in the same
> house with Him who cured the sick and taught His
> disciples [...] in the days of His flesh.[41]

Indeed, it was the presence of Christ in the tabernacle which
brought home to Newman in large part that the Catholic religion

---

[39]   *Apologia*, pp. 194, 234.
[40]   Newman to Henry Wilberforce, 26 February 1846, *LD* xi, p. 129. See also
his letter to Mrs J. W. Bowden, *LD* xi, p. 131; to J. J. Gordon, 7 January
1853, *LD* xv, p. 248; to Richard Stanton, 22 February 1855, *LD* xvi, p 388.
[41]   Newman to Mrs. J. W. Bowden, 1 March 1846, *LD* xi, p. 131.

is a 'great objective fact' in which he could bask, so to speak, after his conversion.[42]

There is not space here to enter into all the difficulties Newman experienced as a Catholic. But through them he found in the Blessed Sacrament his greatest solace and consolation. When the Achilli Trial was about to begin, he asked the president of Ushaw College if 'he could set any convents praying', if possible having 'an Exposition of the Blessed Sacrament on the day of the trial'.[43]

Newman understood the importance of having the Blessed Sacrament reserved and he took great care in that reservation.[44] While in Dublin, establishing the Catholic University as its founding rector, Newman had a little chapel built in the collegiate house which he oversaw, in the hope of receiving permission to reserve the Blessed Sacrament there.[45] He later wrote to his friend, Richard Stanton, about his many blessings in Dublin including his chapel and the Blessed Sacrament reserved there.[46]

The Mass

While it is true that, as a Catholic, Newman seems to speak about the Eucharist mostly in the context of the tabernacle or Exposition of the Blessed Sacrament for adoration, he does speak frequently about the Mass as well. After some hesitation, he decided to study for the priesthood after his conversion and was ordained a Roman Catholic priest on 30 May 1847 at the Propaganda Fide in Rome. His letters and diaries are punctuated with references to the celebration of Mass.

'I propose saying a Mass once a week for your Grace till you return', he wrote to Archbishop Cullen, who was away in Rome.[47]

---

[42]   See *Apologia*, p. 340; *Biography: Newman*, p. 320.

[43]   See Newman to Charles Newsham, 27 May 1852, *LD* xv, p. 92, n. 1.

[44]   See Ellis, *op. cit.*, p. 335, as well as Newman to Darnell, 28 February 1853, *LD* xv, p. 314; Newman to Austin Mills, 27 February 1855, *LD* xvi, p. 393.

[45]   Newman to Cullen, 8 December 1854, *LD* xvi, p. 320.

[46]   Newman to Richard Stanton, 22 February 1855, *LD* xvi, p. 388. See also Newman to Cullen, 23 February 1855, *LD* xvi, p. 389.

We find frequent reference to the offering of Mass as his prayer for people: 'Of course I shall not forget you, nor do I, in mass';[48] 'I had said Mass for you this morning, as I have done before of late';[49] 'I will not forget your intention in my mass';[50] 'I have been saying Mass for you and others several times';[51] 'I hope soon to say Mass for you';[52] 'I trust to say Mass for her the three next days'.[53]

In both his novels, *Loss and Gain* and *Callista*, the Mass figures prominently. In *Callista*, Newman is at great pains to describe the Mass in third-century North Africa, complete with a description of the vestments worn, the placement of the candles, the altar cloth and the position of the celebrant.[54] It is truly remarkable—and has often been remarked upon[55]—how closely the Novus Ordo Mass resembles that which Newman describes in *Callista*.

Remarkable as well, is the description of the Mass in Newman's other novel, *Loss and Gain*.[56] While some concentrate on the few lines which describe the faithful with their own prayers and thoughts while following the actions and words of the celebrant, what is most striking is the manifest passion, not only of the character, but of the author, for the 'greatest action that can be on earth'.

> It is, not the invocation merely, but, if I dare use the word, the evocation of the Eternal. He becomes present on the altar in flesh and blood, before whom angels bow and devils tremble. This is that awful event which is the scope, and is the interpretation, of every part of the solemnity. Words are necessary, but as means, not as ends; they are not mere addresses to the throne of grace, they are

47   Newman to Cullen, 23 February 1855, *LD* xvi, p. 389.
48   Newman to Mrs J. W. Bowden, 18 January 1854, *LD* xvi, p. 16.
49   Newman to Miss M. R. Giberne, 16 January 1849, *LD* xiii, p. 11.
50   Newman to William Monsell, 5 January 1859, *LD* xix, p. 8.
51   Newman to William Maskell, 7 July 1850, *LD* xiv, p. 6.
52   Newman to H. La Serre, 8 January 1868, *LD* xxiv, p. 5.
53   Newman to Mrs Peter Bretherton, 3 July 1865, *LD* xxii, p. 6.
54   *Callista*, pp. 337–41.
55   See for example Ellis, *op. cit.*, pp. 330–1.
56   *Loss and Gain*, pp. 327–9.

instruments of what is far higher, of consecration, of sacrifice. They hurry on as if impatient to fulfil their mission. Quickly they go, the whole is quick; for they are all parts of one integral action.[57]

Newman was, of course, speaking about the Mass as it was celebrated in his day. He was not making any statement about its form of celebration; indeed he had experienced no other form. To concentrate on that aspect of this passage of *Loss and Gain* is to miss the overpowering sense of the work of God through the Church in the Mass and the wonderful sense of participation in that work.

While the above-mentioned passage in *Callista* is descriptive in nature, the passage in *Loss and Gain* is experiential. You know that Newman has lived it. That is palpable. The very cadence of the passage with its repetitive 'quickly they go' and 'quickly they pass' is evocative of the rhythm of the Mass and emphasizes that those participating do not do so 'painfully and hopelessly' as if 'following a hard form of prayer from beginning to end', but rather, are 'like a concert of musical instruments, each different, but concurring in a sweet harmony'.[58]

Thus, though John Tracy Ellis speaks of the Masses in the two novels with a decided anachronistically slant, his conclusion about these two passages is on the mark:[59] 'Yet, both the rite that admitted the participation of the laity and the Mass of *Loss and Gain* that kept them separate, revealed, each in its own way,

---

[57] *Ibid.*, p. 328.

[58] *Ibid.*, p. 329. Once again, we find Newman's delight in not having to build or manufacture his religion, but in being able to rest in an objective religion expressed not only in dogmas and doctrine, but also in liturgy.

[59] To say that the Mass as described in *Loss and Gain* kept the laity separate from the celebration is to miss Newman's point of the passage and to bring into his writings controversies which are a part of our time but were not of his. Newman in fact expresses clearly that the laity are participating in the Mass. A deeper reading of this passage could, perhaps, give insight into what the 'full, conscious, and active participation' (*Sacrosanctum Concilium*, 14) called for by Vatican II really means.

Newman's profound reverence for the eucharistic rite and his appreciation of the graces that accompany it for the souls of those present at the sacred action.'[60]

Conclusion

It is obvious that there are many aspects of the Eucharist in Newman's life which could not be addressed in this short piece, one of the most fascinating being, for example, the subject of church architecture. Nonetheless, it has become clear that the final take-away would remain the same. Newman's respect and love for the Eucharist permeated all of his life as well as his writings about it, both as an Anglican and as a Roman Catholic. He was not an original thinker on the subject, but with It, as with all things, Newman sought the truth.[61]

From the time of his first Communion, Newman had a relationship of profound respect and awe towards the Eucharist. To this was added a personal intimacy with our Lord in the Blessed Sacrament when he became a Catholic, an intimacy which gave him a home and a firm support in times of trial and distress, but above all a great joy and delight, as in the presence of an intimate friend, which indeed he was. One cannot imagine Newman's way into the Roman Catholic Church without the Eucharist playing a role and so it is fitting that in the Blessed Sacrament he especially found his home in the Catholic Church.

> I praise, and bless, and give myself wholly to Him, who is
> the true Bread of my soul, and my everlasting joy.[62]

---

[60]   Ellis, *op. cit.*, pp. 331–2.
[61]   'It was all part of that extraordinary pursuit of truth that was the illuminating principle of his life' (Ellis, *op. cit.*, pp. 339–40).
[62]   *Meditations*, p. 392.

JOHN HENRY NEWMAN ON MARY, MOTHER OF GOD, NEW EVE

FR CARLETON P. JONES, OP

J OHN HENRY NEWMAN was more than willing to defend Our Lady's position in the economy of Christian doctrine and in the devotion of Catholics, but it would not be accurate to call him a Mariologist in the systematic theological sense. It should also be mentioned that Newman had reservations about propagating certain 'foreign' Marian devotions, as the English Ultramontane party were doing in the 1860's through their translations of contemporary Italian and Spanish books. In addition, as is commonly the case with Newman, one is forced to glean his contributions to Marian theology from the complex web of his engagements in contemporary controversy. Most of his writings, including his Marian writings, were of an occasional character, occasioned by controversy.

The occasion for Newman's most extensive treatment of Marian themes was his reply to a book entitled *Eirenicon* that was written and published in the autumn of 1864 by his old friend and former Tractarian collaborator, the Professor of Hebrew at Oxford University, Edward Pusey.[1] The full title of *Eirenicon* was *The Church of England a Portion of Christ's One Holy Catholic Church, and a Means of Restoring Visible Unity.* Pusey was replying to an attack on Anglican ecclesiology by the recently-appointed Archbishop of Westminster, Henry Manning, and, though purporting to be an ecumenical proposal (an *Eirenicon*), Pusey's work was really a counterattack to Manning's which, as

---

[1]   Unless otherwise noted, all the quotations in this essay are taken from Newman, 'A Letter to the Rev. E. B. Pusey, DD, on occasion of his Eirenicon of 1864', in *Difficulties* ii, pp. 1–170.

Newman said, was calculated to make Catholics 'very angry—and justly angry'.[2]

Pusey had offered as typical examples of Roman Catholic Mariology some extremely misleading expressions that were taken out of context from popular devotional writers—as, for example, that no one could be saved who did not have a personal devotion to the Blessed Virgin, or that Mary had the power to 'search the reins and hearts'. Newman said that 'when I read (such expressions) in your volume, they affected me with grief and almost anger'; (p. 103) indeed, these expressions, which tended to confirm Protestant suspicions about Catholic Mariology, were also precisely those most likely to shock genuinely devout Catholics. So when Newman penned his own reply to Pusey's *Eirenicon*, he chided his old friend: 'excuse me—you discharge your olive-branch as if from a catapult'. (p. 7)

Newman had not originally intended to reply to Pusey's book, but in the end he did because he suspected that the Ultramontanes were likely to make the kind of reply that would confirm Protestant prejudices and give scandal to the many recent converts who were under Newman's influence, and even prevent further conversions from the Church of England.

Newman's fear of what the Ultramontane party might reply to Pusey was based on their recent proclamations concerning the *Syllabus of Errors*, which they regarded as an infallible document: W. G. Ward had given it out as the Catholic position, for example, that the Pope's Temporal Power was *de fide* doctrine.[3] And this was not only inflaming old Protestant suspicions of the Pope's designs upon the realm of England, but—more important to Newman's mind—it was imposing an unnecessary burden on the consciences of recent and potential converts to the Catholic Church.

Newman therefore felt obliged to make the kind of reply to Pusey that might stand the chance of helping reasonable Protes-

---

2   Newman to Mrs W. Froude, 16 October 1865, *LD* xxii, p. 76.
3   *Newman: Biography*, p. 576.

tants to recognize their own faith in what the Church undoubtedly professes; and instead of choosing his ground on matters
that were doubtful as to their dogmatic weight, such as the
Syllabus of Errors and the Temporal Power of the Pope, Newman
chose his ground upon the firm tradition in the Church concerning Mary—a tradition which, he was prepared to argue, Anglicans
were bound by their own principles to acknowledge.

Pusey had made his challenge by writing that 'that vast system
as to the Blessed Virgin [...] to all of us has been the special *crux*
of the Roman system'. But Newman was convinced that the
Catholic Marian doctrines were so evidently present in the
Fathers of the Church that there was in fact no reason why they
should be a stumbling block to Anglicans. And so he wrote, in
reply to Pusey, that 'here, let me say, as on other points, the
Fathers are enough for me. I do not wish to say more than they
suggest to me, and will not say less. You, I know, will profess the
same; and thus we can join issue on a clear and broad principle,
and may hope to come to some intelligible result'. (pp. 24–5)

Even if Pusey's *Eirenicon* was somewhat less than irenic, then
Newman was prepared to outdo Pusey in irenicism, all the more
so as he gave a strong defense to Catholic doctrine and appropriate devotion. But this truly ecumenical approach was certainly
not that of the dominant Catholic spokesmen at the time in
England. In fact, Newman's method was severely condemned by
Archbishop Manning in a famous passage that he wrote concerning his now more esteemed fellow convert:

> Whether (Dr Newman) knows it or not, he has become
> the centre of those who hold low views about the Holy See,
> are anti-Roman, cold and silent, to say no more, about the
> Temporal Power, national, English, critical of Catholic
> devotions, and always on the lower side. [...] I see much
> danger of an English Catholicism, of which Newman is the
> highest type. It is the old Anglican, patristic, literary,
> Oxford tone transplanted into the Church. [...] In one
> word, it is worldly Catholicism, and it will have the worldly

> on its side, and will deceive many. Now Ward and Faber
> may exaggerate, but they are a thousand times nearer to
> the mind and spirit of the Holy See than those who oppose
> them. Between us and them there is a far greater distance
> than between them and Dr Pusey's book.[4]

Surely, Manning and the other Ultramontanes would have
regarded Newman's statement that 'the Fathers are enough for
me' as the essence of 'the old Anglican [...] Oxford tone'; and yet
it was the Fathers, not contemporary Catholics, who had per-
suaded Newman to become a Catholic. He had even been so bold
as to say that Oxford had given him his motive to convert.[5]

Newman's side of the dialogue concerning Mary should not
be thought of as an ecumenical strategy in the sense that Manning
feared, of being an attempt to find the lowest common denomi-
nator, but as a genuinely Catholic theological method that is
capable of yielding ecumenical results—not in the sense of
creating a *tertium quid* between Catholic and Protestant positions, but in the sense of expounding Catholic doctrine in a way
that places the burden of proof on the Protestant side by removing their objections to it.

The principal objection, of course, was that Catholic teaching
about and devotion to the Virgin Mother was an unwarranted
addition to the undivided Church's witness in Scripture and
Tradition. Newman's method, therefore, is to identify the basis
for contemporary Catholic faith concerning Mary in the earliest,
most catholic, tradition. Let us look now at Newman's argument,
which is found in section three of his *Letter to Pusey*.

Newman begins with a distinction between faith and devotion,
which he compares to the distinction between objective and
subjective truth: thus, 'by "faith" I mean the Creed and assent to

---

4   Manning to George Talbot, 20 February 1866, cited in E. S. Purcell, *Life
     of Cardinal Manning, Archbishop of Westminster*, vol. ii (London: Mac-
     millan, 1896), p. 323.

5   'Catholics did not make us Catholics; Oxford made us Catholics' (Newman
     to E. E. Estcourt, 2 June 1860, *LD* xix, p. 352).

the Creed; (and) by "devotion" I mean such religious honours as belong to the objects of our faith, and the payment of those honours'. He adds, 'we cannot, indeed, be devout without faith, but we may believe without feeling devotion'. (p. 26) Faith does not vary with time, or between individual believers; but devotion varies considerably. Newman states it as a 'peculiarity of the Catholic religion (that) the faith is everywhere one and the same, but a large liberty is accorded to private judgment and inclination as regards matters of devotion'. It is on this basis that Newman opposes the Ultramontane attempt to make foreign Marian devotions normative in England. To illustrate his meaning, Newman employs a simile:

> The sun in the spring-time will have to shine many days before he is able to melt the frost, open the soil, and bring out the leaves; yet he shines out from the first notwithstanding, though he makes his power felt but gradually. It is one and the same sun, though his influence day by day becomes greater; and so in the Catholic Church it is the one Virgin Mother, one and the same from first to last, and Catholics may have ever acknowledged her; and yet, in spite of that acknowledgment, their devotion to her may be scanty in one time and place, and overflowing in another. (p. 28)

Newman observes, for example, that devotion to the Apostles and Martyrs arose earlier in the Church than devotion to those saints who were 'nearer to our Lord than either Martyrs or Apostles [...] as if these sacred persons were immersed and lost in the effulgence of His glory, and because they did not manifest themselves, when in the body, in external works separate from Him, it happened that for a long while they were less dwelt upon'. (pp. 29–30) Although Newman will not admit that devotion to the Blessed Virgin was ever really lacking in the Church, he points to devotion to St Joseph as the main proof of his point, and as evidence of the fact that Mary's objective title to the Church's honour cannot be measured by the extent or type of honour that any particular age or nation gives to her.

The faith of the Church concerning Mary from first to last—from the earliest period and forever—Newman defines precisely as her being the Second, or New, Eve. The proper starting-point of Catholic Mariology is thus the so-called *proto-evangelion* of Genesis,[6] as it was first interpreted by Justin, Tertullian and Irenaeus, whose witness, Newman firmly states, must be to the faith of the Apostles, because these three Fathers, coming so soon after the Apostles, represent the faith of the whole Christian world at the time. Newman expounds their interpretation of the *protoevangelion* as follows:

> In that awful transaction (referring to the fall of man) there were three parties concerned—the serpent, the woman, and the man; and at the time of their sentence, an event was announced for a distant future, in which the three same parties were to meet again, the serpent, the woman, and the man; but it was to be a second Adam and a second Eve, and the new Eve was to be the mother of the new Adam. 'I will put enmity between thee and the woman, and between thy seed and her seed.' The Seed of the woman is the Word Incarnate, and the Woman, whose seed or son He is, is His mother Mary. This interpretation, and the parallelism it involves, seem to me undeniable; but at all events (and this is my point) the parallelism is the doctrine of the Fathers, from the earliest times; and, this being established, we are able, by the position and office of Eve in our fall, to determine the position and office of Mary in our restoration. (p. 32)

In the course of his discussion of the Fathers—the three pre-Nicene Fathers, and then seven Eastern and Western post-Nicene Fathers—Newman particularly notices one element of the analogy that they make between the first and second Eves: that is, as the fall of man was brought on by Eve's failure to act with faith and obedience, so man's restoration was begun by Mary's personal exercise of these virtues. Newman says, the Fathers 'do not speak of the Blessed

---

6   Genesis 3:15.

Virgin merely as the physical instrument of our Lord's taking flesh, but as an intelligent, responsible cause of it'. (p. 35)

But as mankind fell in Adam, not in Eve, so mankind is restored in Christ, not in Mary. The precise position of Our Lady in relation to her Son is prefigured by Eve's position in relation to her husband: 'as Eve made room for Adam's fall, so Mary made room for our Lord's reparation of it; and thus, whereas the free gift was not as the offence, but much greater, it follows that, as Eve co-operated in effecting a great evil, Mary co-operated in effecting a much greater good'. (p. 36)

Thus, not only is Our Lady's personal, intelligent and free cooperation in our redemption emphasized by the analogy, but so is her subordination to the Second Adam. Newman notes the similarity between the patristic pattern of argument concerning the two Eves and St Paul's (in Romans 5) concerning the two Adams: this similarity in the pattern of argument is strong circumstantial evidence of apostolic precedent for the patristic doctrine. Newman is removing the ground from the Protestant objection to the Catholic faith concerning Mary, which seeks to preserve the prerogatives of Christ by reducing Mary's portion in the Incarnation to mere physical instrumentality. Newman proves that this reduction is unnecessary if one considers Christ in the light of Adam and Mary in the light of Eve.

In his discussion of seven post-Nicene Fathers, Newman shows that their Marian doctrine, which is founded on the same analogy, develops even further the theme of Mary's meritorious cooperation in the redeeming work of Christ. This they do mainly by enhancing the significance of Mary's virginity, considered not as a mere physical condition, but as her free and total disposition of herself to what God asks of her. Noting that the later Fathers speak with more rhetorical exuberance than the earlier ones, Newman takes for example this passage from St Peter Chrysologus, the fifth-century bishop of Ravenna:

> Heaven feels awe of God, Angels tremble at Him, the creature sustains Him not, nature sufficeth not; and yet

one maiden so takes, receives, entertains Him, as a guest within her breast, that, for the very hire of her home, and as the price of her womb, she obtains peace for the earth, glory for the heavens, salvation for the lost, life for the dead, a heavenly parentage for the earthly, the union of God Himself with human flesh. (quoted on pp. 42–3)

Newman comments that 'it is difficult to express more explicitly that the Blessed Virgin had a real meritorious co-operation, a share which had a "hire" and a "price" in the reversal of the fall'. (p. 43) He might have added that it is difficult to avoid those theological conclusions which the Catholic Church has drawn from this patristic testimony in the form of her definitions of the dogmas of the Immaculate Conception and the Assumption. These conclusions Newman specified in two categories: Mary's sanctity and Mary's dignity.

First, as regards Mary's sanctity, Newman says that the analogy with Eve implies that Mary must have possessed at least that original grace with which God endowed our first parents. He writes:

If Eve was raised above human nature by that indwelling moral gift which we call grace, is it rash to say that Mary had even a greater grace? And this consideration gives significance to the Angel's salutation of her as 'full of grace',—an interpretation of the original word which is undoubtedly the right one, as soon as we resist the common Protestant assumption that grace is a mere external approbation or acceptance, answering to the word 'favour', whereas it is, as the Fathers teach, a real inward condition or superadded quality of soul. And if Eve had this supernatural inward gift given her from the first moment of her personal existence, is it possible to deny that Mary too had this gift from the very first moment of her personal existence? I do not know how to resist this inference:—well, this is simply and literally the doctrine of the Immaculate Conception. (pp. 45–6)

It is interesting that Newman identifies the stumbling-block to accepting the Immaculate Conception as the 'common Protestant assumption that grace is a mere external approbation or acceptance, answering to the word "favour"', and not as the scruple that Mary's privilege might seem to exempt her from redemption through Christ. He also makes it clear that the Anglican doctrine of grace does not share what he calls the 'common Protestant assumption'.

In view of what is common between Anglicans and Catholics in regard to the doctrine of grace, Newman observes that it is 'a most strange phenomenon that so many learned and devout men (including Pusey) stumble at this doctrine'. He surmises that 'in matter of fact they do not know what we mean by the Immaculate Conception'—as for example that 'it has no reference whatever to (Mary's) parents, but simply to her own person'. Protestants, he says, may 'fancy that we ascribe a different nature from ours to the Blessed Virgin'—and if this is so, it is because Protestants (not all Anglicans, however) understand original sin to be 'a disease, a radical change of nature, an active poison internally corrupting the soul', whereas Catholics hold that it is only 'the deprivation of that supernatural unmerited grace which Adam and Eve had on their first formation'. No one, including Mary, could 'merit [...] the restoration of that grace; but it was restored to her by God's free bounty, from the very first moment of her existence [...] in order to fit her to become the Mother of her and our Redeemer, to fit her mentally, spiritually for it'. (pp. 47–9)

So much for the Virgin Mother's sanctity. Newman now turns to her dignity, and he presents an argument for believing in her Assumption that I think is among his most remarkable rhetorical achievements. Newman's argument is fashioned to persuade the reader not (as in the case of his argument for the Immaculate Conception) by strict deductive logic, but by demonstrating a convergence of probabilities in the direction of a Catholic conclusion. This most characteristically Newmanian method of religious argument, while certainly more apologetic than theological, is the more powerfully convincing in that it appeals, not only to the reader's logic, but also to his Christian good sense and good will.

He begins modestly by presenting what he elsewhere calls an antecedent probability: that is, if what he has just shown logically about Our Lady's sanctity is accepted, then it is antecedently probable that 'all generations would call (her) blessed'. Invoking what might be called the 'common consent of humankind', Newman observes that there is a necessity of human nature whereby the benefactors of a people or a nation are (as it were) immortalized. This 'necessity' Newman calls 'the hopefulness of our nature', whereby human beings are led to 'make present' to themselves the great deeds of their past. '(How) much more then', he says, 'in the great kingdom and people of God; the Saints are ever in our sight, and not as mere ineffectual ghosts or dim memories, but as if present bodily in their past selves'. (p. 51)

Acknowledging that he is 'following a line of thought which is rather a meditation than an argument in controversy', Newman urges nonetheless that 'it is to the point to inquire, whether the popular astonishment, excited by our belief in the blessed Virgin's present dignity, does not arise from the circumstance that the bulk of men, engaged in matters of this world, have never calmly considered her historical position in the gospels, so as rightly to realize [...] what that position imports'. (pp. 52–3)

Newman ascribes the failure of Protestants to appreciate what Catholics believe about Our Lady's present dignity in part to their habit of 'expending their devotional energies [...] on abstract doctrines, such as justification by faith only, or the sufficiency of Holy Scriptures instead of employ(ing) themselves in the contemplation of Scripture facts, and bring(ing) out before their minds in a tangible form the doctrines involved in them'. (p. 53) If they were not so preoccupied with those abstractions whereby they justify their separateness, Newman says, Protestants would be more open to the proper objects of their Christian faith—which, as Newman never tires of stating, are not abstractions but facts.

Mary's sanctity is just such a fact, plainly evident in Scripture. Then, Newman makes 'what perhaps (may be thought) a very bold step—which is to find the doctrine of Our Lady's present exaltation (to be another fact) in Scripture'. He does not ignore the evidence for Mary's present dignity that can be found in the Church's earliest tradition, and he devotes a couple of pages (pp. 55–6) to the recently-published findings of the Cavaliere de Rossi on the images of the Madonna and Child that are present in the Roman Catacombs. But he uses this evidence as collateral for interpreting St John's vision of the Woman and Child in the twelfth chapter of the Apocalypse.

Newman deals with two objections to interpreting this passage as referring to Our Lady's present dignity. The first is that 'such an interpretation is but poorly supported by the Fathers'. To this, Newman replies that 'Christians have never gone to the Scripture for proof of their doctrines, till there was actual need, from the pressure of controversy;—if in those times the Blessed Virgin's dignity was unchallenged on all hands, as a matter of doctrine' (p. 54), then there would have been no need for the Fathers to comment on St John's vision in support of it. So Newman uses the argument from silence in favour of an early doctrine of Mary's Assumption. The second, more challenging, objection is that the Woman of the Apocalypse more obviously signifies Israel, or the People of God, from whom came the Messiah. To this, Newman replies:

> No one doubts that the 'man-child' spoken of is an allusion to our Lord: [then] why [...] is not 'the Woman' an allusion to His Mother? This surely is the obvious sense of the words; of course they have a further sense also, which is the scope of the image; doubtless the Child represents the children of the Church, and doubtless the Woman represents the Church; this, I grant, is the real or direct sense, but what is the sense of the symbol under which that real sense is conveyed? *Who* are the Woman and the Child? I answer, they are not personifications but Persons. This is true of the Child, therefore it is true of the Woman. (p. 58)

Newman here disputes the method of dealing with the figures of this passage as mere allegories, rather than what he states to be far more usual in Scripture, as types. 'Scripture is not fond of allegories; the sacred writers [...] are not much given to dressing up abstract ideas or generalizations in personal attributes'. The Bible rather tends to take one fact to stand for, or to signify, another. Thus, 'Israel stands for the chosen people, David for Christ, Jerusalem for heaven. [...] So too the structure of the imagery in the Apocalypse is not a mere allegorical creation, but is founded on the Jewish ritual.' Thus, it is not the Woman (a personification) who stands for the Church, but Mary (a person). Returning to his original theme, then, Newman observes:

> Not only Mother and Child, but a serpent is introduced into the vision. Such a meeting of man, woman and serpent has not been found in Scripture, since the beginnings of Scripture, and now it is found in its end. If the dragon of St John is the same as the serpent (of Genesis), and the man-child is 'the seed of the woman', why is not the woman herself she, whose seed the man-child is? And, if the first woman is not an allegory, why is the second? If the first woman is Eve, why is not the second Mary? (pp. 58–9)

The clinching argument for interpreting St John's vision as referring to Our Lady, then, is that it conforms to the typological pattern under which the earliest Church Fathers spoke of Mary, as the New Eve. Such an argument will obviously not convince someone who approaches the Biblical text skeptically, or who methodically spurns whatever light the earliest tradition of the Church might shed upon it—whether this tradition is embodied in the images of the Catacombs or in the writings of the Fathers. But Newman is not trying to convince rationalists or skeptics; he is addressing the faithful Pusey and his followers, assuming their Christian good sense and good will, and inviting them to take their faith beyond the *a priori* boundaries their Protestantism sets for it. So Newman offers this appeal to his old friends:

> If all this be so, if it is really the Blessed Virgin whom Scripture represents as clothed with the sun, crowned with the stars of heaven, and with the moon as her footstool, what height of glory may we not attribute to her? and what are we to say of those who, through ignorance, run counter to the voice of Scripture, to the testimony of the Fathers, to the traditions of East and West, and speak and act contemptuously towards her whom her Lord delighteth to honour? (p. 61)

This concludes what Newman calls 'the rudimental teaching of Antiquity about the Blessed Virgin'. He appends two notes, and it is interesting that he puts them at the end of his doctrinal discussion because in a sense it might be said that they belong at the beginning. The first concerns Our Lady's original title, Mother of God, and the second concerns her intercessory power—two themes most familiar to a Catholic's heart, but most intimidating to a Protestant's. And that, I think, is precisely why Newman puts them at the end: he first disarms his adversary on their common ground, in Scripture and the Fathers of the Church, and then invites his adversary to accompany him to higher ground.

Before I conclude, let me quote two passages that illustrate this higher ground to which Newman is inviting his Anglican friends: they refute, I think, the charge that Manning made against his 'Oxford tone'.

First, concerning Mary's original title, Mother of God:

> It is this awful title, which both illustrates and connects together the two prerogatives of Mary, on which I have been lately enlarging, her sanctity and her greatness. It is the issue of her sanctity; it is the origin of her greatness. What dignity can be too great to attribute to her who is as closely bound up, as intimately one, with the Eternal Word, as a mother with a son? What outfit of sanctity, what fullness and redundance of grace, what exuberance of merits must have been hers, when once we admit the supposition, which the Fathers justify, that her Maker really did regard those merits, and take them into account, when He condescended

> 'not to abhor the Virgin's womb'? Is it surprising then that
> on the one hand she should be immaculate in her concep-
> tion? or on the other that she should be honoured with an
> Assumption, and exalted as a queen with a crown of twelve
> stars, with the rulers of day and night to do her service? Men
> sometimes wonder that we call her Mother of life, of mercy,
> of salvation; what are all these titles compared to that one
> name, Mother of God? (pp. 62–3)

And second, concerning Mary's intercessory power:

> I consider it impossible, then, for those who believe the
> Church to be one vast body in heaven and on earth, in
> which every holy creature of God has his place, and of
> which prayer is the life, when once they recognize the
> sanctity and dignity of the Blessed Virgin, not to perceive
> immediately, that her office above is one of perpetual
> intercession for the faithful militant, and that our very
> relation to her must be that of clients to a patron, and that,
> in the eternal enmity which exists between the woman and
> the serpent, while the serpent's strength lies in being the
> Tempter, the weapon of the Second Eve and Mother of
> God is prayer. (p. 73)

In conclusion, I have chosen to expound the Mariology of
Newman by attending to the first part of only one of his writings,
his *Letter to Pusey*. The second part, concerning Marian devotion,
is not as interesting theologically, being mainly a refutation of
Pusey's charges concerning its excesses. There are several other
writings that I might have considered, but the one I have chosen
is the most important because in it Newman is presenting the
Marian dogmas as belonging to the common patrimony of
Christian faith in such a way as to make it very difficult for Pusey
and his followers to consistently object to them. Newman's
presentation is an excellent example of non-reductive ecumenical
discourse. By following his example, Catholic ecumenists may
hope to introduce into the dialogue with other Christians the

most powerful of all the influences toward reunion: the Blessed Virgin Mary, Mother of God, New Eve, and Mother of the Church.

PART FOUR

Men of Letters

11 TURNCOAT TO TREASURE: NEWMAN AND *PUNCH*

Are you not afraid of this getting into Punch?

J. H. Newman to F. W. Faber, 11 February 1851[1]

SERENHEDD JAMES

1841 WAS A fateful year. The outcry over the publication of John Henry Newman's infamous *Tract 90* brought to a close the Tractarian phase of the Oxford Movement, which he had helped to lead; it also signalled the beginning of the end of the *via media* that he had sought to navigate between what he had up to then regarded as the errors of both Protestantism and Roman Catholicism in the modern era. As Anglican bishops lined up to condemn Newman's doomed, if eloquent, attempt to demonstrate that the Thirty-Nine Articles of Religion—the nearest thing that the Church of England could claim to possess as *sui generis* dogma—could be read in a way that was consonant with the teachings of the Tridentine Church of Rome, he became uneasily aware of the possibility that 'the only way to keep in the English Church [was] steadily to contemplate and act upon the possibility of leaving it'.[2]

The controversies that surrounded *Tract 90* were the second of Newman's 'three blows' in 1841 that sent him on the way to his 'Anglican death-bed'; he later enumerated them in the *Apologia pro Vita Sua*. The first was his study of the Arian heresy, through which he came to realise that 'the pure Arians were the Protestants, the semi-Arians the Anglicans, and that Rome now was what it was then'. The last was the controversy by which the

---

[1]   *LD* xiv, p. 211.
[2]   Newman to J. R. Hope, 17 October 1841, *LD* viii, p. 301.

Church of England (which claimed apostolic succession) entered into an ecumenical arrangement with the Evangelical Church of Prussia (which did not) to establish a shared Protestant bishopric in Jerusalem, the occupants of which See would alternate between the churches.[3]

'It really does seem to me as if the bishops were doing their best to uncatholicize us', Newman wrote to John Keble, 'and whether they will succeed before a rescue comes, who can say?'[4] To Henry Wilberforce he was more forthright: 'I have no call at present to go to the Church of Rome; but I am not confident I may not have some day. [...] All sorts of heresies are promulgated.'[5] The call had in fact already come, as he later realised; at the time Newman instead agonised his way towards its recognition through his preparation for what finally appeared as his *Essay on the Development of Christian Doctrine*. Published in 1845, it was his last major Anglican work; Ian Ker has called it 'one of the great classics of theology'.[6]

While all these lofty wranglings were going on in Oxford, in London a quite different project had been underway. A group of hearty bohemians—with Mark Lemon, Henry Mayhew, and Stirling Coyne at its centre—quietly conceived and launched in the middle of the summer a satirical magazine that would send up all and sundry from a broadly middling standpoint: *Punch, or the London Charivari*. Drawing to some extent on the *Paris Charivari*, it was immediately favourably received; while the French tradition was one of acidic, sharp, and merciless satire— what Tamara L. Hunt calls 'a traditional ritual public shaming'[7]— its London progeny capitalised on the fact that after the passing of the infinitely lampoonable House of Hanover, the Victorian

---

[3]   *Apologia*, pp. 139–43.

[4]   5 October 1841, *LD* viii, p. 286.

[5]   8 November 1841, *LD* viii, p. 321.

[6]   *Newman: Biography*, p. 269.

[7]   Tamara L. Hunt, *Defining John Bull: Political Caricature and National Identity in Late-Georgian England* (Burlington, VT: Ashgate, 2003), p. 4.

age required a gentler approach. As Marion Spielmann noted, *Punch* instead aimed to be 'a budget of wit, fun, and kindly humour, and of honest opposition based on fairness and justice'.[8]

'Society was turning respectable', wrote Richard D. Altick, in his history of *Punch*'s first decade, 'and the family dominated its system of values'. Not only that, but the newly-emergent middle class was literate and often possessed of disposable income; it was therefore an obvious market for anyone selling books and magazines. At the same time a yearning for respectability—or at least its outward maintenance—had begun to pervade English society.

> Many of the savage, tumultuous prints of the Reform era would have been inadmissible to any Victorian household that prided itself on sobriety and decency. It is difficult to imagine a drawing-room table bearing a portfolio of prints with phallic images or *double entendres.*[9]

While it can hardly be forgotten that there remained plenty of private vice, sobriety and decency were essential to a Victorian presentation of public virtue. To these we might add churchgoing; it was a time when new churches seemed to spring up like mushrooms, creating their own problems for later generations, and sabbath observance was also tied to the new social *mores*. This was not, however, why Edward Norman has described the nineteenth century as a 'religious age'.[10]

Norman instead uses that phrase to denote a period of great public debate on religious questions, and particularly in the life of the Established Church; it was inevitable that *Punch* would take a concomitant interest in the ebb and flow of the religious life of the nation. While it was an essentially apolitical organ, needling statesmen on both sides of the Houses of Parliament as the

---

[8] M. H. Spielmann, *The History of Punch* (London: Cassell & Co., 1895), p. 17.

[9] Richard D. Altick, *Punch: The Lively Youth of a British Institution, 1841–1851* (Columbus: Ohio State University Press, 1997), p. 4.

[10] E. R. Norman, *Anti-Catholicism in Victorian England* (London: Allen & Unwin, 1968), p. 19.

occasion arose, Spielmann's description of 'opposition based upon fairness and justice'[11] only went so far, for in matters of religion *Punch* was—at least at the outset—profoundly partisan. Mr Punch found his place 'with [Archbishop] Tait and Spurgeon and John Bull among the defenders of the faith';[12] Andrew Drummond thought that despite his vaunted disdain for abuse of office and patronage, he was still 'one hundred percent Protestant, a pronounced Low Churchman, and unrepentant Erastian' who admired F. D. Maurice and lionised Charles Kingsley.[13]

To ascribe the codification of the idea that the State has authority over the Church entirely to Thomas Erastus is unfair— the blurring of the boundaries between the two has been a perennial problem since the conversion of Constantine—but the eponym has stuck. It was inevitable that *Punch* should come into conflict with a movement that viewed Erastianism with horror; that said, there were elements of overlap of interest, which were conveniently ignored as required. The leaders of the Oxford Movement, gushed Wallace Duthie, 'had been witness too long to the apathy which had drugged the Spiritual Mother of the Race'.

> Bishops and clergy at ease in Sion; churches with closed
> doors; infrequent services; ministrations, save with notable
> exceptions, perfunctory; presented a humiliating picture
> of sluggishness and complacency. And all the while, abuses
> visible to every eye were crying aloud for redress.[14]

To this *Punch* was not blind, and its prime target was the bishops: more than one pun played on 'cant' and 'Cantuar'. Of particular interest was the size of their stipends; in 1847 the Prime Minister, Lord John Russell, dandled a fat episcopal baby against an industrial backdrop of smoking factory chimneys, to illustrate

---

11 Spielmann, *op. cit.*, p.17.
12 D. Wallace Duthie, *The Church in the Pages of Punch* (London: Smith, Elder & Co., 1912), p. 13.
13 A. L. Drummond, *The Churches Pictured by Punch* (London: Epworth Press, 1947), p. 32.
14 Duthie, *op. cit.*, p. 12.

the question 'given a bishop at £8,000 a year with an outlay of £28,000 for a palace, how many curates at £75 *per annum* will it require to feed and house him?'[15] Mr Punch's apathy towards the Tractarians—which stretched back to its earliest days, and later took in the Puseyites and ritualists as well—stemmed not from their drive for a general raising of clerical standards, but from his suspicion that they were, wittingly or otherwise, a fifth column for the Pope.

In considering the particular treatment by *Punch* of New-man—given the space available in this short essay—three obvious moments present themselves for brief scrutiny: his conversion to Catholicism in 1845, his elevation to the cardinalate in 1879, and his death in 1890. To the first, scant attention was paid, and only oblique reference made later; it was less of an individual news story than a *prima facie* example of the trend that Mr Punch deplored: the inevitable defection, as he saw it, of Anglicans who had come under the influence of the apparently ubiquitous popery in the Church of England, which had spewed out of Oxford since the 1830s.

In the wake of the restoration of the Catholic hierarchy in 1850—the 'Papal Aggression' vaunted by the Prime Minister, Lord John Russell, in his infamous letter to the Bishop of Durham[16]— *Punch* had, as Michael Wheeler has put it, 'a field day'.[17] Newman was presented as a salutary reminder of the consequences of Tractarian dalliance, and the *Tracts for the Times* themselves frequently alluded to in laboured Victorian puns.

---

[15] 'An Episcopal Sum', *Punch* 13 (1847), p. 40; 'Lord John's Last', *Punch* 13 (1847), p. 34. The earlier bound volumes were printed without the dates of individual weekly publication; the references that follow give volume, page, and year. A precise date is recorded when available in the later material.

[16] John Russell to William Maltby, *The Times*, 7 November 1850.

[17] Michael Wheeler, *The Old Enemies: Catholic and Protestant in Nine-teenth-Century English Culture* (Cambridge: Cambridge University Press, 2006), p. 15.

> [S]everal children of the Church have proved rebellious
> and difficult to deal with; but of all her children those
> naughty little boys of Oxford, who for years past have been
> pelting the head of their venerable parent with Tracts, have
> certainly turned out the most In-Tractable.[18]

It was a time for many when 'religion was not yet divorced from
questions of national security';[19] the situation was hardly helped
by Wiseman's unintentionally inflammatory pastoral letter 'From
Without the Flaminian Gate' (7 October 1850). A cartoon, 'The
New Oxford Costume', warned of the beguiling dangers that
remained for impressionable students; an undergraduate on his
way to lectures appeared in front of Tom Tower, the Radcliffe
Camera, and Newman's former University Church, clasping a
religious tome to his chest, and wearing a mortarboard balanced
precariously upon a papal tiara.[20]

1850 was also the year of the Gorham Judgement, and the
imposition by the Judicial Committee of the Privy Council of the
heterodox incumbent George Gorham on the orthodox Bishop
Henry Philpotts of Exeter. To many the Church of England
seemed fatally to have failed to make a stand for its Catholic
doctrine of baptismal regeneration in the face of rampant Erastianism; a tranche of high-profile departures followed, including
that of Henry Edward Manning. The restoration of the hierarchy
a few months later reignited what Duthie felt were 'long-smoul-
dering resentments';[21] *Punch* did not forget Newman's role in the
movement that it despised. A small piece, 'The Quickest Way to
Rome', sneered that 'of all roads none will take you there so
quickly as the small Tracts that run through Oxford'.[22]

Newman appeared most explicitly in 'Domestic Scenes—
Served with a Writ', with its conceit of Mr Punch being informed

---

[18]   *Punch* 19 (1850), p. 231.
[19]   R. G. G. Price, *A History of Punch* (London: Collins, 1957), p. 47.
[20]   *Punch* 19 (1850), p. 261.
[21]   Duthie, *op. cit.*, p. 37.
[22]   *Punch* 19 (1850), p. 229.

of the restoration of the hierarchy by Wiseman himself, clad in *cappa magna* with Newman in an Oratorian habit holding up its train. A bog-Irish maid with a cod-Irish brogue was an efficient trope, with *Punch* able and willing to mobilise readers' anti-Catholic and anti-Irish prejudices simultaneously.

> *Mr Punch's Irish maid is heard outside in the passage.*
> O Lor'! O Holy Saints! O Marthyrs, and Stars, and Gyarthers! Oh, Blessed of Heaven! And is it your Holinesses Reverences? (*she goes down on her knees*).
>
> *Mr Punch.* What's that noise, Doodena?
>
> *Doodena.* Av you plaise, Sir, 'tis the Gentlemin wishes to see your Honour.
>
> *Mr Punch.* What are their names, Doodena?
>
> *Doodena.* Av you plaise, Sir, they say their names is Mr Wiseboy and Mr Newboy—and they've brought your Honour a little Bull.
>
> *Mr Punch.* A little *what*? Let the persons in.
>
> *Wiseboy enters, with Newboy holding his tail.*

Inevitably, the scene ended with Mr Punch turning both Wiseman and Newman out of his house; in a moment of latitude he refrains from setting his dog on them.[23] Elsewhere an impending 'Invasion and Subjection of England' was prophesied, 'in which High Mass is to be performed in Westminster Abbey, Father Newman is to preach in St Paul's Cathedral, and all Anglican priests are to be exiled'.[24]

A year later, when *Punch* introduced the character of Lady Blanche, a wealthy young heiress beguiled into becoming a nun and thereby handing her fortune over to the Church, it did so in the form of a faux-medieval quatrain which evoked not-too-distant memories of *The Awful Disclosures of Maria Monk* (1836)

---

[23] *Punch* 19 (1850), p. 243.
[24] *Punch* 20 (1851), pp. 214–15.

and Rebecca Reed's *Six Months in a Convent* (1835). The con-
temporaneous scandal of the sensational *Connelly* v. *Connelly*
case, in which Wiseman played a leading role, also loomed large;
the tale unfolded predictably enough.

> Lady Blanche was a mayden of lofty degree,
> And a pretty good way from her majoryte;
> Lady Blanche was an heiress, and worth, I'll bee bounde,
> Yff a dumpe, at the leest ninetye thousand good pounde [...]
> Then she hadd on the vayle, and the Sisterhoode's clothes,
> Bidding farewell forever to flounces and bowes;
> Thus the Church for a bride did the Lady Blanche win—
> Sister Ursula now—with her land and her tyn.
> Here's success to your priests that for fortunes doe hunte,
> And look out for young damsels with plentye of blunte;
> With no lawes to forbid them, as shown in this tayle,
> About catching an Heiress, and taking the Vayle.

The monastic theme was not an unfamiliar one; pieces like 'The
Convent of the Belgravians' or the 'Monks in Masquerade' of a
fictitious monastery in Pimlico served to remind Protestant
readers of the wild rumours that abounded regarding Catholic
religious life.[25]
    It was on the basis of allegations of serial abuse, taking place
behind high forbidding walls, that Monk and Reed's penny-
dreadfuls had seen such a roaring success; it was no coincidence
that the eminent lawyer of Anthony Trollope's *The Warden*, Sir
Abraham Haphazard, was involved in legislation known as 'The
Convent Custody Bill'.[26] In Lady Blanche's case, the piece was
accompanied by a fine tableau-illustration depicting the unfortu-
nate maiden on her knees, making her vows to a corpulent cleric

---

[25]   'Puseyite Histrionics', *Punch* 19 (1850), p. 215; 'The Convent of the
       Belgravians', *Punch* 19 (1850), pp. 163 & 199.
[26]   Anthony Trollope, *The Warden* (London: Heinemann, 1967), p. 66. See
       also Rene Kollar OSB, *A Foreign and Wicked Institution? The Campaign
       against Convents in Victorian England* (Cambridge: James Clarke & Co.,
       2011).

in a tasselled soup-plate hat—clearly the 'conveniently rotund' Wiseman[27]—surrounded by smirking monks and weeping virgins. The aquiline nose of the thin abbess who cuts off Blanche's flowing locks with shears is unmistakably Newman's own.

Meanwhile, a small side-swipe alluding to the establishment of the London Oratory under F. W. Faber read 'The Largest Depots for Cardinals—Oxford University and the Bishop of London's diocese'.[28] It was at least half a prophecy, but of the two Oxford men who received red hats in the succeeding decades Newman got off lightly.[29] *Punch* regarded and treated Manning with unconcealed hostility for years; it was one thing to have left the Church of England and gone to work quietly in Birmingham, but quite another to have become Archbishop of Westminster.

Duthie observed that in Manning's case 'to the repugnance felt towards the Roman Catholic was added the misliking for one who had put off the habit of an Anglian Archdeacon to put on the soutane of the Roman priest, who, not content with quietly slipping into his place in a new communion, had become the protagonist of the Church of Rome in his native land'.[30] Even then, it could not resist a pun on names; when a furious Pius IX refused to countenance the requested appointment of George Errington as Wiseman's successor in 1865, with the arguments over the *Syllabus of Errors* of the preceding year continuing to rage, it took full advantage of the possibilities to print its own 'Pope's Reply' to the Chapter of Westminster.

> I might, perchance, have shown gentility
> In making Dr E your chief, I own:
> But could you ask Infallibility

---

[27] Dominic Janes, 'The Role of Visual Appearance in *Punch*'s Early Victorian Satires on Religion', *Victorian Periodicals Review* 47:1 (Spring 2014), p. 71.

[28] *Punch* 19 (1850), p. 230.

[29] Eleanor McNees, '*Punch* and the Pope: Three Decades of Anti-Catholic Caricature', *Victorian Periodicals Review* 37:1 (Spring 2004), p. 42.

[30] Duthie, *op. cit.* p. 43.

> To say that it would take an Erring-Tone?
> Besides, while angry gusts our sails are fanning,
> Can you not see St Peter's Barque wants Manning?[31]

Unlike Wiseman, who had controversially been made a cardinal on his appointment—at the time Newman had been 'very uneasy about the excitement it was bound to create'[32]—Manning did not receive the sacred purple until 1875. Newman joined him four years later, but *Punch*'s first reaction was a response to the confusion that prevailed in March 1879 when a rumour began circulating that Newman had declined the honour. It was traced back to a misapprehension of Manning's in his communications with the Vatican about the matter; Ker's assessment is that 'The charitable judgement on Manning's understanding must be that he was guilty of a certain wishful thinking.'[33]

It was not that *Punch* by this stage begrudged Newman the laurels of old age; when he had gone to high table at Trinity the previous year, after his election to an honorary fellowship, and visited Pusey and dropped in at Oriel, the writers had duly delivered another irresistible pun.

> Once more in Oriel! Face to face
> With scenes to ancient memories due:
> Is't a new man in the old place,
> Or is't the old man in a new?[34]

Nor were they displeased that Leo XIII had made the offer, but in the case of his assumed disinclination to accept it they approved of what they presumed was Newman's preference to retain his characteristic independence of thought, which from a Protestant viewpoint they regarded as incompatible with being a Prince of the Church. It was also, naturally, as good an opportunity as any other for a dig at Manning, which Sheridan Gilley

---

[31] 'The Pope's Reply', *Punch* 48 (20 May 1865), p. 205.
[32] *Newman: Biography*, p. 360.
[33] *Newman: Biography*, p. 718.
[34] 'Oxford Revisited', *Punch* 74 (16 March 1878), p. 120.

has described as 'an odious comparison'.[35] 'The Pope, much to his credit, has respectfully offered Dr Newman a Cardinal's Hat. The venerable Doctor, equally to his credit, has respectfully declined the honour.'

> A Cardinal's Hat! Fancy Newman in *that*,
> For the crown o'er his grey temples spread!
> 'Tis the good and great head that would honour the hat,
> Not the hat that would honour the head.
> There's many a priest craves it: no wonder *he* waives it,
> Or that we, the soiled head-cover scanning,
> Exclaim with one breath, *sans* distinction of faith,
> 'Would they wish Newman ranked with Old Manning?'[36]

For Newman there was no such quibbling; his only reticence had been about whether he would be obliged to leave Birmingham to reside at the Vatican. When he was reassured on that point, as Ker observes, he took 'a certain mischievous glee in accepting it', and 'could not help thinking of all those now dead who would have rejoiced at the extraordinary event'.[37] As Newman prepared to travel to Rome, *Punch* caught up with yet another approving if excruciating pun under the heading 'Right Hat on Right Head'.

> Wise Pope to give, and worthy Priest to take
> The Hat, to wear, which duly asks a true man;
> We know the Old Man it will ne'er unmake,
> Though there's no need of it to make a Newman.[38]

It also solemnly intoned that one of the ceremonies involved would be 'that known as "opening and shutting the Cardinal's mouth"', and used the imparting of this ecclesiastical titbit as a vehicle to express its further approbation.

---

[35] Sheridan Gilley, *Newman and His Age* (London: Darton, Longman & Todd, 2003), p. 410.

[36] 'Coronatus, non Pileatus', *Punch* 76 (1 March 1879), p. 89.

[37] *Newman: Biography*, p. 719.

[38] 'Right Hat on Right Head', *Punch* 76 (12 April 1879), p. 157.

In Cardinal Newman's case, the Pope won't find it easy to perform the latter operation. If he opens his mouth, he will do it to good purpose; and if he shuts it, it will be not at any third party's bidding, but because he sees no good reason for opening it.[39]

It then returned to punning and released a couplet after the consistory called 'Newman among the Red Hats (by a *change* of Pope)'.

His virtues are so cardinal and rare,
We wonder how the dickens he got there![40]

Punch responded robustly, however, to Newman's Biglietto Speech, given at the end of the ceremony in which he was formally told that the Pope had raised him to the Sacred College; it is striking for the breadth of its observation, even with the obvious pun of its title, 'A Cardinal Point'. Written from *Punch's* customary Protestant position, it nonetheless opened with an acknowledgement—by then difficult to gainsay—that Newman was the most influential English Catholic of his time.

Most Venerable Cardinal Newman, your Eminence has well earned your Scarlet Hat. It is to yourself, probably, that the Pope owes the reflecting portion of his British converts—or reverts, if you please.

A backhanded compliment followed, crediting Newman's influence to his own personal qualities, rather than any *in esse* truth of the Catholic claims.

A thoughtful man, if any dogma that you subscribe appears nonsense to him, naturally asks himself whether it is the more likely, that you should credit an absurdity, or that he should be an ass. The strongest argument in the view of an enlightened Briton for the creed of your choice is the fact that you chose it. If, instead of going over to Rome,

---

39   'Not so Easy', *Punch* 76 (19 April 1879), p. 174.
40   'Newman among the Red Hats' *Punch* 76 (24 May 1879), p. 229.

you had turned Plymouth Brother, no doubt you would
have had quite a following.

What came next introduced a sour tone, relying on a muddling
conflation of theological and political liberalism; it essentially
accused Newman of hypocrisy while still recognising that, whatever might have been, he had emerged as a theological equal to
the Doctor of Grace.

> Yet where would you, with all your influence, now be, but
> for the working of that very Liberalism in spiritual matters
> against which you testified so eloquently the other day, at
> Rome? You have gone on striving against it 'thirty, forty,
> fifty years'. But suppose you had succeeding in confuting
> that same Liberalism precisely half a century ago. You would
> have effectively prevented Catholic Emancipation. Would
> there then have arisen any Tractarian Oxford Movement?
> Would you ever have written Tract No. 90? Is it probable
> that you would have stuck tight to the 'City of Confusion'?
> At this moment might you not be Archbishop of Canter-
> bury—successor of St Augustine in that see, instead of
> succeeding his namesake at Hippo *in partibus infidelium*?

Men like Newman did not become archbishops of Canterbury,
even in the nineteenth century, but *Punch* ploughed on regardless, missing the nuance of allusion to Erastianism in Newman's
phrase 'the dictum was in force, when I was young, that "Christianity was the law of the land"'.

> When Christianity was in your young days, as you say, 'the
> law of the land', was it not the Christianity of the Church
> by Law Established, and as defined by Parson Thwackum?

Indeed it had been, and the Gorham Judgement had sealed it
forever. The piece closed with a neat comparison with Charles
Darwin's *Origin of Species*, which in 1859 had set a liberal cat
among the theological pigeons, and Newman's *Essay on the
Development of Christian Doctrine*.

> Your Eminence is a Cardinal who has the courage of his
> opinions. Mr Darwin's Theory of 'Development' is not
> exactly yours. Nevertheless with regard to sects, if not to
> species, are you not sufficiently well assured that the
> struggle for existence will result in the survival of the
> fittest? May you live to see it![41]

If the ending was an intimation of 'we shall see', then the horse
had already bolted—and *Punch* knew it. In the coverage of his
cardinalate it is impossible not to see the regard in which it held
Newman, even if it had its qualifications. Leo XIII had told
Newman that 'he judged it would give pleasure to English
Catholics, and even to Protestant England, if I received some
mark of his favour', and among those present in Cardinal
Howard's rooms at the Palazzo Pigna included 'nearly all the
English residents now in Rome, both Catholic and Protestant'.[42]

As Patrick Leary observed in his study of the development of
Punch's mid-Victorian outlook, as early as 1859 the then-proprietor
Frederick Evans was able to direct its gaze: 'Times are altered [...]
and *Punch* alters with the times.'[43] Leary also argued that the tone
of *Punch* was reliant to a great extent on the successive sympathies
of its compilers. In that light, then, the appointment of the regular
contributor Francis Burnand as editor in 1880 cannot be easily
discounted. Burnand declared himself 'hostile to no man's religion',[44] while Shirley Brooks, who had been editor from Lemon's
death in 1870 until his own demise four years later, had been
antipathetic to Catholics in general and Irish ones in particular.[45]

Burnand served as editor for 26 years; furthermore, he was a
convert who had been inspired to join the Catholic Church after

---

[41]   'A Cardinal Point', *Punch* 76 (24 May 1879), p. 233.

[42]   *The Times*, 13 May 1879.

[43]   Patrick Leary, *The Punch Brotherhood: Table Talk and Print Culture in
       Mid-Victorian London* (London: British Library, 2010), p. 124.

[44]   Jane W. Stedman, entry for Sir Francis Cowley Burnand, 1836–1917,
       ODNB.

[45]   Leary, *op. cit.*, p. 121.

reading Newman's *Essay on the Development of Christian Doctrine*. He steered *Punch* away from its nascent anti-Catholicism—notwithstanding its approval of the early policies of Pius IX—although the qualified softening of tone in Newman's own case belonged to the twilight of the editorship of his immediate predecessor, Tom Taylor. A prolific playwright and writer of comedy, by the time he died in 1917 Burnand had also edited Burns & Oates' *The Catholic Who's Who*, and—with shades of Newman's cardinalate—been knighted by Edward VII in the year of his coronation.

Inevitably, *Punch's* direction of travel under Burnand also reflected a general resetting of the public mood as the nineteenth century drew to a close. In Newman's former Church of England, Tractarianism had given way to Puseyism, which had developed a branch of ritualism, before the whole had turned into Anglo-Catholicism writ large; the anonymous author of *Bombastes Religioso, or the Protestant Pope of 1899* concluded that 'an overwhelming majority of the English people are perfectly well satisfied to live and let live, and they care no more what amount of ritual is permitted in any given place of worship within the Queen's dominions than they care how many times the Sultan of Turkey prostrates himself next Friday'.[46]

By the time he died in August 1890, Newman had transcended the memory of the bitter battles of his earlier life and become a national, even international, figure; in the context of his cardinalate, Ker has written of Newman's 'personal victory'[47] over the doubts that had previously lingered on both sides of the Tiber. *Punch* finally accorded him the dignity of a poem-obituary, which it reserved for those of whom it most approved and admired. In his case it took the form of an elegy addressed to Newman himself.

'Lead, Kindly Light!' From lips serene and strong,
Chaste, as melodious, on world-weary ears

---

[46]   *Bombastes Religioso, or The Protestant Pope of 1899* (London: Simpkin, Marshall, Hamilton & Kent, 1899), p. 5.
[47]   *Newman: Biography*, p. 718.

Fall, 'midst earth's chaos wild of hopes and fears,
The accents calm of spiritual song,
Striking across the tumult of the throng
Like the still line of lustre, soft, severe,
From the high-riding, ocean-swaying sphere,
Athwart the wandering wilderness of waves.
Is there not soul-light which so laves
Earth's lesser spirits with its chastening beam,
That passion's bale-fire and the lurid gleam
Of sordid selfishness know strange eclipse?
Such purging lustre his, whose eloquent lips
Lie silent now. Great soul, great Englishman!
Whom narrowing bounds of creed, or caste, or clan,
Exclude not from world-praise and all men's love.
Fine spirit, which the strain of ardent strife
Warped not from its firm poise, or made to move
From the pure pathways of the Saintly Life!

Newman, farewell! Myriads whose spirits spurn
The limitations thou didst love so well,
Who never knew the shades of Oriel,
Or felt their quickened spirits pulse and burn
Beneath that eye's regard, that voice's spell—
Myriads, world-scattered and creed-sundered, turn
In thought to that hushed chamber's chastened gloom
In all great hearts there is abundant room
For memories of greatness, and high pride
In what sects cannot kill nor seas divide.
The light hath led thee, on through honoured days
And lengthened, through wild gusts of blame and praise,
Through doubt, and severing change, and poignant pain,
Warfare that strains the breast and racks the brain,
At last to haven! Now no English heart
Will willingly forego unfeignèd part
In honouring thee, true master of our tongue,
On whose word, writ or spoken, ever hung
All English ears which knew that tongue's best charm.
Not as great Cardinal such hearts most warm
To one above all office and all state

Serenely wise, magnanimously great;
Not as the pride of Oriel, or the star
Of this host or of that in creed's hot war,
But as the noble spirit, stately, sweet,
Ardent for good without fanatic heat
Gentle of soul, though greatly militant,
Saintly, yet with no touch of cloistral cant;
Him England honours, and so bends to-day
In reverent grief o'er Newman's glorious clay.[48]

'Great soul, great Englishman!' As *Punch* in its final tribute now conceded, Newman had triumphed in the end. It was a remarkable close to a remarkable life, and a final burying of the hatchet, while the evocation of the 'pure pathways of the Saintly Life' prefigured history yet to come. 'Saintly, yet with no touch of cloistral cant; him England honours, and so bends to-day in reverent grief o'er Newman's glorious clay.' In the pages of *Punch*, as in the mind of the nation at large, by the time of his death John Henry Newman had moved from turncoat to treasure; from shadows and imaginings into truth.

---

[48]   *Punch* 99 (23 August 1890), p. 95.

12 A 'SAVAGING PEN'? NEWMAN'S *PRESENT POSITION OF CATHOLICS* AND HIS ANGLICAN SATIRE

Andrew Nash

NEWMAN'S *Lectures on the Present Position of Catholics* do not sit comfortably with a certain stereotype of him. Wilfred Ward's view was that in them:

> We have the very curious spectacle of a grave religious apologist giving rein for the first time at the age of fifty to a sense of rollicking fun and gifts of humorous writing, which if expended on other subjects would naturally have adorned the pages of Thackeray's *Punch*.[1]

But was it the first time? Was *Present Position* such a new departure for Newman? A later twentieth-century critic, Owen Chadwick, who though Anglican was generally very sympathetic to Newman, went further and made a more serious charge about these lectures. He saw Newman in these early years of his Catholic life as suffering from 'convertitis' and self-distrust and, instead of pursuing his previous more profound theological work, turning to much less worthy writing. For Chadwick, when Newman critiques Protestant prejudice in *Present Position*, all he is doing is to 'play delightful games' and 'play less delightful games with the counter-prejudices of the convert, even with a savaging pen'. He dismisses Newman's analysis of anti-Catholic publications as 'a refined mind bothering itself with trash' and says that the reader 'is sad to see so delicate an instrument taking its time to

---

[1] Wilfred Ward, *Last Lectures* (London: Longmans, Green & Co., 1918), p. 113.

prove false what no instructed person could believe true'.[2] For Chadwick, this new Catholic Newman had sadly fallen from his previous Anglican heights. In this essay, I shall demonstrate just how inaccurate this view is and what clear continuities there are between Newman's Anglican and Catholic satirical writings.

Ian Ker, in a landmark essay on 'Newman the Satirist',[3] was the first to demonstrate that although Newman's gifts of satire and humour certainly blossomed after his conversion to Catholicism, they were already powerfully present in his Anglican period.[4] He finds Newman first using satire in 1833 in private letters written from Italy to friends back at home, attacking Thomas Arnold's *Principles of Church Reform* (1833) which put forward a plan for religious comprehensiveness in which the various Protestant denominations would share the use of parish churches. Newman makes fun of this, suggesting that there should be *two* Sundays in the week to accommodate them all, with the Jews using the churches on Saturdays and the Moslems on Fridays.[5]

But actually Newman was enjoying using satire long before this. The earliest drawing we have is a sketch of him as the schoolboy chairman of the Spy Club where he is reading aloud to his fellows from his weekly paper, *The Spy*.[6] According to the later reminiscences of his brother Frank, this periodical caused

---

2   Owen Chadwick, *Newman* (Oxford: Oxford University Press, 1983), p. 15.

3   I. Ker, 'Newman the Satirist', *Newman after a Hundred Years*, ed. Ian Ker & Alan G. Hill (Oxford: Clarendon Press, 1990), pp. 1–20.

4   I owe a personal debt of gratitude to Fr Ian for his inspiration and guidance. He acted as a supervisor when I was doing my doctoral thesis on *Present Position*. Many years earlier he had also supervised me when, as an undergraduate at Cambridge, I elected to write a Long Essay on Newman's style in the *Idea of a University* for Part II of the English Tripos. Unable to find a Newman scholar in Cambridge knowledgeable on this subject, the English Faculty sent me to Fr Ian, who was then at the Birmingham Oratory.

5   See *LD* iii, pp. 257–8, 298.

6   This illustration can be found in Maisie Ward, *Young Mr Newman* (London: Sheed & Ward, 1948), between pp. 14 & 15.

friction with some of the other boys because the young John Henry '*quizzed* everybody', that is, in nineteenth-century usage, made fun of them. Here is the early satirist! Newman himself later remembered how both at school and at home he wrote plays for his brothers and sisters: there was a 'mock drama of some kind' in 1812 and 'a satire on the Prince Regent.'[7] As an undergraduate at Oxford, Newman and his friend John Bowden started a periodical, *The Undergraduate*, which got more comic with every issue.[8] In it Newman argued for the setting up of a university debating club: he clearly had a natural enjoyment of public argument. It is perhaps not surprising that his favourite author was Cicero. Newman later described him as 'the only master of style I have ever had';[9] and it is significant that he highlighted Cicero's use of 'raillery' and 'irony' in the article he wrote on him for the *Encyclopaedia Metropolitana* in 1824.[10]

There were no signs of Newman's satirical gifts in his early published writings: we would hardly expect it in his sermons or the *Arians of the Fourth Century* (1833). However, once the Oxford Movement was under way, Newman began to write in a much more robust and satirical style. Ker identifies a number of examples, but there are many more, sometimes in works Newman did not republish in his later collected works, particularly his contributions to the *British Magazine* and the *British Critic*. The latter was edited by Newman himself from 1838 to 1841, and under his editorship it became much more outspoken in style. Newman encouraged contributors such as Tom Mozley whose writing was often more outrageously satirical than Newman's own, even more so after he succeeded Newman as editor.[11] The

---

[7]   Newman, 'Memorandum on Writings 1812–17', *LD* i, p. 10.
[8]   See M. Trevor, *Newman. The Pillar of the Cloud* (London: Macmillan, 1962), p. 29.
[9]   Newman to J. Hayes, 13 April 1869, *LD* xxiv, p. 242.
[10] 'Personal and Literary Character of Cicero', reproduced in *HS* i, p. 294.
[11] See Trevor, *op. cit.*, p. 249.

lively tone of the *British Critic* in these years is the context for
the development of Newman's satire.

The article by Newman on 'Exeter Hall' which appeared in July
1838 will give the flavour.[12] Ker does not mention this in his
survey of Newman's satirical writings, perhaps because Newman
did not reprint it when he later collected other articles in his
Essays Critical and Historical in 1871. It is a review of *Random
Recollections of Exeter Hall, in 1833–1837, by one of the Protestant
Party*, which had just been published. Exeter Hall in London was
the meeting place of the Evangelicals and particularly of the
anti-Catholic societies. The book Newman was reviewing was a
sympathetic account of its proceedings and notable speakers. He
begins his review with an historical account of early Church
synods with their atmosphere of solemnity and reverence which
he contrasts with the practices of the 'New Religion', that is, the
Protestantism of his day. The ancient practice of almsgiving is
contrasted with the modern charity bazaar:

> [...] much might be said of the potent influence exerted on
> such occasions by the young ladies who ofttimes take their
> station at the booths and vend their charity. Aged bishops
> are said, of old time, to have exerted an arm of force, and to
> have compelled others to enjoy the privileges, and under-
> take the duties of the Christian Church;—but now-a-days,
> bright eyes and tasteful bonnets are found more effective,
> and, though we do not pretend to be connoisseurs in the
> matter ourselves, we certainly have read in the public prints
> that, whatever their advantage in the ball-room, our charm-
> ing countrywomen never look so well as in a morning dress.[13]

---

[12]   The late archivist at the Birmingham Oratory, Gerard Tracey, drew my
       attention to this and other un-republished Anglican writings of Newman's
       when I was doing research for my thesis on the *Present Position*. Like many
       other students of Newman, I was greatly helped by Gerard and have happy
       memories of enjoying a pint with him at the nearby Plough and Harrow
       inn.

[13]   'Exeter Hall', *The British Critic* xxiv (July 1838), p. 197.

To be noted here is Newman's gentle mockery of the way that religion has become mixed up with fashion and social occasions. 'The Temple of this new system', he says,

> is Exeter Hall: its holytide is 'the London season;' its chancel is a platform; its cathedral throne is the chairman's seat; its ministers are the speakers; for holy salutations it uses 'Ladies and Gentlemen;' for benedictions it has 'cheers;' for a creed it maintains the utility of combination; and for holy services and godly discipline it proclaims civil and religious liberty throughout the world.[14]

The twenty-first-century reader (particularly in the United States) may not appreciate the nuances of some of Newman's phraseology here. 'The London season' was the time of year from Christmas to mid-summer when the upper classes spent time in the capital, as opposed to their country houses, in order to socialise and especially to find husbands for their daughters. It is therefore absurd that such a secular and class-based period of time should be the 'holytide' of an allegedly religious activity as the meetings in Exeter Hall. The 'utility of combination' means the practical project of various bodies working together—again, a secular concept, as opposed to the church's sense of itself as a single body, or as we would call it today, its ecclesiology. And whereas 'religious and civil liberty throughout the world' is an ideal endorsed by all the Christian churches today, in Newman's time it was a secular goal which was part of the programme of 'liberalism' which Newman saw as antithetical to the Church's teaching of God-given truth.[15] But again, the joke is that it is self-evidently absurd, to Newman, that an allegedly religious institution, Exeter Hall, should be adopting a fashionable secular slogan instead of 'holy services and godly discipline'. And, of

---

[14] *Ibid.*, p. 198.

[15] Newman's political outlook was nuanced but was very conservative by modern standards. When in quarantine on board ship in Marseilles harbour after his Sicily trip in 1833, he would not even look at the French tricolour, emblem of the hated Revolution.

course, 'religious liberty' referred to countries where the Catholic Church was seen as having too much power, not to Protestant England where Catholics had only recently been allowed their civil rights after centuries of persecution. Exeter Hall was famous for its anti-Catholic meetings with their fierce attacks on the Pope and opposition to any extension of the rights of Catholics in England or support for the Catholic Church in Ireland such as the Maynooth grant.

Newman goes on to quote from the book's descriptions of the halls (the building housed two) and detailed accounts of the most celebrated orators. His technique is to let these extracts speak for themselves, bringing out their absurdities or incongruities by italicising key phrases. For example, he quotes passages about the Rev. Mr Stowell, a noted anti-Catholic Anglican clergyman:

> 'His face is large and broad'; 'his eyes blue and laughing', and 'his mouth, which is very wide, *garnished with splendid white teeth*.' We are told that 'his images are striking, sometimes rather coarse, and his style often the most jocular, *even to broad comic effect*;' that 'no speaker more frequently *sets the Hall in a roar*', and that it is a question 'which makes the most noise in proportion, Mr Stowell or his audience.'[16]

Newman's point is the incongruity of such descriptions when the speakers are supposedly speaking on sacred subjects:

> what is there of a religious character in exhibitions, which to a deaf person, or to one who was suddenly introduced to them without knowledge of the societies to which they belonged, taken at greatest advantage, would not differ at all, or scarcely, from those of any other meeting, political or other, which take place in the metropolis? [...] we cannot help coming to the conclusion that, while Exeter Hall has throughout all its floors the dry rot of irreverence, some of its speakers are but stage players at best, and at worst actual drolls and merry andrews.[17]

---

[16]   *Ibid.*, p. 204.

Newman was not alone, incidentally, in finding Exeter Hall grotesque. Before *Punch* became a champion of the campaign against the 'Papal Aggression' of 1850, it had published a seventeenth-century-style cartoon of 'A Prospect of Exeter Hall, Showing a Christian Gentleman Denouncynge ye Pope', together with a mock Pepys' diary entry describing a meeting.[18]

Another article in the *British Critic* which Newman chose not to include in his collected works (and so not discussed by Ker) was 'Elliott's Travels' published in April 1839. This was a review of *Travels in the Three Great Empires of Austria, Russia and Turkey* (2 vols, 1838) by C. B. Elliott. What Newman found funny, and to some extent distasteful, about Mr Elliott's account of his travels was his extreme insularity. The volumes, said Newman,

> do not disclose nearly so much about the countries they advertise, as about Mr Elliott himself; or at least their principal charm lies in the relation existing between the traveller and his adventures, in his exquisite appreciation of the worth of every thing of English manufacture, whether English comfort, or English Ultra-Protestantism, and his consequent annoyance, dejection, or contempt when he meets with things and person moulded upon a different standard.[19]

He quotes many extracts from the book in illustration, letting Elliott speak for himself, so that the reader gets to know Elliott's voice and manner, sometimes drawing attention to Elliott's distinctive obsession with material comfort and his intensely insular attitudes by italicising words and phrases. He also emphasises Elliott's ignorant approach towards the religious sites and persons he visits: 'we are sorry to detect in him, what is a great fault in religious matters, a want of duly realizing what he is doing

---

[17]   *Ibid.*, p. 211. A 'droll' was a jester, and a 'merry andrew' was a clown at a fair.

[18]   *Punch* 16 (1849), p. 206.

[19]   'Elliott's Travels', *The British Critic* xxv (April 1839), p. 306.

or talking about; so that he will use solemn words to round a sentence, speak disrespectfully of sacred subjects'.[20]

This review in itself is of only marginal interest now, but the reader of the later *Lectures on the Present Position of Catholics in England* will immediately recognise Elliott as one of those 'men of contracted ideas, who cannot fancy things going on differently from what they have themselves witnessed at home, and laugh at everything because it is strange',[21] who are so vividly caricatured in Lecture VII. The story Newman tells in that lecture about a country gentleman undertaking a continental tour who thought himself prepared for anything abroad, provided he had 'a good beef-steak every day',[22] had in fact already appeared in the Elliott article. This is perhaps the clearest single example of the way that the Catholic *Present Position* is a continuation of Newman's Anglican *British Critic* satire.

Newman republished most of his Anglican writings which contain satire, collecting them in *Essays Critical and Historical* (2 vols) in 1871.[23] 'The State of the Religious Parties', originally an article in the *British Critic* in April 1839, contains a passage of sustained irony on the Anglican ability to hold mutually contradictory beliefs:

> In the present day mistiness is the mother of wisdom. A man who can set down half a dozen general propositions, which escape from destroying one another only by being diluted into truisms, who can hold the balance between opposites so skilfully as to do without fulcrum or beam, who never enunciates a truth without guarding himself from being supposed to exclude the contradictory, who holds

---

[20]   *Ibid.*, p. 316.

[21]   *Present Position*, p. 295.

[22]   *Ibid.*, p. 296.

[23]   For a more detailed analysis of the articles discussed here, see the Editor's Introduction to my edition of *Essays Critical and Historical*, vol. i (Leominster: Gracewing, 2019). See also the Textual Appendix to my edition which reveals that Newman carefully honed the text of these articles when he republished them, without softening their satire.

> that Scripture is the only authority, yet that the Church is
> to be deferred to, that faith only justifies, yet that it does not
> justify without works [...] this is your safe man and the hope
> of the Church; this is what the Church is said to want, not
> party men, but sensible, temperate, sober, well-judging
> persons, to guide it through the channel of No-meaning,
> between the Scylla and Charybdis of Aye and No.[24]

What attracts Newman's withering satire here is the respectability which masks inconsistency. The same phenomenon is to be
found in *Present Position* in the Protestant father 'in his house,
his family, and his circle of friends, in his occupation, and his civil
and political position, as a good kind father, as a liberal master,
as a useful member of society', who ends up ruthlessly persecuting
members of his own family who have become Catholics.[25]

The subject of Newman's satire is often the habits and attitudes of the middle and upper classes. For example, in an article
on the 'The Anglo-American Church', originally published in
October 1839, Newman noted the danger of attraction of this
episcopalian sister-church of Anglicanism to the 'respectable'
classes in the United States: 'If this view of things is allowed a
footing, a sleek gentleman-like religion will grow up within the
sacred pale'. On the comfortably furnished churches, he comments with irony, 'we think we may say without fear of mistake,
that pews, carpets, cushions and fine speaking are not developments of the Apostolical Succession'.[26] This is the milieu of the
same comfortable bourgeois Protestantism which Newman will
reveal to be so prejudiced in *Present Position*.

This is particularly significant in Newman's article on 'The
Protestant Idea of Antichrist', a review of J. H. Todd's *Discourses
on the Prophecies Relating to Antichrist* (1840), in the *British
Critic* in October 1840. This contains a witty critique of Bishop
Thomas Newton. Newton was the main source for the Anglican

---

[24]   *Essays* i, p. 302.
[25]   *Present Position*, pp. 184–6.
[26]   *Essays* i, p. 350.

tradition of identifying the papacy with Antichrist, yet he himself was a worldly and careerist cleric who lived a life of ease while asserting that the Pope was the Beast of the Apocalypse and that all Roman Catholics were servants of the devil who were going to hell. Newman brings out the incongruity of Newton's comfortable lifestyle by quoting from Newton's own autobiography, again italicising to bring out the incongruities. In this Newton referred to himself in the third person, which only served to make his accounts of the way he obtained promotion in the Church of England through the influence of aristocratic friends sound all the more self-satisfied:

> 'Dr Newton [...] had the honour of being in some measure known to the Earl of Bute, having baptized one or two of his children, and having sometimes met him at Leicester House, when as chaplain he had been in attendance upon the Princess of Wales. *He had also presented to him the three volumes of his Dissertations on the Prophecies, having obtained the favour of his lordship to present them to the Prince of Wales.* Upon the death of Bishop Sherlock, Lord Bute told a noble lord, a particular friend of Dr Newton's, *that he would certainly be the new bishop,* and would be obliged to no minister for his promotion: it was entirely the doing of the king himself and the Princess of Wales ... He' [the Duke of Newcastle] 'had been so long used to shuffle and cut the cards, that he well knew how to pack them in such a manner as to have the *honours*' [for instance, the see of London] 'dealt to his particular friends.'[27]

Newman quotes Newton's own account of his getting married, which reveals that the bishop's motives were entirely financial and practical. From 'his *old principle* of avoiding as much as possible the *trouble* of housekeeping', Newton had been boarding with friends, but

> 'the breaking up of the family naturally engaged him to *think seriously again of matrimony* [...] And *especially*,' he

---

[27]   *Essays* ii, p. 135.

continues, '*when he had some prospect of a bishopric*, fresh *difficulties* and *troubles* opened to his view; there would be a better table and public days to be kept; and he plainly foresaw that he must either fall a prey to servants or must look out for some clever sensible woman to be his wife, who had some knowledge and experience of the world, who was a prudent manager, who could do the honours of his table in a becoming manner [...]' He was at this time fifty-seven, and 'it was happy for him', he adds, 'that such a woman was in his eye', one whom 'he had known from a little child in a white frock, and had observed her through all the parts of her life.'[28]

To modern readers, this is distinctly unpleasant, even creepy. But even allowing for an earlier age in which it was not uncommon for older men to marry younger women whom they had known as children, Newton's reasons for choosing his bride are distinctly unromantic. One is reminded of Mr Casubon's deciding to marry Dorothea in *Middlemarch*.

The picture which emerges is that of a cleric whose worldly lifestyle sat incongruously with stern denunciation of the Papacy as Antichrist. Newman summed up:

A man so idolatrous of comfort, so liquorish of preferment, whose most fervent aspiration apparently was that he might ride in a carriage and sleep on down, whose keenest sorrow that he could not get a second appointment without relinquishing the first, who cast a regretful look back upon his own dinner while he was at supper, and anticipated his morning chocolate in his evening muffins, who will say that this is the man, not merely to unchurch, but to smite, to ban, to wither the whole of Christendom for many centuries, and the greatest part of it even in his own day.[29]

Such satirical use of food was to be a feature of Newman's other critiques of the culture of Establishment Protestantism; it recurs

---

[28]   *Ibid.*, p. 138.
[29]   *Ibid.*, pp. 138–9.

in his depiction of the Prejudiced Man in Lecture VII of *Present Position* and is in fact an important feature of his satire there.[30] It is not that Newman had an ascetic objection to food; it is the incongruity of the combination of a comfortable self-indulgent lifestyle with vehement anti-Catholic self-righteousness. Newman makes his point even more strongly by contrasting Newton's life with the selfless dedication of Catholic saints such as St Charles Borromeo; yet such a man was, by Newton's theory, a follower of Antichrist. Newman asks of those who 'so confidently and solemnly pronounce Christian Rome to be Babylon',

> Do they know what they say? [...] Do they *in faith* make over the millions upon millions now and in former times who have been in subjection to the Roman See to utter and hopeless perdition? Do they in very truth look upon them as the direct and open enemies of God, and children of Satan?[31]

It is the *unreality* of the Protestant view which Newman so effectively attacks here. This unreality and inconsistency is a recurrent target of his satire.

This article is a precursor of *Present Position* in a number of ways. For instance, discussing the evidence which Protestant polemicists use to support the Pope being called Antichrist, Newman reveals a number of historical inaccuracies. Newton had stated that the Pope '*is styled* and *pleased* to be styled our Lord God the Pope', but this turns out to be based on a gloss of a canonist which occurred in the course of an argument, 'the object of which was to prove that the Pope's words were to be obeyed, *because, as all law, civil inclusive, they were the decision of God*'.[32] This is the kind of mistake which the imaginary Russian Count in Lecture I of *Present Position* makes when he reads Blackstone's *Commentaries on the Laws of England* and interprets it as

---

[30]   *Present Position*, pp. 295–6. See my Introduction to my edition of *Present Position* (Leominster: Gracewing, 2000), pp. lxii–lxvi for a full analysis of this element in the lectures.

[31]   *Essays* ii, pp. 147–8.

[32]   *Ibid.*, p. 128.

containing outrageous blasphemies, such as the legal principle that 'the King can do no wrong', which he takes to be a statement of the monarch's personal perfection.[33]

Very close in style to *Present Position* was Newman's article on 'Private Judgment' in the *British Critic* (July 1841). Here he satirises the inconsistency of the Protestant claim to believe in the right of private judgement in religious matters (as opposed to the Catholic principle of authority):

> If a staunch Protestant's daughter turns Roman, and betakes herself to a convent, why does he not exult in the occurrence? Why does he not give a public breakfast, or hold a meeting, or erect a memorial or write a pamphlet in honour of her, and of the great undying principle she has so gloriously vindicated? Why is he in this base, disloyal style muttering about priests, and Jesuits, and the horrors of nunneries, in solution of the phenomenon, when he has the fair and ample form of Private Judgment rising before his eyes, and pleading with him?[34]

Newman's use of concrete details is effective here—the public breakfast, meeting, memorial or pamphlet—and the indirect imitation of the Protestant father's mutterings, 'priests, and Jesuits and the horrors of nunneries'. This passage, which Ker quotes, was in fact preceded by one which is an even closer precursor of *Present Position*. Here is the Anglican Newman in this 1841 article on the subject of how people react to converts:

> A convert is undeniably in favour with no party; he is looked at with distrust, contempt, and aversion by all. His former friends think him a good riddance, and his new friends are cold and strange; and as to the impartial public, their very first impulse is to impute the change to some eccentricity of character, or fickleness of mind, or tender attachment, or private interest. Their utmost praise is the reluctant confession that 'doubtless he is very sincere'.

---

[33]   *Present Position*, p. 30.

[34]   *Essays* ii, p. 340.

Churchmen and Dissenters, men of Rome and men of the Kirk, are equally subject to this remark. Not on extraordinary occasions only, but as a matter of course, whenever the news of a conversion to Romanism, or to Irvingism, or to the Plymouth sect, or to Unitarianism, is brought to us, we say, one and all of us, 'No wonder, such a one has lived so long abroad'; or, 'he is of such a very imaginative turn'; or, 'he is so excitable and odd'; or, 'what could he do? all his family turned'; or, 'it was a re-action in consequence of an injudicious education'; or, 'trade makes men cold', or 'a little learning makes them shallow in their religion'.[35]

And here is the Catholic Newman, in *Present Position*, on how a Protestant father reacts to the news of his child's conversion to Catholicism:

'Such a base, grovelling, demoralising religion, unworthy of a man of sense, unworthy of a man! I could have borne his turning Drummondite, Plymouth-Brother, or Mormonite. He might almost have joined the Agapemone.[36] I would rather see him an unbeliever; yes, I say it deliberately, Popery is worse than Paganism. I had rather see him dead. I could have borne to see him in his coffin. I cannot see him the slave of a priest. And then the way in which he took the step: he never let me know, and had been received before I had had a hint about it'; or 'he told me what he meant to do, and then did it in spite of me'; or, 'he was so weak and silly', or 'so head-strong', or 'so long and obstinately set upon it'. 'He had nothing to say for himself', or 'he was always arguing'. 'He was inveigled into it by others', or 'he ought to have consulted others, he had no right to have an opinion. Anyhow he is preferring strangers to his true friends; he has

---

[35] *Essays* ii, p. 339.

[36] The Agapemone, the 'abode of love', was a community in Spaxton, Somerset, founded by a defrocked Anglican clergyman, Henry Prince, who had declared himself divine. It consisted mostly of wealthy upper-class women who had to give the community their money and become his supposedly spiritual 'brides'. It became known for its sexual immorality.

> shown an utter disregard of the feelings of his parents and
> relations; he has been ungrateful to his father.'[37]

So parallel are the style and structure of these two passages that
the fundamental continuity of Newman's Anglican and Catholic
satire is evident.

Surprisingly, Ker does not include the satiric gem which
Newman republished in *Essays Critical and Historical*, his article
on 'Selina, Countess of Huntingdon', which had appeared in the
British Critic (October 1840). This was a review of the recently
published biography of this aristocratic patron of Methodism.
Newman begins with a generous appreciation of her: 'she devoted
herself, her name, her means, her time, her thoughts, to the cause
of Christ'. However, her biography was a blend of hagiography
and snobbery, and Newman has great fun with this:

> Selina, Countess of Huntingdon, being the second daugh-
> ter of Washington, Earl Ferrers, was noble both by birth
> and marriage; and it will not be the fault of her biogra-
> phers, if posterity is not fully aware of this fact. Before
> opening the volume, we encounter her arms, with coronet,
> supporters and motto, in gilt, upon the side of it. We open
> it, and are met with her portrait, with the coronet above
> it, and her arms below, not however as before, but accord-
> ing to a second device. Then comes the title-page, and here
> a third representation of her arms presents itself, and
> according to a third device; and we are informed, in
> addition, that the memoir which is to follow is the work
> of 'a *member* of the noble houses of Huntingdon and
> Ferrers'. This is but a specimen of the whole book.[38]

The volume's Introduction not only gives 'a minute account of
the ancestral peculiarities' of the lady's family but also 'contains
genealogical notes [...] so copious that, put together, they would
go far to make up a Lodge or Debrett'. Newman suggests, a touch
mischievously, that such worship of rank is because Methodism

---

[37] *Present Position*, p. 187.
[38] *Essays* i, p. 390.

has discarded the authority of bishops: 'Disbelieving the existence of a divine priesthood, it will ever gaze with awe and reverence at the high station or splendid connections or noble birth of the children of men.' And he goes on to quote (using italicisation again, in this case to bring out the unconscious snobbery) the book's account of how a certain Dr Haweis had been deprived of his curacy for his Methodist leanings,

> *yet* he had had influence, *and was of a good family*, long resident in Cornwall, and well known as Haweis of St Coose. His mother, Miss Bridgman Willyams, was the only daughter of, etc. Her mother was a sister of the last Baron Sandys of the Vines, etc. etc., whose eldest sister, Hester, was granddaughter and heiress of, etc. etc. etc.

It is quite clear, he comments, that the aristocratic biographer

> has been taught by his own people, that whatever excuse may be made for a bishop's acting vigorously towards snobs or *parvenus*, none at all of any sort or kind can be made for his curbing the zeal of well-connected ranters or gentleman-like heretics: the very idea of which argues a degree of presumption which need but be recorded to receive the deserved condemnation of an impartial posterity.[39]

This irony Newman surely learnt from Gibbon—the final sentence, in particular, is exactly his style. Another superb passage is Newman's comment on a saying of Frederic, Prince of Wales, whose court Lady Huntingdon attended and whom she hoped to persuade to the Methodist cause. Asking on one occasion where the Lady was and being told that she was praying with beggars, the Prince apparently said, '"When I am dying, I think I shall be happy to *seize the skirt* of Lady Huntingdon's mantle, *to lift me up* with her to Heaven."' Newman goes on:

> Such a speech in a royal mouth surely gives a favourable impression of the speaker; such is *our* judgment of it; but we marvel that the Calvinistic biographer of Lady Hunting-

---

[39]   *Ibid.*, p. 392.

don allows it to pass without a protest. Surely he must feel in his heart, that, under the language of Scripture, it savours of what he considers the leaven of Popery, that it interferes with the doctrine of justification by faith only, ascribes to Lady Huntingdon works of supererogation, tends to saint-worship, and encourages the notion that the intervention of one man can be of service to the soul of another.[40]

With the use once again of ironic italicisation, Newman illustrates the extraordinary confusion of obsequiousness and piety in the Methodist leader Whitfield's attitude to Lady Huntingdon: Whitfield wrote that he was '"quite astonished at her ladyship's condescension, *and* the unmerited superabounding grace and goodness of Him who has loved me" etc'.[41] Newman also plays on the idea that Lady Huntingdon's rank became a theological substitute for episcopal authority: 'the rulers of the Church did not understand her mission, and Lady Huntingdon became acting bishop instead of them', quoting from the biography a letter by Whitfield which describes her as having

'five clergymen under her roof, which makes her ladyship look *like a good archbishop, with his chaplains around him* [...]. We have the sacrament every morning, heavenly conversation all day, and preach at night. This is to live at court indeed!'[42]

He finds passages in the biography which show her issuing instructions and reprovals to various clergymen, which he introduces with 'Thus she speaks *ex cathedrâ*,—Selena Episcopa'. He concludes, 'Might not this be a translation from St Basil, bating the proper names, or the allocution of some Pope, whose legates had been insulted?'[43]

---

[40] *Ibid.*, pp. 400–1.
[41] *Ibid.*, p. 393.
[42] *Ibid.*, p. 413.
[43] *Ibid.*, pp. 413–14.

Newman had struck a rich vein for satire—some of his material was simply a gift. For instance, the biography makes much of the Rev. Mr Madan, who, as well as being from a most well-connected family, became a zealous Methodist preacher. The biographer waxes eloquent in heavily Scriptural language about his gifts and virtues in passages which Newman quotes in detail. And then, in a technique which the French critic Fernande Tardivel was to note was later used in *Present Position*,[44] Newman builds up to a climax which brings the whole edifice crashing down as this alleged modern saint is revealed as an advocate of men being allowed to have several wives:

> At a later date, this gentleman, thus paralleled to St John and St Barnabas, baptized with fire and enlightened in the nature of regeneration, actually wrote a book, called 'Thelyphthora, or a Treatise on Female Ruin', in which he advocates polygamy, as an expedient for setting things straight.[45]

Newman's most sustained satire in his Anglican writings, according to Ker, is the Tamworth Reading Room letters which he wrote anonymously as 'Catholicus' for *The Times* in 1841. These attacked the speech made by Sir Robert Peel at the opening of a new public library in Tamworth. Peel had taken a wholly utilitarian line, presenting the knowledge provided by such an educational institution as effecting moral improvement in people, being, in effect, a substitute for religion. Newman's satirical techniques here are indeed sophisticated. In her unpublished critical edition of *The Tamworth Reading Room*, Nina Burgis analyses Newman's techniques. For instance, she comments on his mockery of Peel:

> This treatment ensures that the reader identifies himself with 'Catholicus' who is witty and sensible and whose seriousness is never solemn. An invitation to the reader to

---

[44] Fernande Tardivel, *La Personalité Littéraire de Newman* (Paris: G. Beauchesne, 1937), p. 289.

[45] *Essays* i, p. 419.

> share the writer's superiority to another's foolishness or
> ignorance is not very frequent in Newman [...] In the
> 'Tamworth Reading Room' [it] functions as a rhetorical
> means to enlist support for his views.[46]

The stance of Newman himself as the speaker was also to be an
important part of his rhetorical strategy in *Present Position*: starting
with a pose of innocence, he makes the spokesmen of Protestantism
whom he quotes or invents look foolish. Burgis also notes that one
of the grounds on which Newman attacks Peel is that he is speaking
'on a subject to which he had never given any deep thought and in
consequence he was "unreal", as we are, in Newman's words, "when
we speak on a subject with which are minds are not familiar."'[47] This
is precisely the ground on which he attacks the prejudiced Protestant who thinks he understands Catholicism but in reality does not
(in Lecture VIII of *Present Position*).

Newman's use of 'parallelism or antithesis in the constituents
of phrases and sentences' is noted by Burgis. She adds the
comment that in his longer works 'such verbal patterning is less
frequent although sometimes more elaborate than in *The Tamworth Reading Room*'.[48] There is certainly very subtle use of such
verbal patterning in *Present Position*. Far from its being 'less
frequent', it is in fact a notable feature of the lectures' style. Here
is a typical pair of balanced sentences, from Lecture VI:

> Tame facts, elaborate inductions, subtle presumptions, will
> not avail with the many; something which will cut a dash,
> something gaudy and staring, something inflammatory, is
> the rhetoric in request; he must make up his mind then to
> resign the populace to the action of the Catholic Church,
> or he must slander her to her greater confusion.[49]

---

[46] Nina F. Burgis, 'An Edition of Newman's *Tamworth Reading Room* with
introduction and textual and expository apparatus' (London University,
M.A. thesis, 1964), p. 162.

[47] *Ibid.*, p. 176. (The Newman quotation is from *Parochial and Plain* v, pp.
34–5.)

[48] *Ibid.*, pp. 183–4.

Many similar examples could be quoted.

Another of the stylistic features which Burgis notes in *The Tamworth Reading Room* is the way that Newman draws on 'the colloquial and even slang to give a nicely judged informality and directness to his tone and an edge to his attack [...] this extension of his diction to words and turns of phrase belonging to the spoken word rather than the written language'. This colloquial tone is indeed strongly marked in *Present Position* (although Newman's textual revisions of the Fourth Edition toned it down). Burgis makes the interesting observation that Hurrell Froude's letters to Newman share this characteristic of colloquialism.[50] After Froude's death, his papers and letters were edited by Keble and Newman and published as his *Remains* (4 vols, 1838–39). Newman commented that 'His letters approach to conversation' and praised their 'unaffectedness, playfulness, brilliancy' and the way they expressed Froude's 'utter hatred of pretence and humbug'.[51] The later papers showed Froude's 'leaning to Popery, nay his bitter hatred of our Reformers'[52] and were an important influence on Newman who, when he first read them, recorded that they 'quite made my head whirl, and have put things in quite a new light'.[53] I suggest that their 'uncompromising anti-Protestantism' and lively style were in fact a remote influence on *Present Position*. Burgis makes a further interesting comment on a feature of *The Tamworth Reading Room*: Newman's 'embodying of his theme with the *personae* of Peel and 'Catholicus' as representatives of opposed views running through the series [of letters]'.[54] This is just how *Present Position* works, with Newman embodying his theme of anti-Catholic prejudice in a series of Protestant

---

[49] *Present Position*, p. 225.
[50] Burgis, *op. cit.*, p. 191.
[51] Newman to F. Rogers, 5 July 1837, *LD* vi, p. 9.
[52] Newman to Keble, 27 August 1837, *LD* vi, p. 118.
[53] Newman to F. Rogers, 31 August 1837, *LD* vi, p. 120.
[54] Burgis, *op. cit.* p. 190.

opponents, some of them imaginary in this case, while others are real, whom he shows to be ignorant or prejudiced.

In his discussion of *The Tamworth Reading Room* Ker analyses Newman's satirical techniques, quoting a number of examples of the way that Newman makes Peel look ridiculous.[55] Peel had claimed that knowledge of the sciences not only was 'the means of useful occupation and rational recreation' but also contributed to 'the moral improvement of the community'. So, Newman asks:

> *how* these wonderful moral effects are to be wrought under the instrumentality of the physical sciences. Can the process be analyzed and drawn out, or does it act like a dose or a charm which comes into general use empirically?[56]

I would add a further extract from this passage which uses the technique of dramatised characters which we later also find in *Present Position*:

> To know is one thing, to do is another; the two things are altogether distinct. A man knows he should get up in the morning,—he lies a-bed; he knows he should not lose his temper, yet he cannot keep it. A labouring man knows he should not go to the ale-house, and his wife knows she should not filch when she goes out charing; but neverthe-less, in these cases, the consciousness of a duty is not all one with the performance of it.[57]

These down to earth examples are typical of Newman's satire. They make Peel look ridiculous because they show how unreal-istic his theory of 'moral improvement' is when applied to ordinary life. The more ordinary Newman's examples, the more unreal Peel's theory is revealed to be. Hence Newman's deliberate touches of colloquialism: 'lies a-bed, 'ale-house', 'filches', 'goes out charing'. There is also a passage in which Newman makes fun

---

[55] Ker, 'Newman the Satirist', pp. 12ff.
[56] *Discussions*, pp. 261–2.
[57] *Ibid.*, p. 262.

of the way that scientific knowledge is presented by Peel as a distraction from the ills of human nature:

> When a husband is gloomy, or an old woman peevish and fretful, those who are about them do all they can to keep dangerous topics and causes of offence out of the way, and think themselves lucky, if, by such skilful management, they get through the day without an outbreak. When a child cries, the nurserymaid dances it about, or points to the pretty black horses out of the window, or shows how ashamed poll-parrot or poor puss must be of its tantrums. Such is the sort of prescription which Sir Robert Peel offers to the good people of Tamworth.[58]

This has the distinctive feature of Newman's best satire in *Present Position*: the imitating of a speaker's voice, in this case the nurserymaid's baby-language of 'the pretty black horses', 'poll-parrot' and 'poor puss'. Like Burgis, Ker notes Newman's use of a colloquial tone of voice in *The Tamworth Reading Room*[59] in passages such as:

> Such is this new art of living, offered to the labouring classes,—we will say, for instance, in a severe winter, snow on the ground, glass falling, bread rising, coal at 20d, the cwt., and no work.[60]

I agree with Ker that the humour comes from the incongruity of the idea that such down to earth problems will be alleviated by the solace of scientific knowledge gained in a reading room. What is effective about a passage like this is not only the colloquialism but also the sentence structure with its verbal patterning ('glass falling, bread rising') and rhythm, leading to the emphatic climax 'no work.' In *Present Position* Newman was to use just such patterning.

The full picture of Newman's pre-1845 satire enables us to see *Present Position* in a truer perspective than that of Wilfred Ward

---

[58]   *Ibid.*, p. 264.
[59]   Ker, 'Newman the Satirist', p. 13.
[60]   *Discussions*, pp. 262, 264, 268.

or Chadwick. What emerges is that the 1851 lectures were certainly not just the product of a zealous convert's newly-sharpened wit at the expense of his former co-religionists. He was not descending to some unworthy ridicule for the sake of Catholic polemic. Newman's awareness of the absurdities of the Protestant mind-set went back much further. His satire of the comfortable English Protestant establishment, both clerical and lay, had been well-established, and he was already adept at the techniques which he went on to use in *Present Position*—and indeed later in the combative sections of the *Apologia*—in a more fully developed and sustained way. If Newman's was a 'savaging pen', it was one which he had used as an Anglican for many years.

13 NEWMAN, GIBBON AND THE CRITERIA OF STYLE

EDWARD SHORT

I N A FRAGMENT of autobiography, John Henry Newman
wrote that, as a schoolboy, although 'in no respect a preco-
cious boy', he 'attempted original compositions in prose and
verse from the age of eleven, and in prose showed a great
sensibility and took much pains in matters of style'.[1] Later, even
after years of composing some of the most brilliant prose ever
written, he would describe these pains as comparable to those of
child-birth. 'Did you ever hear me say', he asked his Tractarian
friend Frederic Rogers, 'what I am ever saying, that with me the
composition of a book is a child-birth?—It is so indeed. It takes
a vast deal out of me, and I dread it. I have hardly ever written
except from necessity.'[2] Yet Newman inaugurated what would
become this unremitting labor in his schooldays, when, as he
recalled, he 'devoted to such literary exercises and to such books
as came in his way, a good portion of his play-time; and his
school-fellows have left on record that they never, or scarcely
ever, saw him taking part in any game', an admission that would
not have endeared him to the muscular Christian Dr Arnold.[3]

In this essay, I shall look at how Newman came to understand
what he regarded as the criteria of style, especially in his lifelong
reading of Gibbon, to show how much his own style expressed
his faithful, affectionate, practical nature.

In his teens, Newman's delight in style only deepened. 'For
myself when I was fourteen or fifteen, I imitated Addison; when

---

[1]   AW, p. 29.
[2]   Newman to Frederic Rogers, 18 January 1866, LD xxii, p. 129.
[3]   AW, p. 29.

I was seventeen, I wrote in the style of Johnson; about the same time I fell in with the twelfth volume of Gibbon, and my ears rang with the cadence of his sentences'.[4] Later, the author, who would define style in *The Idea of a University* (1873) as 'a thinking out into language',—'thought and speech' being 'inseparable from each other'—came to recognize that style was only as good as the truth of its thought.[5] Thinking in writing, deploying style, required accountability. A good example of how Newman took this to heart can be found in one of his letters. 'I begin to have serious apprehensions lest any religious body is strong enough to withstand the league of evil, but the Roman Church', he wrote his sister Jemima in February of 1840.

> At the end of the first Millenary it withstood the fury of Satan—and now the end of a second is drawing on. It has [[possesses]] *tried* strength; what it *has* endured during these last centuries! and it is stronger than ever. We [that is to say, the Anglican Church] on the other hand have never been tried and come out of trial without practical concessions. I cannot see that we *can* receive [[sustain]] the assault of the foe. We are divided among ourselves, like the Jews in their siege. So that it seems to me as if there were coming on a great encounter between infidelity and Rome, and that we should be smashed between them. Certainly the way that good principles have shot up is wonderful—but I am not clear that they are not tending to Rome—not from any necessity in the principles them- selves, but from the much greater proximity between Rome and us, than between infidelity and us—and that in a time of trouble we naturally look about for allies. I cannot say enough of the wonderful way in which the waters are rising here—and one should be very thankful. The Heads of Houses promise soon to be fairly carried off their legs, and to be obliged to fast and scourge themselves for good

---

[4]   *Idea*, p. 322.
[5]   *Idea*, p. 276.

> company's sake. All this is a miserable prose, a regular talk
> worth nothing at all, and sure to be falsified by the event.[6]

The very fact that Newman should have interpolated what he regarded as preferable verbs here into the holograph of the original letter—*possesses* for *tried*, *sustain* for *receive*—shows how the fastidious archivist in him deferred to the even more fastidious stylist, even after the actual letters had been posted. Yet while he might have been right enough about the Anglican Church not being up to the task of withstanding the 'league of evil' gathering force in mid-Victorian England, his utter misapprehension of the likely response of the Heads of Houses to the long-simmering Romanizing of the Tractarians fully justified his referring to his speculations here as 'a miserable prose'. The staunch advocate of the dogmatic principle could not have been more wrong about the readiness of Anglican bishops to rally to the defense of dogma, even reluctantly, when the broad church Establishment saw fit to jettison it.

II

One can see a good deal of Newman's evolving attitude to style in his treatment of Gibbon. After reading him at length in the summer of 1819, the aspiring author in Newman wrote to his friend John Bowden of the historian in the most effusive of terms.

> You must excuse my talking on book subjects, but, having been stationary all the vacation, I have no others to discourse upon; and Herodotus, Thucydides, and Gibbon have employed me nearly from morning to night. A second perusal of the last historian has raised him in my scale of merit. With all his faults, his want of simplicity, his affectation, and his monotony, few can be put in comparison with him; and sometimes, when I reflect on his happy choice of expressions, his vigorous compression of ideas, and the life and significance of his every word, I am prompted indignantly to exclaim that no style is left for

---

[6]   Newman to Mrs John Mozley, 25 February 1840, *LD* vii, pp. 245–6.

> historians of an after day. O who is worthy to succeed our
> Gibbon! *Exoriare aliquis!* and may he be a better man![7]

Here, one might say, was a would-be writer encountering the
work of an altogether accomplished writer and finding himself
incapable of expressing anything other than emulous praise. Yet,
as he matured, Newman's view of Gibbon grew less laudatory. If
it began in callow adulation, it ended in a kind of puzzled sorrow.
While it might have been the case that Newman regarded
Gibbon's literary gifts highly, he could scarcely have failed to see
a certain aptness in Protestant England producing as its one
ecclesiastical authority a historian who might be objectionable
on any number of matters relating to the early Church, but who
was at least right in recognizing the impostures of Rome.[8] What
Newman found particularly deplorable in Gibbon was the ruinous
historicist example he set in falsifying the rise of Christianity by
refusing to credit the role faith, hope and charity had played in
its unfolding, a falsification only compounded by the undeniable
allure of his style.[9] Evelyn Waugh, in his favorite novel, *Helena*
(1950), would echo Newman's concerns about the influential
mischief of Gibbon's style. In the novel, my readers will recall,
Waugh has the Christian apologist Lactantius (240–320), 'the
greatest living prose stylist,' say to Helena, the mother of the
Emperor Constantine:

> Suppose in the years to come, when the Church's troubles
> seem to be over, there should come an apostate of my own
> trade, a false historian, with the mind of Cicero or Tacitus
> and the soul of an animal. [...] A man like that might make

---

[7]   Newman to John Bowden, October 1819, *LD* i, p. 67. *Exoriare aliquis
       nostris ex ossibus ultor* (Virgil, *Aeneid*, IV, 625) 'Let an avenger arise from
       my bones.'

[8]   'It is notorious that the English Church is destitute of an ecclesiastical
       History; Gibbon's is almost our sole authority for subjects as near the heart
       of a Christian as any well can be.' (Newman, 'Milman's View of Christian-
       ity', 1841, *Essays* ii, p. 186)

[9]   *Grammar*, pp. 462–3.

it his business to write down the martyrs and excuse the persecutors. He might be refuted again and again but what he wrote would remain in people's mind. [...] That is what style does—it has the Egyptian secret of the embalmers. It is not to be despised.[10]

As to the historicist fallacy that Gibbon wrote *The Decline and Fall of the Roman Empire* to commend—a fallacy still very much credited in our own addled age—Newman is withering.

It is undeniable that the records of former ages are of primary importance in determining Catholic doctrine; it is undeniable also that there is a silence or a contrariety abstractedly conceivable in those records, as to an alleged portion of that doctrine, which would be sufficient to invalidate its claims on our acceptance; but it is quite as undeniable that the existing documentary testimony to Catholicism and Christianity may be so unduly valued as to be made the absolute measure of Revelation, as if no part of theological teaching were true which cannot bring its express text, as it is called, from Scripture, and authorities from the Fathers or profane writers,—whereas there are numberless facts in past times which we cannot deny, for they are indisputable, though history is silent about them.[11]

Newman cites Gibbon's resolutely external approach to the rise of Christianity as a cautionary example of what follows when historians of Christianity misapply historical evidence, or its absence, to sacred history. 'Gibbon argues against the darkness of the Passion from the accident that it is not mentioned by Pagan historians', he writes, which he sees as tantamount to arguing 'against the existence of Christianity itself in the first century, because Seneca, Pliny, Plutarch, the Jewish Misha, and other authorities are silent about it.' Protestants rejected transubstantiation and the Arians the Divinity of Christ on the same

---

[10]   Evelyn Waugh, *Helena* (Harmondsworth: Penguin, 1963), p. 80.

[11]   *Idea*, pp. 94–5.

ground—'that extant writings of certain Fathers do not witness those doctrines to their satisfaction'.[12]

Of course, in warning of the Socinian errors of historicism, Newman never disparages the place of history *per se* in understanding sacred history. 'The evidence of History,' he reaffirms, 'is invaluable in its place; but, if it assumes to be the sole means of gaining Religious Truth, it goes beyond its place. We are putting it to a larger office than it can undertake, if we countenance the usurpation; and we are turning a true guide and blessing into a source of inexplicable difficulty and interminable doubt.'[13] Möhler would break from Tübingen, the *fons et origo* of historicism, to embrace this vital truth; those still captivated by Baur and Strauss have yet to grasp it.

Newman's mining of history in the lectures of his *Anglican Difficulties* to delineate the false pretensions of the English National Church may never have been forgiven him by many of his erstwhile Anglican friends, but it remains a bravura testament to his respect for history as well as his prowess as a stylist—especially a satirical stylist.[14] Although, over the years, historians have made valiant efforts to try to rehabilitate the *via media*, no one could look to Newman to bless their strenuous enterprises. The *via media*, he says, in the last and final lecture of *Anglican Difficulties*,

> is an interposition or arbitration between the extreme doctrines of Protestantism on the one hand, and the faith of Rome which Protestantism contradicts on the other. At the same time, though it may be unwilling to allow it, it is, from the nature of the case, but a particular form of Protestantism. I do not say that in secondary principles it may not agree with the Catholic Church; but, its essential idea being that she has gone into error, whereas the

---

[12] *Idea*, p. 5.

[13] *Idea*, p. 95.

[14] See *Certain Difficulties Felt by Anglicans in Catholic Teaching*, vol. i, ed. Edward Short (Leominster: Gracewing, 2021).

essential idea of Catholicism is the Church's infallibility, the Via Media is really nothing else than Protestant'[15]

The most eloquent advocate of the *via media* finally proved its most unanswerable critic.

Another element in Gibbon's falsification of the rise of Christianity that Newman naturally found objectionable was his relentless mockery of the development of Christian doctrine. 'The strange transformations of the Eucharist from the sign to the substance of Christ's body,' he writes in his celebrated history, 'I have purposely abandoned to the curiosity of speculative divines.'[16] That Gibbon poured so much of his ironical wit into this mockery has given his style a perennial appeal for those who prefer witty scoffing to any sympathetic engagement with the supernatural realities integral to the emergence of the new faith, though for Newman it is precisely Gibbon's abandonment of such considerations that rendered his work so evasive and unsatisfactory.[17] Even Leslie Stephen, the staunchest of agnostics, admitted that by refusing to enter into the beliefs of the early Christians, or their martyrdoms, Gibbon could hardly claim that he had accounted for what had caused the rise of Christianity. For Stephen, Gibbon had left the question that ought to have animated his massive work unanswered. 'From his pages little can be learnt as to the true significance of the greatest religious convulsion that has transformed the world's history.'[18]

If Gibbon was dismissive of Christian dogma, he was appreciative of the ceremonials of the new faith, seeing them, as the historian Peter Brown recognized, as more than merely impressive. In the *Decline and Fall*, Gibbon remarks how 'Experience had shewn [Pope Gregory the Great] the efficacy of these solemn

---

[15] *Difficulties* i, p. 377.

[16] Edward Gibbon, *The Decline and Fall of the Roman Empire*, ed. J. B. Bury (London: Methuen, 1909), ch. xlix, p. 261. Hereinafter, *Decline and Fall*.

[17] See *Grammar*, pp. 456–63.

[18] Leslie Stephen, *History of English Thought in the Eighteenth Century*, 2 vols (London: Smith Elder, 1876), vol. i, p. 449.

and pompous rites, to soothe the distress, to confirm the faith, to mitigate the fierceness, and to dispel the dark enthusiasm, of the vulgar'.[19] Yet the quote Brown deploys to illustrate his point shows another aspect of Gibbon's style that Newman could not have found winning: its inveterate snobbery, a trait utterly foreign to Newman, who famously confessed that what he was after in his own writing was a style that would convert both 'philosophers and factory girls' by acquainting them with what he considered the cogency of 'antecedent probability', the insight which he derived, in part, from Bishop Butler's famous dictum, 'Probability is the guide of life.'[20] Gibbon's disdain for the ordinary run of men extended even to those he met as Captain of the Hampshire Grenadiers, a post his father insisted he take when he came back from Lausanne sufficiently Protestant but too French for his sire's liking.[21] 'The loss of so many busy and idle hours was not compensated by any elegant pleasure,' the historian complained in retrospect; 'and my temper was insensibly soured by the society of our rustic officers who were alike deficient in the knowledge of scholars and the manners of gentlemen.'[22]

Newman's lack of snobbery was of a piece with his profound appreciation of God's relation to the lowly. He is eloquent about this in his early sermon, 'Religious Joy', where, speaking of Our

---

[19]   Gibbon quoted in Peter Brown, 'Gibbon's Views on Culture and Society in the Fifth and Sixth Centuries', *Daedalus* (Summer, 1976), p. 77. *Decline and Fall*, ch. xlv, p. 38.

[20]   *The Theological Papers of John Henry Newman on Faith and Certainty*, ed. Hugo M. de Achaval SJ & J. Derek Holmes, vol. i (Oxford: Oxford University Press, 1976), p. 19. See also Ian Ker's splendid encapsulation of Newman's discovery of the epistemological uses of Butlerian probability *vis-à-vis* religious certainty—what Newman called 'the clue, the "Open Sesame" of the whole subject', *Newman: Biography* (rev. ed. 2009), pp. 620–1. Butler's famous phrase appears in the introduction of *The Analogy of Religion* (1736).

[21]   Gibbon *père* had sent his son to Lausanne to repatriate him to the Protestant religion after he 'poped' at Oxford.

[22]   *The Memoirs of the Life of Edward Gibbon*, ed. George Birkbeck Hill (London: Methuen, 1900), p. xvii.

Lord's Nativity, he writes: 'There are two principal lessons which we are taught on the great Festival which we this day celebrate, lowliness and joy.'[23] And speaking of the first, he shows how entirely untainted he was by the sort of disdain for lowliness that characterized alike Gibbon and his ancient Romans. Asking why God in the form of his only-begotten Son should have appeared to the lowly shepherds of Bethlehem, he answers:

> [...] for their poverty's sake and obscurity. Almighty God looks with a sort of especial love, or (as we may term it) affection, upon the lowly. Perhaps it is that man, a fallen, dependent, and destitute creature, is more in his proper place when he is in lowly circumstances, and that power and riches, though unavoidable in the case of some, are unnatural appendages to man, as such. Just as there are trades and callings which are unbecoming, though requisite; and while we profit by them, and honour those the more who engage in them, yet we feel we are glad that they are not ours; as we feel grateful and respectful towards a soldier's profession, yet do not affect it; so in God's sight greatness is less acceptable than obscurity. It becomes us less.[24]

Here is a good example of how Newman's supple prose captures the music of his thought. Music and style, for Newman, were always inseparable. As he wrote in *Idea*, the appeal of style was very much like the appeal of music.

> How real a creation, how *sui generis*, is the style of Shakespeare, or of the Protestant Bible and Prayer Book, or of Swift, or of Pope, or of Gibbon, or of Johnson! Even were the subject-matter without meaning, though in truth the style cannot really be abstracted from the sense, still the style would, on that supposition, remain as perfect and original a work as Euclid's elements or a symphony of Beethoven. And, like music, it has seized upon the public mind; and the literature of England is no longer a mere

---

[23] 'Religious Joy', 1825, *Parochial and Plain* viii, p. 244.
[24] *Parochial and Plain* viii, pp. 246–7.

letter, printed in books, and shut up in libraries, but it is a living voice, which has gone forth in its expressions and its sentiments into the world of men, which daily thrills upon our ears and syllables our thoughts, which speaks to us through our correspondents, and dictates when we put pen to paper.[25]

When Frederic Rogers and Dean Church made Newman a gift of a violin, after being estranged from him for twenty years after his conversion, Newman wrote to Church: 'I really think it will add to my power of working, and the length of my life. I never wrote more than when I played the fiddle. I always sleep better after music. There must be some electric current passing from the strings through the fingers into the brain and down the spinal marrow. Perhaps thought is music.'[26] Here is the music of Newman's own thought, which recalls something he had said twenty years before in his great sermon, 'The Theory of Developments in Religious Doctrine' (1843), which illuminates the attention he paid to underlying realities, to what one might call the music of the supernatural. Speaking of 'musical sounds, as they are exhibited most perfectly in instrumental harmony', Newman wrote:

> There are seven notes in the scale; make them fourteen; yet what a slender outfit for so vast an enterprise! What science brings so much out of so little? Out of what poor elements does some great master in it create his new world! Shall we say that all this exuberant inventiveness is a mere ingenuity or trick of art, like some game or fashion of the day, without reality, without meaning? We may do so; and then, perhaps, we shall also account the science of theology to be a matter of words; yet, as there is a divinity in the theology of the Church, which those who feel cannot communicate, so is there also in the wonderful creation of sublimity and beauty of which I am speaking. To many men the very names which the science employs are utterly incomprehensible. To speak

---

[25]   *Idea*, p. 313.
[26]   Newman to R.W. Church, 11 July 1865, *LD* xxii, p. 9.

of an idea or a subject seems to be fanciful or trifling, to speak of the views which it opens upon us to be childish extravagance; yet is it possible that that inexhaustible evolution and disposition of notes, so rich yet so simple, so intricate yet so regulated, so various yet so majestic, should be a mere sound, which is gone and perishes? Can it be that those mysterious stirrings of heart, and keen emotions, and strange yearnings after we know not what, and awful impressions from we know not whence, should be wrought in us by what is unsubstantial, and comes and goes, and begins and ends in itself? It is not so; it cannot be. No; they have escaped from some higher sphere; they are the out-pourings of eternal harmony in the medium of created sound; they are echoes from our Home; they are the voice of Angels, or the Magnificat of Saints, or the living laws of Divine Governance, or the Divine Attributes; something are they besides themselves, which we cannot compass, which we cannot utter,—though mortal man, and he perhaps not otherwise distinguished above his fellows, has the gift of eliciting them.[27]

Here, we have the beauty of Newman's style, in all of its refulgence and grace,[28] and yet it is also a good example of that style's pronounced colloquial character, which struck Gerard Manley Hopkins. 'What Cardinal Newman does is to think aloud', the poet recognized, 'to think with pen and paper [...] He seems to be thinking "Gibbon is the last great master of traditional English prose; he is its perfection; I do not propose to emulate him; I begin all over again from the language of conversation, of common life."'[29] Regardless of whether we agree that Newman thought

---

[27] *Development*, pp. 346–7.

[28] 'I think I never have written for writing sake; but my one and single desire and aim has been to do what is so difficult—viz. to express clearly and exactly my meaning'. Asked about influences on his style, Newman replied, 'the only master of style I have ever had [...] is Cicero', whose 'great mastery of Latin is shown especially in his clearness' (Newman to John Hayes, 13 April 1869, *LD* xxiv, pp. 241–2).

[29] Gerald Manley Hopkins to Coventry Patmore, 20 October 1887, *The*

Gibbon 'the last great master of traditional English prose', this was a shrewd insight. Certainly, for all of his dazzling attainments, Newman paid very close attention to 'common life': it was an expression of his respect for the importunate claims of reality. Consequently, the limpidity of his prose is of a piece with the naturalness, sincerity, and humility of his personality. Dean Church, the author of what remains the best history of the Oxford Movement, made a number of observations in his obituary of Newman in *The Guardian*—an Anglican paper in the nineteenth century—which nicely corroborate Hopkins's point.

> It is common to speak of the naturalness and ease of Cardinal Newman's style in writing. It is, of course, the first thing that attracts notice when we open one of his books; and there are people who think it bald and thin and dry. They look out for longer words, and grander phrases, and more involved constructions, and neater epigrams. They expect a great theme to be treated with more pomp and majesty, and they are disappointed. But the majority of English readers seem to be agreed in recognising the beauty and transparent flow of language, which matches the best French writing in rendering with sureness and without effort the thought of the writer. But what is more interesting than even the formation of such a style—a work, we may be sure, not accomplished without much labour—is the man behind the style. For the man and the style are one in this perfect naturalness and ease. Any one who has watched at all carefully the Cardinal's career, whether in old days or later, must have been struck with this feature of his character, his naturalness, the freshness and freedom with which he addressed a friend or expressed an opinion, the absence of all mannerism and formality; and where he had to keep his dignity, both his loyal obedience to the authority which enjoined it and the half-amused, half-bored impatience that

---

Collected Works of Gerard Manley Hopkins, 7 vols (Oxford: Oxford University Press, 2013), vol. i, ed. R. K. R. Thornton & Catherine Phillips, pp. 898–9.

he should be the person round whom all these grand doings centred. It made the greatest difference in his friendships whether his friends met him on equal terms, or whether they brought with them too great conventional deference or solemnity of manner. He was by no means disposed to allow liberties to be taken or to put up with impertinence; for all that bordered on the unreal, for all that was pompous, conceited, affected he had little patience; but almost beyond all these was his disgust at being made the object of foolish admiration. He protested with whimsical fierceness against being made a hero or a sage; he was what he was, he said, and nothing more, and he was inclined to be rude when people tried to force him into an eminence which he refused. With his profound sense of the incomplete and the ridiculous in this world, and with a humour in which the grotesque and the pathetic sides of life were together recognised every moment, he never hesitated to admit his own mistakes.[30]

These are the qualities that make the *Apologia pro Vita Sua* (1864) such an enthralling book. Far from being an exercise in self-vindication, as some have charged, it is full of the most guileless honesty. After all, it is the tale, for the most part, of how Newman had allowed himself to become involved in an Anglo-Catholic fantasy that he would spend a good deal of his Catholic life repudiating.[31] If we recognize that Newman's style is the natural efflorescence of his thought, we will also see that that

---

[30] Richard William Church, 'Cardinal Newman's Naturalness', *Occasional Papers*, 2 vols (London: Macmillan & Co., 1897), vol. ii, pp. 480–1.

[31] The error that attaches Anglicans to their Anglican Church, Newman told the audience of his King William Street lectures is 'an error for many reasons too dear to be readily relinquished. But at length, either the force of circumstances or some unexpected accident dissipates it; and, as in fairy tales, the magic castle vanishes when the spell is broken, and nothing is seen but the wild heath, the barren rock, and the forlorn sheep-walk, so is it with us as regards the Church of England, when we look in amazement on that we thought so unearthly, and find so commonplace or worthless.' (*Difficulties* i, p. 6)

thought is the expression not only of an extraordinarily versatile but a most truthful personality.

The stylist in Gibbon, conversely, is at once highly ornate and invariably impersonal. As the classicist Gilbert Highet nicely put it: '*The Decline and Fall of the Roman Empire* is a perpetual peroration.'[32] V. S. Pritchett, the short story writer and critic, got at something of the essence of the matter when he observed that, for Gibbon, 'style was the ugly, short man's form of power. His shocking health as a child and youth, though astonishingly restored when he was sixteen years of age [...] inscribed on his heart and instincts the detachment, the reserve, the innate melancholy of invalid habits.'[33] Accordingly, there is no unbuttoning in Gibbon, no intimacy, no warmth. And little stylistic variety. The grand stylist never leaves his stilts. As aesthetes, we can revel in the exquisite finish and elaboration of his prose, and marvel at its grand, remorseless march, but we never do so because it is the expression of any open-hearted or even particularly intriguing personality. This is one of the reasons why he is never interested in any of the ordinary people moving across his landscape. In his grand scheme, they never figure as anything other than a mob.

Newman, like Chesterton, had a soft spot for the mob.[34] Indeed, he shows his affectionate esteem for the faith of the lowly in his moving portrait of his character Callista, a third-century young Greek girl martyred under the Emperor Decius, about whose conversion he writes with such ennobling sympathy:

> O what a new world of thought she had entered! it occupied her mind from its very novelty. Everything looked dull and dim by the side of it; her brother had ever been dinning into her ears that maxim of the heathen,

---

[32]   Gilbert Highet, *The Classical Tradition: Greek and Roman Influences on Western Literature* (Oxford: Clarendon Press, 1949), p. 348.

[33]   V. S. Pritchett, 'Gibbon and the Home Guard', *Collected Essays* (London: Chatto & Windus, 1991), p. 4.

[34]   See *Chesterton: Biography*, pp. 84–5.

'Enjoy the present, trust nothing to the future.' She indeed could not enjoy the present with that relish which he wished, and she had not any trust in the future either; but this volume spoke a different doctrine. There she learned the very opposite to what Aristo taught—viz., that the present must be sacrificed for the future; that what is seen must give way to what is believed. Nay, more, she drank in the teaching which at first seemed so paradoxical, that even present happiness and present greatness lie in relinquishing what at first sight seems to promise them; that the way to true pleasure is, not through self-indulgence, but through mortification; that the way to power is weakness, the way to success failure, the way to wisdom foolishness, the way to glory dishonour. She saw that there was a higher beauty than that which the order and harmony of the natural world revealed, and a deeper peace and calm than that which the exercise, whether of the intellect or of the purest human affection, can supply. She now began to understand that strange, unearthly composure, which had struck her in Chione, Agellius, and Cæcilius;[35] she understood that they were detached from the world, not because they had not the possession, nor the natural love of its gifts, but because they possessed a higher blessing already, which they loved above everything else. Thus, by degrees, Callista came to walk by a new philosophy; and had ideas, and principles, and a sense of relations and aims, and a susceptibility of arguments, to which before she was an utter stranger. Life and death, action and suffering, fortunes and abilities, all had now a new meaning and application. As the skies speak differently to the philosopher and the peasant, as a book of poems to the imaginative and to the cold and narrow intellect, so now she saw her being, her history, her present

---

[35] In the novel *Callista*, Chione is the Christian slave who befriends the heroine, Agellius the heroine's suitor, and Caecilius a portrait of Cyprian of Carthage, later St Cyprian. For an excellent critical introduction to *Callista* (1856), see Ian Ker, *Newman on Vatican II* (Oxford: Oxford University Press, 2014), pp. 3, 134–7, 140, 142, 154, 156–8, 161.

condition, her future, in a new light, which no one else could share with her. But the ruling sovereign thought of the whole was He, who exemplified all this wonderful philosophy in Himself.[36]

By contrast, for the Enlightenment historian, the very fact that Christianity won the sympathies of poor, needy, uneducated people, whom most men of sense would naturally shun, was proof of its contemptibleness. Speaking of the conversion of the Roman senate under Constantine, Gibbon could scarcely conceal his contempt.

> The hasty conversion of the senate must be attributed either to supernatural or to sordid motives; and many of these reluctant proselytes betrayed, on every favorable occasion, their secret disposition to throw aside the mask of odious dissimulation. But they were gradually fixed in the new religion, as the cause of the ancient became more hopeless; they yielded to the authority of the emperor, to the fashion of the times, and to the entreaties of their wives and children, who were instigated and governed by the clergy of Rome and the monks of the East.[37]

In this regard, Gibbon was the quintessential eighteenth-century rationalist, not only leery but disdainful of dogmatical religion. One can hear something of Gibbon's insouciant attitude to these consequential matters in the former master of Eton College, George Lyttelton, sharing his view of Christianity with his correspondent Rupert Hart-Davis: 'One could hardly fail to be interested in a subject at once so fundamental and so fantastic, but I am generally too busy to spend too much time on it.'[38] Centuries of Protestant England haunt that throwaway admission. Gibbon, for all of his cosmopolitanism, was cut out of the

---

[36] *Callista*, pp. 36–8.

[37] *Decline and Fall*, ch. xxviii, pp. 204–5.

[38] *The Lyttelton Hart-Davis Letters: Correspondence of George Lyttelton and Rupert Hart-Davis*, 6 vols (London: John Murray, 1978–1984), vol. i, p. 79.

same cloth. His theme, after all, is never so much how Christianity rose as how Rome fell. And for the decided historian, that the fall of Rome should be blamed on the Christians' 'barbarism and religion' was never in dispute, even though it is Christianity that preserved and renewed the legacy of Rome.[39] Highet, after serving as a Colonel in British Intelligence in the Second World War, had no illusions regarding this:

> The history of nearly every Roman province shows how the successive waves of savages that broke over the walls of the empire were resisted by Christians and, even when they burst the dikes and flowed in, were, at last, through Christian teaching and example, calmed and controlled and civilized. Perhaps it was inevitable for Gibbon in the eighteenth century to believe that Christian fanaticism was one of the most dangerous of all evils, and to despise Christianity for inspiring it. A more complete explanation is that, even if Christian creeds sometimes gave an outlet to the forces of savagery, Christianity was always exercised to repress them or to canalize them. And to us in the twentieth century, who have seen the barbarities of highly organized contemporary pagan peoples and who are likely to see more, Christianity is very clearly a greater thing than Gibbon could understand, one of the greatest constructive social forces in human history.[40]

Some of Gibbon's disinclination to bother with dogma might have been a reaction against his impulsive 'poping' as an undergraduate at Magdalen, when, as he said: 'The blind activity of idleness encouraged me to advance without armour into the dangerous

---

[39] *Decline and Fall*, ch. lxxi, p. 321. Gibbon pinched his famous précis of his history—'I have described the triumph of barbarism and religion'—from Voltaire, who complained that 'Deux fléaux détruisirent enfin ce grand colosse, les barbares et les disputes de religion' (Two scourges ruined this great colossus [Rome]: the barbarians and rows over religion). Voltaire, *Essai sur les mœurs et l'ésprit des nations* (II), *Œuvres complètes de Voltaire* xxii (Oxford: Voltaire Foundation, 2009), p. 212.

[40] Highet, *The Classical Tradition*, pp. 353–4.

maze of controversy.'[41] But mostly it was of a piece with his thoroughgoing rationalism. Nevertheless, for Newman, Gibbon's apostasy was as much a failure of faith as of the humility required of good style, though it was characteristic of his generosity that he should extol the historian's industry. 'You must not suppose I am going to recommend his style for imitation, any more than his principles,' he told his young scholars in Dublin;

> but I refer to him as the example of a writer feeling the task before him, feeling that he had to bring out into words for the comprehension of his readers a great and complicated scene, and wishing that those words should be adequate to his undertaking. I think he wrote the first chapter of his History three times over; it was not that he corrected or improved the first copy; but he put his first essay, and then his second aside—he recast his matter, till he had hit the precise exhibition of it which he thought demanded by his subject.[42]

In other words, Gibbon had to be given credit for being at least willing, as Newman himself had been willing, to subject himself to the extravagant pains of composition. Newman began and cast aside the *Grammar of Assent* (1870) nineteen times over twenty years before finally alighting on what he deemed 'the precise exhibition' of his theme in that vertiginous book. Where Gibbon failed to meet the demands of 'literary workmanship' was in not rising to the demands of his subject, for 'the mere dealer in words cares little or nothing for the subject he is embellishing, but can paint and gild anything whatever to order, whereas the artist, whom I am acknowledging, has his great or rich visions before him, and his only aim is to bring out what he thinks or what he feels in a way adequate to the thing spoken of [...]'[43]

In his discourses to the students of the Catholic University, Newman elaborated still further on what the stylist must possess in order to meet the demands of his subject.

---

[41]   *The Memoirs of the Life of Edward Gibbon*, p. 67.

[42]   *Idea*, p. 285.

[43]   *Idea*, p. 285.

> A great author, Gentlemen, is not one who merely has a
> *copia verborum*, whether in prose or verse, and can, as it
> were, turn on at his will any number of splendid phrases
> and swelling sentences; but he is one who has something
> to say and knows how to say it. I do not claim for him, as
> such, any great depth of thought, or breadth of view, or
> philosophy, or sagacity, or knowledge of human nature, or
> experience of human life, though these additional gifts he
> may have, and the more he has of them the greater he is;
> but I ascribe to him, as his characteristic gift, in a large
> sense the faculty of Expression.[44]

Gibbon certainly had this 'faculty of Expression.' Quoting the
tribute that the poet Prudentius (348–413) had paid to Julian the
Apostate after the emperor's death, Gibbon remarked, in his best
derisive manner: 'The consciousness of a generous sentiment
seems to have raised the Christian poet above his usual medioc-
rity.'[45] What Gibbon lacked was something rather more fundamental. Newman speaks of the successful stylist having 'but one
aim, which he keeps steadily before him, and is conscientious and
single-minded in fulfilling. That aim is to give forth what he has
within him; and from his very earnestness it comes to pass that,
whatever be the splendour of his diction or the harmony of his
periods, he has with him the charm of an incommunicable
simplicity.[46] Gibbon may put us in mind of many things but 'an
incommunicable simplicity' is not one of them.

   In the *Grammar of Assent*, while exonerating Gibbon of the
charge of 'mere ingenuity', Newman would again fault him for
failing to do justice to his august subject, 'his account of the rise
of Christianity' being 'the mere subjective view of one who could
not enter into its depth and power'.[47] Consequently, Newman
never returned to the style that had so dazzled his youth without

---

[44]   *Idea*, p. 291.
[45]   *Decline and Fall*, ch. xxii, p. 455, note 87.
[46]   *Idea*, p. 292.
[47]   *Grammar*, p. 373.

a certain exasperation. Gibbon's literary gifts notwithstanding, he was still representative of the fallen nature of all literature. As Newman told his charges in the Catholic University: 'Man's work will savour of man; in his elements and powers excellent and admirable, but prone to disorder and excess, to error and to sin. Such too will be his literature; it will have the beauty and the fierceness, the sweetness and the rankness, of the natural man'.[48] Nothing illustrated this more strikingly than English literature.

> We may feel great repugnance to Milton or Gibbon as men; we may most seriously protest against the spirit which ever lives, and the tendency which ever operates, in every page of their writings; but there they are, an integral portion of English Literature; we cannot extinguish them; we cannot deny their power; we cannot write a new Milton or a new Gibbon; we cannot expurgate what needs to be exorcised. They are great English authors, each breathing hatred to the Catholic Church in his own way, each a proud and rebellious creature of God, each gifted with incomparable gifts.[49]

In Newman's last published reflections on Gibbon, one can hear the critic in him, or perhaps, one should say the priest, almost wishing that the historian had somehow found a way to perceive the Christian reality that he could not perceive. There is a kind of solicitude in Newman's strictures, a pastoral solicitude. Here, he is not being so much censorious as lamenting aloud the gifted historian's failure to see the real import of his theme. 'It is very remarkable that it should not have occurred to a man of Gibbon's sagacity to inquire, what account the Christians themselves gave of the matter,' he wrote.

> Would it not have been worth while for him to have let conjecture alone, and to have looked for facts instead? Why did he not try the hypothesis of faith, hope, and charity? Did he never hear of repentance towards God, and faith in

---

[48]   *Idea*, p. 316.
[49]   *Idea*, p. 309.

> Christ? Did he not recollect the many words of Apostles, Bishops, Apologists, Martyrs, all forming one testimony? No; such thoughts are close upon him, and close upon the truth; but he cannot sympathize with them, he cannot believe in them, he cannot even enter into them [...][50]

Instead, Gibbon delivered himself up to the direction of what Newman nicely called a 'godless intellectualism', which prevented him from writing any fair or illuminating history of Christianity.[51] For Newman, this same 'intellectualism' was at the root of the limitations and incoherence of the merely humanist university. Unconverted, neither Gibbon nor the university could hope to accomplish their true ends. In *Callista*, Newman dramatizes the power of conversion by having his heroine at one point tell Caecilius that she cannot enter into his Christian faith because, like so many of Newman's countrymen, she is not ready to abjure what Christians call sin and 'must live and die where I have been born,' to which the convert replies:

> Do *I* deserve anything but evil? Is it not the Power, the Mighty Power of the only Strong, the only Merciful, the grace of Emmanuel, which has changed and won me? If He can change me, an old man, could He not change a child like you? I, a proud, stern Roman; I, a lover of pleasure, a man of letters, of political station, with formed habits, and life-long associations, and complicated relations; was it *I* who wrought this great change in me, who gained for myself the power of hating what I once loved, of unlearning what I once knew, nay, of even forgetting what once I was? Who has made you and me to differ, but He who can, when He will, make us to agree?[52]

That this same power of conversion, this 'Mighty Power', somehow eluded the author of the *Decline and Fall* was indeed

---

[50]   *Grammar*, pp. 462–3.
[51]   *Idea*, p. 196.
[52]   *Callista*, pp. 223–4.

'remarkable'.[53] The good fortune of Caecilius might very well have been that of Edward Gibbon.

III

There were many good prose stylists in nineteenth-century England—Emily Eden, Sydney Smith, Lamb, Hazlitt, Froude, Jane Austen, Macaulay, Ruskin, Trollope, Thackeray, Dickens, Arnold, Henry James—but none of them had anything like Newman's range or richness. Why this should have been the case can be attributed to two things. First, Newman was Newman, a man of altogether rare sanctity, acuity, wit and zest. Secondly, unlike Gibbon and indeed all of the splendid stylists I have just named, he saw the world *sub specie aeternitatis*, and seeing the world in this light, he understood the relationship between Our Lord and Saviour and the fallen world he came to redeem—the very thing poor Gibbon got so terribly wrong—and what is more he could bring the reality of that relationship home as no one else. He was a great stylist not because he had a better command of language than the other stylists but because he had an incomparably better theme and he saw to it that his style did the theme justice.

Here, to illustrate my point, I shall conclude with a moving passage from his sermon, 'Ignorance of Evil' (1836), in which he considers how different our state is from the one for which God made us. 'He meant us to be simple, and we are unreal', Newman writes.

> He meant us to think no evil, and a thousand associations, bad, trifling, or unworthy, attend our every thought. He meant us to be drawn on to the glories without us, and we are drawn back and (as it were) fascinated by the miseries within us. And hence it is that the whole structure of society is so artificial; no one trusts another, if he can help

---

53   For an interesting case for Gibbon *not* having been apostate—a case Newman would have found fascinating, if unconvincing—see Paul Turnbull, 'The "Supposed Infidelity" of Edward Gibbon', *The Historical Journal* 25:1 (March 1982), pp. 23–4.

it; safeguards, checks, and securities are ever sought after. No one means exactly what he says, for our words have lost their natural meaning, and even an Angel could not use them naturally, for every mind being different from every other, they have no distinct meaning. What, indeed, is the very function of society, as it is at present, but a rude attempt to cover the degradation of the fall, and to make men feel respect for themselves, and enjoy it in the eyes of others, without returning to God. This is what we should especially guard against, because there is so much of it in the world. I mean, not an abandonment of evil, not a sweeping away and cleansing out of the corruption which sin has bred within us, but a smoothing it over, an outside delicacy and polish, an ornamenting the surface of things while 'within are dead men's bones and all uncleanness'; making the garments, which at first were given for decency, a means of pride and vanity. Men give good names to what is evil, they sanctify bad principles and feelings; and, knowing that there is vice and error, selfishness, pride, and ambition, in the world, they attempt, not to root out these evils, not to withstand these errors;—that they think a dream, the dream of theorists who do not know the world;—but to cherish and form alliance with them, to use them, to make a science of selfishness, to flatter and indulge error, and to bribe vice with the promise of bearing with it, so that it does but keep in the shade.[54]

None of us with any knowledge of ourselves or of our world could possibly dispute any of this without perjuring ourselves. And yet Newman writes his sermon not simply to remind us of our troubles, our ineradicable troubles, but to help us to take arms against them. The essence of Newman's style is practicality; it is only incidentally a style for aesthetes; at heart, it is designed to inspire action; to enlist and encourage doers—faithful doers. And thus, he concludes:

---

[54] *Parochial and Plain* viii, pp. 265–6.

But let us, finding ourselves in the state in which we are, take those means which alone are really left us, which alone become us. Adam, when he had sinned, and felt himself fallen, instead of honestly abandoning what he had become, would fain have hid himself. He went a step further. He did not give up what he now was, partly from dread of God, partly from dislike of what he had been. He had learnt to love sin and to fear God's justice. But Christ has purchased for us what we lost in Adam, our garment of innocence. He has bid us and enabled us to become as little children; He has purchased for us the grace of *simplicity*, which, though one of the highest, is very little thought about, is very little sought after. We have, indeed, a general idea what love is, and hope, and faith, and truth, and purity, though a poor idea; but we are almost blind to what is one of the first elements of Christian perfection, that simple-mindedness which springs from the heart's being *whole* with God, entire, undivided. And those who think they have an idea of it, commonly rise no higher than to mistake for it a mere weakness and softness of mind, which is but its counterfeit. To be simple is to be like the Apostles and first Christians. Our Saviour says, 'Be ye harmless', or simple, 'as doves.' And St Paul, 'I would have you wise unto that which is good, and *simple concerning evil*.' [Rom 16:19] Again, 'That ye may be *blameless and harmless*, the sons of God, without rebuke, in the midst of a crooked and perverse nation.' [Phil 2:15] And he speaks of the 'testimony of' his own 'conscience, that in *simplicity* and godly sincerity, not with fleshly wisdom, but by the grace of God', he had his conversation in the world and towards his disciples. Let us pray God to give us this great and precious gift; that we may blot out from our memory all that offends Him; unlearn all that knowledge which sin has taught us; rid ourselves of selfish motives, self-conceit, and vanity, littlenesses, envying, grudgings, meannesses; turn from all cowardly, low, miserable ways; and escape from servile fears, the fear of man, vague anxieties of conscience, and superstitions. So that we may have the boldness and frankness of those who are as if they had no sin, from having been cleansed from it; the uncontaminated hearts, open countenances, and untroubled eyes of those who neither suspect, nor conceal, nor shun, nor are jealous; in a word, so that we may have confidence in Him, that we may stay on Him, and rest in the thoughts of Him, instead of plunging amid the thickets of this world; that we may bear His eye and His voice, and know no knowledge but the knowledge of Him and Jesus Christ crucified, and desire no objects but what He has blessed and bid us pursue.[55]

---

[55] *Parochial and Plain* viii, pp. 267–8.

14 THE DIM BEAST IN THE BRIGHT JUNGLE. NEWMAN AND HENRY JAMES

FR JAMES REIDY

ST JOHN HENRY Newman and Henry James, both of whom are recorded as being themselves exemplars of personal refinement, can also be considered together as moralists who arrived at the same conclusion about the equivocal character of an ideal they both revered: that of the liberally educated and aesthetically cultivated personage, the gentleman. What Newman had to say about the concept of a gentleman in the *Idea of a University* is almost identical with a theme James dealt with more than once in his stories, and particularly in his late novel *The Ambassadors*, which can be seen simply as a novelist's illustration of what Newman wrote.

Readers have been surprised at what is found in the eighth chapter of the *Idea*. In section 10 they encounter that definition of a gentleman which is so celebrated and was once so often anthologized. The surprise comes from reading the famous long paragraph in its context, because one sees that Newman's main object has not been to describe and recommend an incomparably fine ideal of human formation. On the contrary, he has his doubts about this ideal, and not merely because it might be hopelessly high. The burden of the chapter is to point out serious limitations in that product of a university education which here and elsewhere in the *Idea* he so persuasively sketches.

Since, Newman insists, education is not the same thing as virtue, it is possible that certain moral defects can co-exist with personal refinement in the character of the gentleman. For one thing, the conscience of educated men is liable to become 'not the word of a Lawgiver, as it ought to be, but the dictate of their own minds and nothing more'. And this leads them to be 'engrossed in notions of what is due to themselves, to their own dignity and their own consistency'. In short, 'their conscience has become a mere self-respect'. But there are more pleasing and interesting forms of this moral malady, Newman goes on to say, one being the substitution of taste, or what is called a moral sense, for conscience. 'Men of an imaginative and poetical cast of mind find it especially congenial to accept the notion that virtue is nothing more than the graceful in conduct.' We can conclude that in this case genuine morality is endangered because it is possible to sin gracefully. 'The splendors of a court, and the charms of good society, wit, imagination, taste, high breeding, the prestige of rank, and the resources of wealth, are a screen, an instrument, and an apology for vice and irreligion.' Gentlemanly formation becomes under these circumstances 'the religion of civilization'.[1]

It is possible to feel a certain ambiguity in Newman's argument in that by now we are not sure what our attitude should be toward the ideal he has before so winningly described. It should be pointed out that what Newman says here is a corollary to a thesis that he felt necessary to demonstrate to those who might expect the wrong thing from Catholic university education, namely that knowledge is its own end and that its liberal character excludes direct utilization for practical moral ends. In the section of the *Idea* where that argument occurs, he anticipates succinctly the question we are considering here:

> Liberal Education makes not the Christian, not the Catholic, but the gentleman. It is well to be a gentleman, it is well to have a cultivated intellect, a delicate taste, a candid, equitable, dispassionate mind, a noble and courteous bearing in the conduct of life;—these are the connatural qualities of a large knowledge. But they are no guarantee for sanctity or even for conscientiousness, they may attach

---

[1]   *Idea*, p. 182.

to the man of the world, to the profligate, to the heathen,—
pleasant, alas, and attractive as he shows when decked out
in them.[2]

The 'alas' points up any ambiguity there might be in the case. The
notable thing is that such an eloquent summing up of attributes
made only for the sake of an antithesis shows how Newman was
devoted to his ideal but at the same time forced to be ironical
with it. He feels that he has almost to take back something of what
he has said. As Andrew Meszaros explains: '

> Newman's famous portrait of the gentleman has caused
> not a little consternation among his readers. Newman's
> *laudatio* of the gentleman seems like a solid endorsement,
> and yet he is quite clear that the intellectual qualities of
> the refined gentleman can be used for ill ... [They bear] no
> relationship to moral improvement.[3]

So here is the argument in the *Idea* that coincides with a major
theme in the fiction of Henry James, one that is included among
his celebrated ambiguities. In James's stories we are confronted
with people and a culture both of which appeal with the force
Newman has given to his portrait of the gentleman. James himself
is obviously taken with such subjects, yet he is suspicious of them,
thereby perhaps causing some 'consternation' in his readers, and
herein lies the drama of several of his stories. James, too, felt it
necessary to compromise about culture and set out to show the
clay feet of certain very appealing characters.

On taking up James's books for the first time we might not
expect this kind of concern at all. His reputation for snobbishness
and devotion to an esoteric code of life and art may have
conditioned a reader for anything but the moral attitude found
in his fiction. That James was intensely devoted to a high cultural
ideal is sufficiently clear from his early expatriation, his 'escape'

---

[2]   *Idea*, pp. 120–1.

[3]   Quoted from 'A Philosophical Habit of a Mind: Newman and the University' on pp. 261 of this volume.

to Europe. 'What I pointed out as our vices', he wrote of his native land, 'are the elements of the modern with culture left out'.[4] And in his book on Hawthorne he lists, rather wistfully, some of the things America lacks: she has no court, no aristocracy, no church, no country gentlemen, no manors, no old country houses, no cathedrals, no literature, no museums, no pictures, no public schools, no great universities—no Oxford, no Eton, no Harrow.[5]

So James went to Europe because Europe meant art, intellect, and supreme human refinement and because her culture, and the human character formed in her traditions became for him an ideal on the whole equivalent to that in the pages of the *Idea of a University*. Lionel Trilling says that James is one with the likes of Shakespeare, Scott, and Dickens 'who saw the lordliness and establishment of the aristocrat and the gentleman as the proper spirit of man'.[6]

What is personal in James appears in the moral make-up of his characters. In the novels and stories, we find men and women who have their creator's cast of mind in that they live by aesthetic values, or, more simply, good taste. But since James makes a great issue of the possible drawbacks to this way of life, it is only one aspect of his ideal. As one commentator puts it, 'James's fascination with a baronial society was a very condition of his literary existence [...] It contributed, though, to his characteristic irony, that effect of a world of confused splendor and terror, of a bright jungle concealing a dim beast.'[7] What the beast represents comes out roughly in the terms Newman gave us: pride and the glossing of immorality by external graces.

In James's fiction, Newman's demonstration becomes a moral dialectic revolving around the opposed dualities of culture and

---

[4]   Quoted in F. W. Dupee, *Henry James* (New York: Doubleday & Co., 1956), p. 64.

[5]   H. James, *Hawthorne* (New York: Harper & Brothers, 1901), p. 3.

[6]   *The Liberal Imagination* (New York: Doubleday & Co., 1957), p. 80.

[7]   *The Question of Henry James. A Collection of Critical Essays*, ed. F. W. Dupee (New York: Henry Holt & Co., 1945), p. xvi.

conscience, of sensibility and character. In one way or another, in the framework of the so-called International theme of America versus Europe, James is preoccupied with this conflict in *Daisy Miller, The Europeans, The American,* and *The Portrait of a Lady.* Where we meet his most complex and fascinating treatment of it is in *The Ambassadors.*

In *The Ambassadors* the possible deficiencies of the gentlemanly ideal constitute the central situation. For what is at issue in this novel we might invoke another Victorian, Matthew Arnold, and consider his terms 'Hebraism' and 'Hellenism' as he defines them in *Culture and Anarchy.* The latter means 'spontaneity of consciousness', or the sense of the beautiful cultivated by education; the former means 'strictness of conscience', or the sense of morality cultivated by religion. Arnold observes that the world 'at one time feels more powerfully the attraction of one of them, at another time the other; and it ought to be, though it never is, evenly and happily balanced between them'.[8] This is the lesson James's hero, Lambert Strether, is forced to learn before James is finished with him.

At the beginning of the novel, Strether, representing a New England brand of Hebraism, comes out from America on behalf of Mrs Newsome, a widow with whom he is connected by business and a prospect of marriage, to bring back her son Chadwick who is suspected of having lost his virtue amidst the temptations of Paris.[9] Two things happen to Strether. First, he is confronted with a shock of sweetness and light that threatens to overpower a sensibility starved of these things in the life of Woollett, Massachusetts. Second, he becomes devoted to the cause of Chad Newsome, who does not want to go home. He

---

[8]   M. Arnold, *Culture and Anarchy* (1867; Cambridge: Cambridge University Press, 1950), p. 130.

[9]   H. James, *The Ambassadors* (New York: Barnes & Noble Classics, 2007). Quotations from the novel will be from this edition and noted parenthetically in the text.

recognizes in this young man a brilliant incarnation of the qualifies that he himself has missed in his own life.

While a reader suspects that Strether's mission is a witch hunt with the expectation of discovering some Left Bank wanton who has bewitched Chad and is keeping him from home, it turns out that the witch he meets is not a bohemian but a highly cultivated lady whose relationship with Chad is to all appearances innocent, though she is separated from her husband. Not only is it apparently a virtuous relationship but one that, far from corrupting him, has contributed to an exquisite personal formation of the young man.

It is James's dialectic in the novel to give all possible force and attraction to culture as represented by the marvellously formed Chad and his new home Paris. The lady in question, Mme de Vionnet, is drawn by James as a perfect daughter of the graces, one who could succeed in making a gentleman out of Chad from materials known to have been quite raw when he left America. At this point, we might recall Newman's words to explain the impression the novel gives us of Chad Newsome.

> Hence it is almost a definition of a gentleman to say he is one who never inflicts pain. He is mainly occupied in merely removing the obstacles that hinder the free and unembarrassed action of those about him. The true gentleman carefully avoids whatever may cause a jar or a jolt in the minds of those with whom he is cast;—all clashing of opinion, or collision of feeling, all restraint or suspicion [...] his great concern being to make everyone at their ease and at home.[10]

Certainly Strether's errand is painful to all concerned, but it is Chad's accomplishment to meet the situation with a sincere and winning urbanity that calms all tension and disarms the ambassador from Woollett. When Chad sees Strether for the first time, in a theater box on the latter's first night in Paris, before either

---

[10]   *Idea*, p. 185.

can speak, the youth merely 'projects his fineness' by 'an air of good confidence, by a careful, manly, polite bearing, and by a modest bashfulness'. The moment strikes Strether in a way that makes him feels it is 'one of the things in life that count'. Chad knew how 'to come into a theater box at 10 p.m. in a way that was wonderful' (p. 116).

Later with Strether at a cafe, Chad is 'altogether easy about the present occasion, in fact, altogether easy about everything. He sits with a receptive attitude like that of a person who has been gracefully quiet while the messenger at last reaching him has run a mile through the dust.' (p. 121) The effort is Strether's, which Chad smooths down, giving the older man the opportunity to contemplate the changes wrought in him since he was last seen in America. Eyes, smile, color are clearer. He has a form and surface, his voice a tone, to suggest that he 'had been put into a firm mold and turned successfully out' (p. 124). He has improved, and this fact is strongly present to Strether throughout the story as he observes repeatedly and under various conditions the rare qualities of which he has the first vision in this scene. Chad is 'always sleek, gay, and easy, and has always the right Word on his lips' (p. 237). The conflict about Chad's situation increases as Mrs Newsome clamors for her son, but Strether's sense of mission has given way to a deep curiosity. He knows a splendid thing when he sees it.

All is not clear in Strether's mind, however, and early in the book James poses the crucial issue: 'Strether asked himself if he weren't dealing with an irreducible pagan.' The boy is a gentleman for certain, but 'it didn't in the least, on the spot, spring up helpfully for him that a person couldn't at the same time be both' (p. 130).

Meanwhile, there is Paris and what it represents to reinforce the impression Strether received of Chad. James is sparing of description, yet the total suggestion of what Strether sees and feels as he wanders and muses is strong. He senses immediately the deep charm of the capital of mind and art, and little by little it subdues the inhibitions of Woollett. He buys lemon-colored volumes from the bookstalls, wondering how much he has missed of the intellectual currents of the day. He is attracted to Chad's expatriate friends for their enthusiasm, their 'good humored poverty and romantic association', and the way they 'twanged with a vengeance the aesthetic lyre' (p. 108).

In his preface to the novel James refers us to the second chapter of the fifth book to find his theme, and indeed these pages make his meaning clear. The scene is a garden party in the Faubourg Saint-Germain given by a sculptor named Gloriani. 'Much is ideally and enchantingly implied in a Paris garden', James tells us in the preface; 'there are values infinitely precious sealed up there'. And these he makes converge piercingly on Strether: 'the tall bird haunted trees, all of a twitter with the spring and the weather, and the high party walks, with the air everywhere of cessation, of survival, and transmission of rich things'. A noble old home faces the secluded garden. And walking there are distinguished people of the cast of refinement and imagination—artists, dramatists, and critics—that flourish in the climate of Paris. 'The spread flare, unequalled supreme of the aesthetic torch lights this wondrous world', thinks Strether. The sculptor himself appears to him 'with the light, the romance, of glory'. In contact with that element as he had never been before, Strether opens the windows of his mind and drinks in the sun of 'a climate not marked in his old geography' (p. 155).

Since he has not experienced such moments in his life before, pangs of regret stab him. And this prompts some passionate words to a friend of Chad's: 'Live all you can, it's a mistake not to. It doesn't so much matter what you do in particular so long as you have your life. If you don't have that, what have you had?' (p. 169)

A kind of sacredness in the way of life epitomized here is apparent from the religious atmosphere James creates in this and other scenes of the book. The house and garden of Gloriani were formerly a convent, 'a convent of mission, a nursery of young priests' (p. 155). Here Strether feels that he is somehow on trial, just as Chad Newsome is said to have been on trial in Paris and been 'saved' by Mme de Vionnet (p. 214). Once, while in a mood of deference to Woollett, Strether feels that he has been sacrificing to strange gods; his hands are 'imbrued with the blood of alien altars' (p. 335).

By such means James suggests the religion of civilization. That his hero succumbs is perfectly just, we feel, because of the beauty of what is represented and implied in these pages. But a suspicion remains as we await the outcome of Strether's mission. It occurs, as we would expect, in the form of a conflict of the aesthetic values posited by the novel with the moral code, yet it is a triumph of Jamesian subtlety that while the conflict is resolved in favor of morality, it somehow leaves the virtues of aestheticism in higher relief.

While taking a turn in the country around Paris to think out a solution of the problem whether or not he should after all send Chad home to his worried mother, Strether makes a painful discovery that proves Mrs Newsome's fears to be only too justified. 'Strictness of conscience' comes into the mix with 'sweetness and light' when Strether sees Chad and Mme de Vionnet boating on the river and sees further that they are staying together at the inn where he is having supper.

The first thing this sudden knowledge of an adulterous relationship does is to shock Strether into a realization of an old truth: things are seldom what they seem. Chad, Mme de Vionne, and Paris turned out to be magnificently different from what he had been prepared for, but now he knows that in one respect the worried mother at home was right after all. Seeing serious wrong here, the sense of it begins to color his view of everything around him. As he now walks through Paris his once 'too interpretive innocence' senses something 'more acute in manners, more sinister in morals, more fierce in the national life' (p. 406). This is an impression of the lovely city not experienced before. Sensing 'the smell of revolution, of blood' (p. 409), he begins to be more aware of terrible things of the past and sinister things of the present that go just as much as all the charming things to make the city what it is.

Yet there is a hesitancy and an indistinctness about Strether's attitude toward the new situation, and with this I think James is making the chief point of the novel. With Chad and the lady, Strether's relations definitely change. He does not need to speak the disapproval that he nonetheless conveys, but on the other hand he is not at all indignant at the hypocrisy so nicely contrived for so long. He even pities Mme de Vionnet for the enigma of her situation, one indication that his admiration continues. And going to see Chad once more he reflects that he is still committed to the boy, that 'had come up four flights, counting the entresol, at midnight, and without a lift, for Chad's life' (p. 429). That life still embodied the gentlemanly and aristocratic ideal that Strether had come to see as the 'proper spirit of man'. And so he does not condemn its embodiment in Chad; he leaves it behind and goes sadly home to America. But while he cannot connive at evil in Paris, it is clear that he will by no means take up again with humdrum respectability in Woollett and marry Mrs Newsome.

He is too much changed by contact with a culture truly not what it seems to Puritan Woollett. And while it is possible that the muddy waters of the situation left behind will clear, that Chad will come home to be the advertising executive his mother wants him to be, none of this is at all definite, and Strether departs not only without any direct protest to the dubious young man, but even with a parting admonition that he not on any account soon desert the woman who has done so much for him. 'I feel how much more she can do for you. She hasn't done it all yet. Stay with her at least till she has' (p. 432).

At the beginning of the story Strether becomes friends with one Maria Gostrey, an American tour guide he met on first arriving in Europe. She explains to him that she is a 'general guide to "Europe"' (p. 33). He shares with her the purpose of his mission and they discuss how it is going at various stages. She on her part identifies with Chad and his expatriate friends and wholeheartedly approves of them. 'We're abysmal—but may we never be less so!' (p. 310). Just how morally abysmal in Chad's case she has concealed from Strether because she does not want to hurt him with the knowledge. At the very end of the story, she invites Strether to stay with her, which he sees as an 'offer of exquisite service, of lightened care, for the rest of his days' and it 'might well have tempted' being in fact an invitation from the 'general guide to Europe' to enjoy for as long as he lives the sweetness and light that has so captured his heart, but he will have none of it. Strictness of conscience dictates that, as he says, he should 'not out of the whole affair have got anything for myself' (p. 441).

No doubt his attitude toward Chad Newsome is an instance of a tentativeness in James's stories that can be exasperating (though quite fascinating in the spooky enigma of *The Turn of the Screw*) and is here abetted by the complicated writing style of his late period. Yet, for James this can just as well be a reluctance to come out with the obvious in a situation too complicated to be obvious. Here, as he sees it, a flat moral condemnation is not adequate to the whole of a situation, and instead, as he tells us in his preface, 'the precious moral of everything' is 'that [his hero] now at all events *sees*.' The novel is simply a 'demonstration of this process of vision'.

So what James is showing us in Lambert Strether is a man who has an experience that convinces him of the incomparable richness of the graces, the amenities, and the beauty of European civilization. Though he laments that he has missed these things in his own life to the extent that he feels he really has not lived, nevertheless he knows that they cannot gloss evil or make it good. He has simply learned that they are of consummate worth in a world that has too little of them. Because culture can be mixed up with evil, it is sometimes an ambiguous value, and this is how James deals with it. Yet he implies that it is a sign of wisdom to acknowledge its worth in spite of the limitations of circumstance. This, then, is what his hero sees.

It might be tempting to dismiss the complexity of *The Ambassadors* as a muddled compromise, in the manner of Van Wyck Brooks who says censoriously that 'while James upheld his moral standard, the glamor [of Europe] filled his imagination'.[11] That there is much truth in this, *The Ambassadors* and other Jamesian stories clearly demonstrate. James was smitten with the glamor, but, of course, there is more to Europe than glamor, like the Faith, the heart of European civilization, and this James almost entirely missed. What he did not miss is that character of the gentleman eulogized by Newman as the inheritance of the ages and such an ideal as to inspire the great novelist to celebrate it in the pages of *The Ambassadors*. James was not taken in by it, his eyes closed to its very real defects, any more than Newman had been. He was dramatizing one of the ironies of life, that high civilization and moral deformity can co-exist so as sometimes to confuse and always to sadden the just.

---

[11]   Van Wyck Brooks, *New England: Indian Summer* (New York: E. P. Dutton, 1940), p. 294.

PART FIVE

Contributions to the Academy

15 A PHILOSOPHICAL HABIT OF MIND: NEWMAN AND THE UNIVERSITY[1]

ANDREW MESZAROS

THE VICTORIAN SCHOLAR George Malcolm Young claimed that if he could preserve only two books on education, they would be Aristotle's *Ethics* and John Henry Newman's *Idea of a University*. He claimed that the 'the rest might, with no loss to humanity and possibly some advantage, be pulped'.[2]

In his letters, Newman reveals that this work of his was his most difficult to write. And of all the discourses on university education that Newman wrote—all but one of which would later be collected and published together as the first half of *The Idea of a University*—it was what later became the fifth discourse that caused him the most anxiety and sleep loss. In that discourse, he was attempting to explain that the goal of a university education is the cultivation of the intellect. Seeking a second opinion, he asked an Oratorian confrère of his to look at it. The confrère strongly criticized it on the grounds that it failed to attribute a religious end to a university education. Upon confronting this criticism, Newman could just picture the very same coming from the Irish episcopate: 'Here we've invited an eminent English Churchman,' they might say, 'to establish a *Catholic University* here in Ireland over against the secular Queen's Colleges, those

---

[1] This is an abridged version of an article that appeared under the same name in *Logos: A Journal of Catholic Thought and Culture* 24:2 (2021), pp. 42–72.

[2] G. M. Young, 'Newman Again', *Last Essays* (London: Rupert Hart-Davis, 1950), p. 96.

"godless colleges", the ones that exclude theology on principle—
and he's telling us that the goal of this Catholic university is not
religious, but secular; not moral, but intellectual?!'

Newman's solution was to draft an introduction that would
clarify his position so as both to appease the Irish bishops who
had brought him to Ireland, and to stay true to his idea of a
university, which was neither a seminary, nor a finishing or
technical school, but a place for the communication and pursuit
of universal knowledge for its own sake. In that introduction, he
clarified that the *direct end* of a university is intellectual, the
indirect end religious.

In what follows, I will treat both the direct and the indirect
end of the university. I hope, however, to do more than simply
present these ends of Newman's university. I will argue that the
indirect end of the university—the moral and religious formation
of the students—is not *simply* superadded to the direct, intellectual end of the university, but is integral to that intellectual
pursuit. To understand this intellectual goal of the university, it
might be helpful to consider first what the ideal graduate of
Newman's university does *not* look like.

Two Intellectual Pitfalls

For Newman, any education that is unbalanced risks promoting
two highly undesirable intellectual characteristics. The first is
what he calls 'viewiness'. He describes this as a superficial
knowledge where facts are not related to other facts or subject
areas, where there is no tracing what is known to higher causes
or principles, where there is no 'connected view or grasp of
things'.[3] It is all breadth and no depth. The person who succumbs
to viewiness is the 'one who is full of "views" on all subjects of
philosophy, on all matters of the day. It is almost thought a
disgrace not to have a view at a moment's notice on any question
from the Personal Advent to the Cholera or Mesmerism.'[4] The

---

[3]   For more about 'viewiness' see *Idea*, p. xviii.

viewy one is not so much a person who has views (which is in itself not a bad thing) but someone who holds them in a rash, half-informed, and unserious way. The best illustration of this is offered by Newman himself in his description of the character Sheffield in *Loss and Gain*:

> he [Sheffield] was 'viewy', in a bad sense of the word. He was not satisfied intellectually with things as they are; he was critical, impatient to reduce things to system, pushed principles too far, was fond of argument, partly from pleasure in the exercise, partly because he was perplexed, though he did not lay anything very much to heart.[5]

A variation on viewiness appears in Newman's addresses in 'University Subjects', the second half of the *Idea*, where Newman describes what he calls the 'inaccurate student'. The inaccurate student is one who seems to know something about a great many things, but those things are flawed, or superficial, and, when tried, wanting; when pushed, found unstable. The 'inaccurate student' is 'viewy' insofar as he finds it hard to focus on one idea or to pay attention to details in reading. Those with an inaccurate mind might be pleasant in conversation and comment on a given topic with flare here and there, but due to intellectual sloth, they will lack 'consistency, steadiness, or perseverance'. On a practical level, says Newman, among other things, 'They will not be able to make a telling speech, or to write a good letter. [...] They cannot state an argument or a question [...] or give sensible and appropriate advice under difficulties.'[6]

And such a juvenile habit—viewiness or inaccuracy—is exacerbated, observes Newman, by the nineteenth century's cultural obsession with periodical literature: the more frequently things have to be published, the more young people are demanded to offer a 'view' on this, that, or the other. It promotes in them what

---

4   *Idea*, p. xx.
5   *Loss and Gain*, pp. 19–20.
6   *Ibid.*, pp. 341–2.

Newman calls a 'reckless originality of thought'.[7] The Victorian could not imagine a twenty-four-hour news cycle, nor could he fathom how vacuous much of the 'round table' discussions are on television; he did not know what Twitter or a meme is, or what it means to be 'woke'. But Newman nevertheless sees the danger posed to intellectual formation by the demands of a culture's voracious appetite for media. This obsession with having views on things is, according to Newman,

> owing in great measure to the necessities of periodical literature, now so much in request. Every quarter of a year, every month, every day, there must be a supply, for the gratification of the public, of new and luminous theories on the subjects of religion, foreign politics, home politics, civil economy, finance, trade, agriculture, emigration [...] the journalist lies under the stern obligation of extemporizing his lucid views, leading ideas, and nutshell truths for the breakfast table.[8]

Viewy or inaccurate persons cannot draw a connection between their opinions on a certain matter, and the deeper principles upon which they are based. They might not know what the principles are, or they may have none. They might be very certain about a given position but fall flat when under sustained critique. And with secularism's side-lining of once-respected institutions that provided a common framework of intellectual 'givens', once, long ago, taken for granted, the viewy persons are hopelessly thrown back on themselves to establish these principles. According to Newman, 'They can give no better guarantee for the philosophical truth of their principles than their popularity at the moment, and their happy conformity in ethical character to the age which admires them.'[9] In other words, viewiness is beholden to a culture that constantly clamors for views and input, and avails of a kind of pop-philosophy that assures the reader or listener that what

---

[7]   *Ibid.*, p. xxi.

[8]   *Ibid.*, p. xx.

[9]   *Ibid.*, p. xxii.

is being said is 'informed' and 'thoughtful'. In this context, viewiness goes hand-in-hand with inaccuracy; the demand for constant input means we have no time for—no stomach for—and consequently, no capacity for, attention to detail and nuance.

Now the opposite of viewiness, for Newman, is the second educational risk for a university: namely, bringing forth the 'man of one idea'. The 'man of one idea' or man of one science, is one whose specialization becomes the sole vantage point for viewing reality. The major interest of the man of one idea becomes the interpretative key for everything. Its principles become 'the measure of all things'. The principle might be 'all material being is made up of atoms'; or 'a free market allocates goods and resources most efficiently', or 'we ought to pursue social justice'. These might be true, but on their own become incredibly misleading. Persons of one idea are incapable of seeing reality from a different perspective. Whatever they say, though in its own place true, is 'sure to become but a great bubble, and to burst'. More nefariously, when in discourse with those who do not have a wider perspective than they, 'They persuade the world of what is false by urging upon it what is true'.[10] That is to say, the world is easily deceived by them, for what they say is not false and actually boasts of great success, usually corroborated by technological and medical progress whose impressiveness is its own justification.

The man of one idea is also simply tedious and, in the long run, an exceedingly tiresome conversationist. I say 'in the long run' because the astrophysicist might dazzle someone at table with a great deal of incredible information that would fascinate anyone who is at all curious about the universe; but over a longer period of time, if this astrophysicist is a man of one idea, he will inevitably sound tiresome when confronted with different subject matters.

The man of one idea and the viewy man are two types, two extremes that Newman seeks to avoid. Instead, one ought to seek accuracy without hyper-specialization, and universal knowledge without superficiality. It seems, then, that we are at risk of

[10]   *Ibid.*, pp. 77–8, 83, 94.

spreading the butter either too thin or too thick, for, as Newman says, 'a thorough knowledge of one science and a superficial acquaintance with many, are not the same thing' and 'a smattering of a hundred things or a memory for detail, is not a philosophical or comprehensive view'.[11]

However, it is not Newman's main aim to spread the perfect amount of cognitive butter perfectly evenly over the entire surface of knowable reality; it is not about the student knowing a *medium amount* about all subjects. His solution is, rather, to develop a habit of mind that he calls philosophical. It is a much more manageable goal, but one for which a university is particularly fit.

Newman's Ideal: a Philosophical Habit of Mind

For Newman, the university is a 'school of universal learning',[12] and its end is to develop and perfect the intellect. The intellect is made for knowledge and so university education should not simply impart knowledge but capacitate the intellect to acquire knowledge in the future. To that end, one needs to develop a habit that capacitates one for learning in different situations, when confronting different questions, when confronted with different kinds of evidence and different methods. Such a capacity is a virtue, or what Newman calls a habit of mind, and this virtue that attends to bearings of different kinds of knowledge Newman calls 'philosophical': a 'philosophical habit of mind'.

We can break down this phrase, starting with 'habit of mind', and then the qualifier, 'philosophical.' The phrase 'habit of mind' and its equivalents are dotted throughout Newman's entire corpus, beginning with his earliest sermons as an Anglican fellow at Oriel College, Oxford. A 'habit of mind' can also be referred to as an 'intellectual habit',[13] a 'frame of mind',[14] and a certain

---

[11]   *Idea*, p. 144. See also p. 77.
[12]   *HS* iii, p. 6. For this definition, Newman appeals to the Studium generale.
[13]   Tract 45, p. 2, *Tracts*.
[14]   *Parochial and Plain* iv, p. 123.

temper. By considering his usage of 'habit of mind', we can infer some things about what Newman means by it.

First, for Newman, a 'habit' is essentially the same as Aristotelian virtue. It is a stable disposition that inclines the person to act in a certain way. An *intellectual* habit, or habit of *mind*, is, for Newman, a habit that disposes the mind to infer and judge in a certain way.

All habits, including intellectual ones, grow and become more stable, permanent and continuous. It might fail on occasion, but the inclination still perdures. By contrast, a one-off exhibition of a certain kind of behavior does not make it a habit. A habit endures. It is abiding. Its stability and steadiness give the mind a certain 'property', 'character', or 'temper'.[15]

Second, a habit of mind is dynamic in the sense that it moves the mind in a certain direction. That is to say, the habit disposes the mind to judge one way rather than another, and such successive judgements of one kind or another propel the mind forward in one direction or another. Hence, Newman sometimes uses the word 'course' interchangeably with 'habit', 'course' here meaning a path or a route to be taken: there is a 'religious *course* of mind' or a secular one.[16]

Third, habits of mind, like other habits, are not taught, but formed and cultivated over long periods of time. This cultivation can be pursued conscientiously, as it is done in the university. But elsewhere, Newman also admits that habits of mind can be formed to a great extent by external circumstances, such as how one is raised, what one is taught, and what one is exposed to as a child.[17] The implication is that students coming to university are not blank slates.

The student who goes off to university already has an intellectual habit, but it is the university's task to refine or recalibrate it.

---

[15] *Justification*, pp. 225, 240, 243. See also *Apologia*, p. 21; *Grammar*, pp. 210–20.

[16] *Parochial and Plain* viii, pp. 222–3; *Grammar*, pp. 245–6; *Difficulties* i, pp. 350–1.

[17] *Present Position*, pp. 229–30.

As Newman writes, 'The bodily eye, the organ for apprehending material objects, is provided by nature; the eye of the mind, of which the object is truth, is the work of discipline and habit.'[18]

Fourth, habits of mind entail the regular belief of certain principles. A habit of mind disposes the individual to think this way or that way by virtue of some prior, deeply ingrained principles to which he or she assents. Such principles, for Newman, are capable of being put into a proposition: for example, 'No miracle can be considered to be true unless proved' or 'That which is necessary for salvation is to be found in scripture alone.' Such principles belong to what Newman calls the Protestant habit of thought. To this might be added the principle of private judgment.[19] Of course, as with any habit of mind, more principles could be enumerated.[20]

Entailed in this fourth point is the fifth and obvious point: namely, that depending on the principles assented to, one begins to cultivate a *certain kind* of habit of mind. So Newman speaks not only of a *Protestant*, but of all sorts of habits of mind, including a Christian habit of mind, a religious habit of mind, a secular habit of mind, and an experimental habit of mind, among others. Religious faith, for Newman, is a habit of mind, as is methodical doubt. One can also have a 'despondent, or liberalistic, or sceptical habit of mind'.[21] If it seems difficult to distinguish between kinds of habit of mind on the one hand and simple character traits on the other this is because they are closely related. Habits, including intellectual habits, determine the kind of person who possesses them. To be hyperbolic, one could say with Ovid that 'mind is the man'.[22]

---

[18]   *Idea*, p. 152.

[19]   *Miracles*, pp. 176–7; *Present Position*, pp. 303–4; *Difficulties* i, pp. 349–52; *Mixed Congregations*, pp. 194–7.

[20]   For example, *Present Position*, p. 189.

[21]   *Essays* i, p. 207.

[22]   Ovid, *Metamorphoses*, book xiii, line 567.

One's intellectual habits give the human person a horizon or a worldview, a frame of reference, a ruling idea, an attitude, a mental disposition, a vision of reality according to particular principles and presuppositions. So it is, for example, that a Christian habit of mind inclines the individual to associate the visible world with the invisible. Thus habituated, the Christian might confront the same phenomena as the secularist but interpret them very differently. For example, a serious Christian who is aware of a past sin or disobedience and is confronted with its negative consequences is capacitated to see in them a kind of divine chastisement or judgment. Someone possessed of a secular habit of mind, however, would not only refuse to interpret events in this way, but would be incapable of doing so. He has not the disposition for it because contrary principles underpin his habit of mind.

Unlike the religious or Christian habit of mind, as opposed to the secular or skeptical, other habits of mind are not necessarily contradictory and can co-exist. Hence, when Newman applies the distinction between real and notional assent to matters of religion, he distinguishes between a religious habit of mind and a theological one. The religiously habituated approach their objects devotionally through impressions on the imagination; the theologically habituated approach the same object, but with a host of abstractions and inferences underlying it. The one with a theological habit of mind assents to God's being and attributes as a theological truth; the one with a religious habit of mind assents to the same reality as a fact. These two habits, for Newman, not only co-exist but are dependent on each other. They are, in his words, 'two concurring and coincident courses of thought'.[23] This is possible because the principles belonging to the religious and theological habits of mind, though different, are not antagonistic.

This same coincidence and concurrence can take place between the philosophical habit of mind on the one hand and a more particular habit of mind pertaining to one's specific course

---

[23]   *Grammar*, p. 99.

of study, so long as that specific habit of mind does not work on principles contrary to the philosophical.

So, if a habit of mind is an intellectual virtue, a stable disposition of the mind that inclines the person to think and judge in a certain way, according to certain principles, which propels that same person in a definite intellectual direction, then what is a philosophical habit of mind? It is, to put it simply, the acquired ability of interpreting and making judgments about reality as one complex, but coherent whole, or, in Newman's words, the 'philosophical contemplation of the field of Knowledge as a whole'.[24]

While Newman's *Idea* is perhaps most well-known for its defense of the liberal arts, its repudiation of a utilitarian view of the academy, and its argument for the rightful and indeed natural inclusion of theology in an institution that pursues universal knowledge, perhaps the most important philosophical presupposition underlying all of this is Newman's claim that reality is one. It is important to note Newman's claim that the intellect can approach that one reality not through an intuitive vision but only piecemeal and, hence, only through individual disciplines or branches of knowledge; and further, 'that these branches are not isolated and independent one of another, but form together a whole or system',[25] a circle of knowledge. Excluding one branch 'is likely to lead to distortion, imbalance, and misrepresentation, either by omission or exaggeration of key perspectives'.[26]

So it is that, while Newman's inclusion of theology at the university has garnered perhaps the most scholarly attention and controversy, it is actually his inclusion and understanding of the role of philosophy, or what he calls the 'science of sciences', that gets to the crux of what he understands a university to be about. Philosophy examines the scope and limits of each subject by

---

[24]   *Idea*, p. 180.

[25]   *Ibid.*, p. 214.

[26]   John Sullivan, 'Newman's Circle of Knowledge and Curriculum Wholeness in "The Idea of a University"', *Receptions of Newman*, ed. F. D. Aquino & B. J. King (Oxford: Oxford University Press, 2015), p. 99.

relating them ultimately to one single, coherent reality or *being* in its height, depth, length, and breadth. Newman explains:

> the comprehension of the bearings of one science on another, and the use of each to each, and the location and limitation and adjustment and due appreciation of them all, one with another, this belongs, I conceive, to a sort of science distinct from all of them, and in some sense a science of sciences, which is my own conception of what is meant by Philosophy, in the true sense of the word, and of a philosophical habit of mind, and which in these Discourses I shall call by that name.[27]

The philosophical habit of mind, then, is about seeing things as part of this whole or system. He also calls this a 'form of Universal Knowledge'. It might come as a relief that universal knowledge, for Newman, is not tantamount to knowing everything about all things. He is simply claiming that the exactness and trustworthiness of the knowledge that each distinct discipline conveys is proportional to the extent to which we are trained to locate each discipline in its rightful place. Universal knowledge, for Newman, is 'the power of viewing many things at once as one whole, of referring them severally to their true place in the universal system, of understanding their respective values, and determining their mutual dependence'.[28] If you know where an individual piece belongs in a puzzle, you have a better, more exact and trustworthy idea of what is depicted on that piece when you examine it individually.

Newman calls 'the perfection or virtue of the intellect by the name of philosophy, philosophical knowledge, enlargement of mind, or illumination'. He also calls it a certain kind of 'comprehensiveness'. The philosophical person is the one who can discriminate 'between truth and falsehood', sift 'out the grains of truth from the mass', and arrange 'things according to their real value'.[29]

---

[27] *Idea*, p. 52.

[28] *Ibid.*, p. 137.

[29] *Ibid.*, pp. 125, 151.

'Such a power', Newman says, 'is the result of a scientific formation of mind; it is an acquired faculty of judgment, of clear-sightedness, of sagacity, of wisdom, of philosophical reach of mind, and of intellectual self-possession and repose'. He calls it a 'philosophical condition of mind'.[30] Newman's use of the word 'condition' coheres well with his other analogies for the university. One's physical condition is helped by the doctor or hospital; one's material condition is enhanced by work, or the almshouse; one's spiritual condition is the remit of the Church; and one's intellectual condition is developed by the university.

To achieve this, the university must provide a forum for the representatives of all the sciences.

> Though [the students] cannot pursue every subject which is open to them, they will be the gainers by living among those and under those who represent the whole circle. [...] They learn to respect, to consult, to aid each other [... The well-formed student] apprehends the great outlines of knowledge, the principles on which it rests, the scale of its parts, its lights and its shades, its great points and its little, as he otherwise cannot apprehend them. [...] A habit of mind is formed which lasts through life, of which the attributes are, freedom, equitableness, calmness, moderation, and wisdom; or what in a former Discourse I have ventured to call a philosophical habit. This then I would assign as the special fruit of the education furnished at a University.[31]

For Newman, different methods in disciplines supply different habits of mind. The co-existence of different but non-contradictory habits of mind is crucial for understanding what Newman is seeking to cultivate at the university. The historian might be using moral proof and reasoning from antecedent probability; the geometrician would reason more deductively. The student of English might be developing a more liberal habit of mind, the aspiring engineer a more experimental one. The challenge of the

---

[30] *Ibid.*, pp. 152, 218.
[31] *Ibid.*, pp. 101–2.

university is to develop a philosophical habit in all students, while letting the more particular intellectual habits flourish as well.

It is not that Newman expects every student to be an expert across the board. He simply believes that the student of English literature, for example, will benefit from not only knowing that a School of Engineering exists, but also from *talking to* engineering students, living with them, and taking courses in other subjects, especially philosophy. Because the university does not *in principle* exclude any branch of knowledge, it alone can offer that locus of intellectual exchange necessary to develop a philosophical habit of mind.

Contrary to the undisciplined, viewy graduate on the one hand, and the narrow-minded specialist on the other, the philosophically habituated knows that each method in its own sphere is good; she knows one method is not adequate to all inquiries. And so the philosophically habituated knows, further, that she has to be nimble enough to oscillate between the various methods and exercises of mind in order to enjoy some kind of vision of the whole. Her mental functions have to work together, in 'concert', to use Newman's expression. The philosophically habituated mind, then, is able to assemble, correct, and combine pieces of knowledge 'by the employment, concentration, and *joint action of many faculties and exercises of mind.* Such a *union and concert* of the intellectual powers, such an enlargement and development, such a comprehensiveness, is necessarily a matter of training'.[32] The university is the training ground.

The Philosophical Foundations for a Philosophical Habit of Mind

The word 'idea' is significant in Newman's corpus. In his *Essay on the Development of Christian Doctrine* he says Christianity itself is an 'idea' which, like other great ideas—such as democracy, Judaism, Gnosticism, and Protestantism—develops in history. An 'idea'

---

[32] *Idea*, p. 151. The italics are mine.

for Newman, is something that seizes the imagination and mobilizes men. For Newman, all institutions are animated by an idea: 'Ideas are the life of institutions'.[33] If the key idea of Christianity is the Incarnation, the leading idea of a university is unity.

In his original fifth discourse, not published in the *Idea*, Newman makes much ado about an 'idea' animating an institution. He adopts Aristotle's teaching that the rational soul is not only the animator, but also the form of the human body. The 'idea' of unity—or the unity of knowledge—not only gives life to the university but makes it what it is. Like a soul that not only animates a foot or hand, but renders that foot or hand a *limb* or a part of a living body, so too the idea of unity not only catalyzes the pursuit of knowledge but renders this or that individual subject discipline a *branch* of knowledge or part of a whole.[34] The idea or principle that unites all the disciplines into a unified endeavor, that 'imparts to each a dignity by giving it a meaning', which 'moulds, inspires, individualizes a whole', is the idea that 'all branches of knowledge are one whole'.[35]

This idea—let us call it the unity of knowledge—assumes a host of other presuppositions or more foundational principles which Newman took for granted (even if many today do not). They are by implication the necessary principles for developing a philosophical habit of mind. These would include, but are not limited to:

1. Reality is intelligible.

2. The intellect is made for reality, and capable of knowledge of the whole.[36]

3. Truth does not contradict truth.

---

[33]   *Campaign*, p. 361.

[34]   *Ibid.*, pp. 359–66.

[35]   *Ibid.*, p. 260.

[36]   In the words of Josef Pieper, 'Education concerns the whole man, man *capax universi* capable of grasping the totality of existing things' (*Leisure: The Basis of Culture*, trans. A, Dru (San Francisco: Ignatius, 2009), p. 39)

4. There is a Truth that transcends all truths, a Being that transcends all beings, a foundational ground for all knowledge that unifies it because it is the cause of it.

5. This first cause is author both of a reality that is intelligible, and of human subjects who are intelligent. In other words, God underlies both reality and the humans who come to know it, for God is, in the words of one Newman commentator, 'the Source and Guarantor of universal knowledge and of its coherent intelligible unity, the philosophical ground of knowledge'.[37]

6. God is also the divine author of our natures, including those laws governing how it is that our human nature comes to know. That we reason one way in morals and another way in physics is under God's providence; discursive proof here, moral proof there. The variety is as God designed it. It is in the nature of things.

7. The world is on a providential course, pregnant with the meaning intended for it by its creator.

The list could be filled out more, but this is simply an indication of the principles involved and presupposed when Newman says that 'knowledge is one'.

Just as *sola scriptura* is one principle among many of the Protestant habit of mind, the philosophical habit of mind works according to its own. One who conducts theological investigations according to *sola scriptura* will arrive at radically different conclusions to one who does not. Similarly, one who works according to these enumerated principles of a philosophical habit will think, learn, and judge differently than one who does not. When confronted with the infinitely disparate kinds of phenomena, whether physical, emotional, cultural, and so forth, and the myriad of truths—biological, chemical, ethical—the one with the

---

[37] Jane Rupert, 'Newman and the Tyranny of Method in Contemporary Education', *John Henry Newman: Doctor of the Church*, ed. Philippe Lefebvre & Colin Mason (Oxford: Family Publications, 2007), p. 87.

philosophical habit of mind is able to integrate them into one whole; he or she is able to see how one thing impacts another thing, how one informs another, how apparently disparate things are able to co-exist and cohere in a unified whole.

The philosophically habituated is on the lookout for ways to harmonize the truths of faith and reason; when confronted with new knowledge, new information, new evidence, new discoveries, he is able to appropriate that new knowledge not passively but actively, in such a way that he situates it coherently in a larger vision of reality.

When the political economist moves beyond an analysis of the market and the efficient allocation of goods and begins talking about the substance of the pursuit of happiness, the intellectual radar of the philosophically habituated will be activated. The same goes with the physician, who might be competent to tell you what to do to be healthy, but does not have the right, in Newman's view, to say that bodily health is the *summum bonum* or that the good life is beyond reach without such health.[38] The philosophically habituated can tell at what point Richard Dawkins's biology stops being biology and trespasses into the philosophical. But being able to do so depends on drawing students' attention to these key principles enumerated above.

There is no doubt that Newman's man of philosophical habit, like Aristotle's perfect orator, is an ideal, and seems an unachievable aspiration. At times, Newman speaks almost hyperbolically about him.[39] The man of philosophical habit is Newman's ideal graduand, as Dwight Culler points out, like Plato's ideal ruler or Aristotle's ideal orator.[40] It is, in the concrete, only partially and imperfectly realizable. But this ought not discourage the educator.

What is essential to developing that habit is adhering to those fundamental philosophical principles enumerated above and

---

[38]   *Ibid.*, pp. 87–8.

[39]   *Ibid.*, p. 113.

[40]   A. D. Culler, *Imperial Intellect: a Study of Newman's Educational Idea* (New Haven: Yale University Press, 1955), p. 189.

getting into the habit of viewing and investigating reality according to these principles.

Newman was in many ways a realist, not only philosophically but also in the colloquial sense. While he had high ideals, he knew that here below we work with what we can. For many, such as those who are already working, a full-time university education is impossible. That is why Newman initiated the evening lectures for the workers of Dublin. He could thereby initiate a process of enlarging their minds too. While a philosophical habit of mind in full bloom cannot be democratized, Newman sought to expose its main contours—its principles in action—to the general public, showing that he was thoroughly practical and did what he could to prompt and cultivate this philosophical habit wherever and however he could.

Now we turn to the indirect end of Newman's university, the moral and religious end.

Newman's beau ideal: *Sagacity and Sanctity*

Newman's famous portrait of the gentleman has caused not a little consternation amongst his readers. Newman's *laudatio* of the gentleman seems like a solid endorsement, and yet he is quite clear that the intellectual qualities of the refined gentleman can be used for ill. A philosophically habituated gentleman who does not take seriously his moral and religious duties can be dangerously crooked. And what is more, Newman is quite clear that intellectual training bears no relationship to moral improvement. For Newman, trying to tackle the giant moral deficits of human passion and pride with knowledge and reason is like quarrying granite with a razor, or mooring a vessel with silk thread.[41]

According to Newman, the university's direct end is the cultivation of the intellect. Its indirect end, however, includes attention to the holistic formation—moral and spiritual—of the human person. A Catholic university has the indirect end of

---

[41]   *Idea*, p. 121.

serving the Church in this way.[42] In a parallel fashion, we can say with Angelo Bottone that, although the intellectual pursuit suffices for the *esse* of the university, for its integrity, perfection or *bene esse*, the moral-spiritual pursuit is necessary.[43]

The complementarity between the intellectual pursuit on the one hand, and religious, moral, and spiritual formation on the other is embodied in Newman's ideal constellation of a university that lives within its constituent colleges or houses of residence. The university and its professors embody progress, dynamism, bustling creativity, and confront the world in all the challenges it poses. The college and its tutors, on the other hand, are dedicated to catechesis, discipline, the formation of good habits, moral character, and the fine-tuning of intellectual habits.[44]

Newman has the students matriculated not only into a university, but into a routine that cultivates self-discipline and virtue, embodied in the college or residence hall. There is a time for rising and a time for study. He provides for the students' spiritual discipline and edification by offering daily morning mass and scheduling notable speakers to preach at the university church. He provides for wholesome recreation by purchasing for the students a billiard table so that they can bypass the more questionable establishments for entertainment.

Academically, Newman's idea of the tutor is one who attends to both the intellectual and moral development of students; he is not simply an academic but a resident assistant. Newman wants his students to excel not only in sagacity, but also in sanctity. After the pattern of a medieval ideal, the university is 'to fit men for this world while it trained them for another',[45] and such fitness and training obviously requires something more than intellectual

---

[42]   *Ibid.*, pp. 459–60.
[43]   A. Bottone, *The Philosophical Habit of Mind: Rhetoric and Person in John Henry Newman's Dublin Writings* (Bucharest: Zeta, 2010), pp. 67–9.
[44]   *HS* iii, pp. 228–9.
[45]   *HS* iii, p. 152. See also *Idea*, p. 177.

prowess. He wants, as he phrased it in a different context, 'clear heads and holy hearts'.[46]

In the Catholic University church, Newman used the different liturgical feast days or gospel passages as occasions for reminding his students—nay, drilling into his students—that, while it is indeed a privilege for the students to be studying and pursuing knowledge, this very knowledge will not get them any closer to holiness, and that ultimately it is much more important to be a saint than a scholar. Saying as much risks giving an inaccurate, or at least impoverished, view of what exactly a Catholic University is for Newman, for it might be understood—wrongly—that all universities are essentially the same, that academically they are on a par, but that the Catholic ones are merely better equipped for religious edification and the cultivation of moral virtue.

Such a view, though not false, is impoverished. On the contrary, a Catholic university makes a difference not only in the arena of the 'extra-curriculars' of morals and religion, but also precisely within the academic sphere. And it is not because Catholic universities include theology and others do not, although this too is relevant. It is not even the *ease* with which Catholic universities include theology, philosophy, and the liberal arts. The question then arises, What difference does a Catholic university make?

Conclusion: The Difference a Catholic University Makes

The difference a Catholic university makes is that it has the capacity to help students assent to key principles—such as the Being of God and his attributes—without which a philosophical habit is impossible. Their assent, furthermore, would not only be notional, but also real.[47]

What is distinctive about a Catholic university, according to Newman, is not the spiritual and moral resources that keep

---

[46] *Via Media* i, p. lxxv.

[47] *Grammar*, pp. 98–124.

students out of trouble and are sprinkled on top of an already complete intellectual formation as icing on a cake. Such a view compartmentalizes the perfection of the intellect from human flourishing. Rather, these spiritual and moral resources provided by a Catholic culture or ethos on campus—such as regularly available liturgy, spiritual direction, and mentorship, opportunities for service and charity, living arrangements conducive to the development of virtue, and fruitful recreational activities—play an integral part in academic excellence and in avoiding the pitfalls of 'viewiness' and monomania.

Students benefiting from such a Catholic ethos can taste and see the goodness of the Lord (Ps 34:8), who is the ground of the unity of knowledge: the creator and goal of all things, and the ground of their intelligibility. At a Catholic university, the biology major who hears a lecture on genetics can also sing the words of Psalm 139. In short, a Catholic ethos helps cultivate not simply a notional, but a vital, imaginative, or real assent to those first principles necessary for the cultivation of a philosophical habit of mind.

It is fitting, then, that Newman's Catholic University in Ireland followed Louvain in taking as its motto *Sedes Sapientiae*. The university is 'a seat of wisdom, a light of the world, a minister of the faith, an Alma Mater of the rising generation'.[48] A Catholic university's students know that this wisdom has become flesh, and so they perceive, and indeed experience, an unprecedented connection between the visible and the invisible. For the community of Catholic scholars, the chasm between astrophysics and English literature is not so large if one knows that the far larger chasm between the created and uncreated has already been connected by wisdom itself.

---

[48]   *HS* iii, p. 16.

16 NEWMAN AND THE IDEA OF A TUTOR

PAUL SHRIMPTON

JOHN HENRY NEWMAN was invited to become the founding rector of the Catholic University in Ireland in July 1851. Soon after accepting the invitation he announced his intention to combine the professorial and tutorial systems in his plans, adding that 'the principal making of men must be by the Tutorial system'.[1] A year later, he explained that at Oxford the 'real working men were, not the Professors, but the Tutors',[2] and that he wished this to be the case in Dublin as well.

What did Newman mean by the word 'tutor', and why did he set such store by the role? In the course of exploring the richness of Newman's idea of a tutor, it is inevitable that some of the shortcomings of the modern academy will be exposed. Though it might seem like a 'lost cause' to revisit the tutorial system, which, because of its expense, has only been fully incorporated into the undergraduate teaching system at Oxford and Cambridge, the Covid pandemic has given us an opportunity to pause and rethink. Certainly, it has made us reconsider our priorities, heightening our awareness of the importance of the personal dimension in education. Is it not an ideal time to reflect on the role of the tutor, as envisaged by Newman? It looks inevitable that the 'new normal' will see increased reliance on online lectures and that as a result higher education will be further

---

[1] 'Report on the Organization of the Catholic University of Ireland', October 1851, *Campaign*, p. 85.

[2] Newman to Cullen, 14 August 1852 (not sent), *Campaign*, pp. 276–7. Known as the 'Statement of 14th August, 1852' this letter can be regarded as one of the six foundational documents of the Catholic University.

impoverished by seeing the human element diminished, but it also offers an opportunity for the academy to rethink its mission and to compensate by introducing counterbalances into the system: the possibility that university lecturers might be able to spend more time in tutorial or small-group work, once released from some of their duties in the lecture hall. By revisiting Newman's arguments for the need of this type of teaching, this great Christian humanist can open our minds to its benefits and instruct us on its workings.

When invited to establish a university in Ireland, Newman was in his early fifties and had spent most of his life immersed in education: firstly as a schoolboy and student; then as a tutor, lecturer, examiner and dean of discipline at Oxford; next as an Anglican clergyman, spiritual guide and preacher; and, latterly, as a seminarian and Catholic priest. He was thus able to draw on the wealth of nearly half a century's experience in order to map out his vision of a university that would promote human flourishing in general, and intellectual development in particular. He was also able to draw on contemporary ideas of tutoring and to assess their worth.

At the start of the nineteenth century, before the public schools had been reformed, the sons of the well-to-do were often tutored at home. The role of the private tutor was assumed to cover the education of the whole person: physical, intellectual, social and moral; and since the moulding of a boy's character required authority over him, the tutor was granted standing so that he could act *in loco parentis*. In times when the age of majority was twenty-one, the private tutors of wealthy young men would follow their charges to university, or else a new private tutor would be engaged.

When Newman began his studies at Trinity College, Oxford he was assigned to the junior of the college's two tutors, Thomas Short, who, as soon as he realised he had a genuine scholar on his hands, lent Newman a book and invited him to breakfast. At the time, each college functioned as a mini-university and college tutors acted as lecturers. Undergraduates were expected to attend 'college lectures' for two or three hours a day, during which a tutor would typically oversee a group of up to fifteen students translating Latin and Greek texts, to which he might add a commentary of a grammatical, historical or philosophical nature. It was an unwieldy system, as the tutors were expected to tackle too many subjects and the pace was reduced by the presence of many backward and idle students. In consequence, a parallel, semi-official system had emerged, in which private coaches were engaged by serious students for individual or small-group tuition, or else engaged as 'cram coaches' by idle students in a last-minute attempt to salvage a degree. In student parlance, the private coach was either a 'class-coach' or a 'pass-coach', the former indicating that everyone who aimed at honours was virtually obliged to supplement the regular college instruction with that of a private tutor.

In his first year Newman made enquiries about engaging a private tutor, but dropped the matter on account of the expense, then changed his mind when he won a college scholarship, worth £60 p.a. At the start of his second year, he and his closest friend John Bowden engaged the services of James Ogle, who had recently graduated from Trinity and, like other private coaches, was combining tutoring with his own reading until he succeeded in gaining a fellowship. The two undergraduates were tutored for two hours a day until Ogle became a college tutor at Trinity, after which he could only give them one hour a day. Not being *au fait* with the private-tutor system, Newman did not continue the extra tuition into his third year, during which he overworked to such an extent that he broke down in Finals. Instead of the First predicted of him, he gained a mere Pass in Classics and failed in Mathematics.

Newman later attributed his failure to a lack of tutorial guidance which left him almost entirely to his own devices; he came to realise that in Oxford 'at that time the very idea of study was new' and that just a handful of colleges had adjusted to the demands of the honours system, which had been recently intro-duced; only they possessed the real tutors, shared the tradition, and—crucially—supplied the examiners.[3] Oriel, Balliol and Christ Church belonged to this charmed inner circle, but Trinity did not. The whole episode taught Newman the need for individual tutorial guidance.

Despite the disappointment in Finals, Newman stayed on in Oxford and joined the ranks of the private tutors, while preparing to compete for college fellowships. At first he struggled to attract tutees on account of his poor degree, but once he landed a fellowship at Oriel College, in April 1822, he had more than he could handle. Newman then followed the usual academic route of being ordained as a clergyman in the Church of England. It was from the Oriel Fellows that Newman received the sort of education that was sorely missing at Trinity—and indeed at most colleges. The provost Edward Copleston assigned the task of drawing the timid young graduate out of his shell to two of the Fellows, Richard Whately and Edward Hawkins, who effectively acted as tutors to Newman. Whately took him walking and riding, and conversed with him at length. He was, as Newman recounts, 'the first person who opened my mind, that is, who gave it ideas and principles to cogitate on'[4] and taught him to think for himself. As for Hawkins, Newman records his intellectual debt by saying that he 'was the first who taught me to weigh my words and to be cautious in my statements'.[5] Twelve years apart, they were like pupil and tutor rather than colleagues, and never more so than when Hawkins carefully checked through Newman's first sermons and gave him helpful criticism.

At the time Newman was not only combining his Oriel fellowship with parochial duties but acting as tutor and dean of the dozen undergraduates at Alban Hall, an independent academic hall of the University. He now began to think that his calling might be for college rather than parish, or even missionary, work. When offered a tutorship at Oriel in 1826 he accepted. Not only did he resign

---

[3]   Newman's memoir, 13 June 1874, *AW*, p. 51.

[4]   Newman to Monsell, 10 October 1852, *LD* xv, p. 176.

[5]   *Apologia*, p. 8.

from Alban Hall, but he also gave up the curacy of his parish, justifying his decision on the grounds that the tutorship was a spiritual office and a way of fulfilling his Anglican ordination vows. What might appear as an excuse for merely indulging academic inclinations was, in Newman's case, the result of several years of discernment, coupled with a conviction that the seventeenth-century idea of the college tutor could be revived. In the Laudian statutes of 1636, which were still technically in force, the role of the tutor was more associated with pastoral care than with secular instruction; and although the tutor's main task had become that of a college lecturer, enough of the old associations lingered on to convince most people that the task should continue to be undertaken by unmarried clergymen.

Reforming the Tutorial System in Oxford

Newman typically threw himself into his new role. Before a month had elapsed he became worried by the 'considerable profligacy' among the undergraduates, many of whom were 'men of family', and by the lack of 'direct religious instruction' for them, and in his zeal he set about doing battle with the privileged young men whom he considered to be the ruin of the place.[6] By all accounts his first year in office was a stormy one, as Newman set about reforming with a vigour born partly of principle and partly of inexperience. Despite the resistance he encountered, which took the form of gossip and the occasional student prank, Newman stuck resolutely to his task. And, though the college authorities did not support his efforts to tame the unruly, he succeeded in winning over the studious element by his unstinting application as a tutor.

By the time he became a college tutor, Newman realised that the use of the private tutor system in parallel with the college lectures was what explained the success of colleges like Oriel, but he disliked the arrangement and as a college tutor sought to make

---

[6]   Newman's diary, 7 May 1826, *LD* i, p. 286n.

it redundant. In the tutorial system then operating at Oriel, each student was assigned to a tutor who in theory was supposed to oversee his work, arrange the distribution of his lectures, assist him in his difficulties, and oversee his religious instruction: but this was far from the reality. The students were usually assigned their college lectures irrespective of who their tutor was; and the normal relation between tutor and undergraduate was distant and largely nominal.

Rather than fall in with the way things were done, Newman set about his duties in a very different fashion. To the more disciplined and promising students he offered 'his sympathy and help in College work',[7] and he laid it down as his rule that he would give without charge whatever additional instruction was necessary for those of his pupils who wished to read for an honours degree. Declaring that the system of private tutors brought students unnecessary expense, he undertook to combine in his own person the teaching offices of public tutor and private. But that was not all: he also assumed into his role as college tutor the pastoral responsibility that, at the time, was an additional function of the private tutor, and this rendered Newman's approach more potent still. He read with his pupils, went for walks with them, breakfasted and dined with them, and (in Newman's own words) 'cultivated relations, not only of intimacy, but of friendship, and almost of equality, putting off, as much as might be, the martinet manner then in fashion with College Tutors, and seeking them in outdoor exercise, on evenings, and in Vacation'.[8] Within two years he acquired 'such a devoted body of pupils as Oxford had never seen', at least since the Middle Ages, according to his tutee Thomas Mozley, who likened him to 'a father, or an elder and affectionate brother'.[9]

---

[7]   Newman's memoir, 13 June 1874, *AW*, p. 90.

[8]   Newman's memoir, 13 June 1874, *AW*, p. 90.

[9]   Mozley, *Reminiscences: Chiefly of Oriel College and the Oxford Movement*, vol. i (London: Longman, Green & Co., 1882), pp. 136, 181.

In Newman the undergraduates found a teacher who took the trouble to master his subject matter, by entering into it not just with his intellect but with his whole personality, giving life to the matter under consideration rather than merely conveying it by rote and rule. However dull the material might be—such as the logic they had to cover—Newman had the knack of breathing life into it. From the testimony of his pupils we know that he challenged each of them to think for himself, to understand what he was reading, and to articulate his ideas; to compare and contrast, to challenge and contradict, to reduce an argument to its simplest form, to test it against historical examples, to recast it in his own words or in a different style, and to make comparisons with the present day. In combining the roles of public and private tutor Newman found himself overwhelmed,[10] and the strain of it all seems to have contributed to his collapse in November 1827 while acting as University Examiner in Classics.

In January 1828 new college appointments meant that as a tutor Newman was now second to senior, and no longer isolated but supported by two like-minded men, Hurrell Froude and Robert Wilberforce; they shared his view that secular education could, if conducted properly, become 'a pastoral cure'. The younger tutors were in perfect harmony with Newman's interpretation of the Laudian statutes, which stressed the pastoral role of tutors and maintained (as Newman put it) that 'a Tutor was not a mere academical Policeman, or Constable, but a moral and religious guardian of the youths committed to him'.[11] They joined Newman in offering the more deserving pupils as much time and attention as the best private tutors; and in doing so the Oriel tutors provided 'the germ of the modern tutorial system' at Oxford.[12]

---

[10] He told his mother, 'Here we are "all droning, droning, droning, all treading in the tutorial mill"' (4 May 1827, *LD* ii, p. 14).

[11] Newman's memoir, 13 June 1874, *AW*, p. 91.

[12] M. G. Brock, 'The Oxford of Peel and Gladstone, 1800–1833', *History of the University of Oxford*, 8 vols (Oxford: Oxford University Press, 1997), vol. vi, ed. M. G. Brock & M. C. Curthoys, p. 61.

In the absence of any system for religious training at Oxford, Froude, Newman and Wilberforce made use of the great pre-Christian treatise on morals, Aristotle's *Ethics*, as the basis for a course in ethical studies through reflection and discussion on the motives and principles of action and on the formation of moral habits and character. They also made use of Bishop Butler's *Analogy of Religion* (1736), the authoritative modern text complementing the *Ethics*. This emphasis by the Oriel tutors could be considered as an early manifestation of the revival of character formation, which began in the 1820s in the reformed public schools and then spread to other schools and Oxford and Cambridge over the next forty years.[13]

These broader educational objectives come to the surface in the brief records Newman kept on his tutorial pupils, where it is clear that he had in mind more than the mere mastery of texts or intellectual progress. To monitor pupils on a university course where there were few set texts and reading was tailored to individual needs, Newman kept a record of the reading he set his pupils, the plan of study he devised for each of them, and how they coped with it; the warnings they received from him and the provost; and how they performed in exams. But there is more, because throughout Newman intersperses comments on academic ability with shrewd character descriptions.[14]

Also clear from these notes is that Newman took stock of each student and adjusted his demands accordingly. Those who were academically able or well-grounded were not allowed to coast unchallenged or to idle their time away, while weaker students were coaxed along and offered support. Where the chemistry of affinity and friendship led to a greater bonding, Newman would exert himself further. Not all students felt comfortable with the close attention Newman offered them, however, and he sometimes had to step back. His patience and paternal instincts are

---

[13]   S. Rothblatt, *Tradition and Change in English Liberal Education* (London: Faber & Faber, 1976), p. 133.

[14]   These can be found in his 'Memorandum Book about College Pupils', BOA, A6.15.

evident in his dealings with the ups and downs of undergraduate life. Newman could be sternly demanding of his pupils, especially if he saw they were wasting their talents and could take a strong reprimand. On one occasion he reproached Henry Wilberforce, a younger brother of Robert, for wasting two terms: 'Beware of repenting indeed of idleness in the evening, but waking next morning thoughtless and careless about it'.[15]

To make sense of these strictures, we need to recognise that, for Newman, university was a place of transition from boyhood to adulthood and therefore entailed responsibilities for the maturing individual, as well as greater freedom. While providing an emancipatory experience, college life brought with it the baggage of rituals, disciplinary restrictions, domestic requirements, academic duties, and shared living, all of which served a formative purpose. At one and the same time tutors needed to be kind and understanding to their charges, while remaining firm and demanding. This degree of formative attention to the needs of students, which involved considerable give and take, was not part of the repertoire of other Fellows. Newman's high-minded stance inevitably grated with those who adhered to the old order and gave rise to tensions.

Hawkins, who had become provost of Oriel in 1828, generally approved of these initiatives and backed up his tutors, but in January 1829 Newman introduced a major change to the lecture system, which effectively made official what three of the four tutors had been doing unofficially: as Newman summarised it, the 'bad men' were left in large classes (according to the existing system) while 'the better sort' were placed in small classes and 'principally with their own tutors quite familiarly and chattingly'.[16] The guiding aim was to give each tutor control over and responsibility for his own pupils. However, Newman did not inform the provost of the initiative. When Hawkins learnt of it, he instructed the tutors to revert to the old system, but they objected and argued

---

[15]   9 July 1827, *LD* ii, p. 23.
[16]   Newman to Rickards, 6 February 1829, *LD* ii, p. 117.

their corner. The quarrel which ensued was fiercely contested, but in the end Hawkins had his way and in June 1830 he effectively dismissed the three tutors, by depriving them of pupils. Much ink has been spilt on the affair, about the causes, what was at stake, and how to interpret the outcome. The dispute concerned the tutors' role—strictly disciplinary in the provost's view, fully pastoral in theirs—but a number of other interconnected issues came into play, such as the weakening of the provost's control over the undergraduate curriculum and the shift in responsibility from the tutors as a body to the tutors as individuals. On a practical level Hawkins was uneasy with what he saw as the proselytising influence of his tutors and feared that the college might lose its connections with wealthy families. The dispute was also affected by the personalities involved: Hawkins had become over-jealous of his authority and autocratic in his management of the college, while Newman, for his part, had begun to show 'an unbecoming truculence and insubordination'[17]—and made a serious error of judgement (as he admitted afterwards) in keeping Hawkins in the dark. Yet the key issue at play in the dispute is still very much with us today: in his opposition to the three tutors Hawkins personified an impoverished view of education, one which pays only lip service to its pastoral dimension and to the close interaction of students and teachers.

A decade before the tutorial row, Newman had composed a ditty about Oriel for *The Undergraduate*, the magazine he had begun with his friend Bowden. It included a stanza which is unconsciously prophetic of his future work:

> As we all have the good of the college at heart,
> The men are divided and each has a part;
> The lecture we give to the general stock,
> But each has besides a particular flock;
> And them we are gratis to superintend,
> And act as a sort of tutorial friend.[18]

---

[17]   Quoted in A. D. Culler, *Imperial Intellect: a Study of Newman's Educational Idea* (New Haven: Yale University Press, 1955), p. 69.

Although Newman ceased being a tutor in 1831, paradoxically his influence on the University's tutorial system seems to have grown rather than declined. The explanation for this surprising turn of events forms part of the story of the Oxford Movement, which spread in grass-roots fashion to the junior men of the University through the more personalised form of tuition initiated by the Oriel tutors and continued by their tutees, immediate successors and followers. The largely oral character of Oxford academic tradition at the time meant that the new approach was discussed among tutors and students and subject to cross-pollination and development out of sight of the general public. It was undoubtedly fostered by the intercollegiate dining club which Newman founded in April 1828 with the aim of bringing young academics together— mainly tutors—and which met fortnightly until 1833.[19] While the spread of Tractarian ideals and principles was readily fostered by what Newman called 'the force of personal influence and conge- niality of thought',[20] the educational value of the new tutor–pupil relationship was prized by many who were unsympathetic to the Tractarian cause; and during the decades after Newman's dismissal a growing number of tutors came to regard their office as a pastoral one—a trend given impetus in 1837 when the Hebdomadal Board re-enacted the section of the Laudian Code on the tutor's moral and religious responsibilities—and saw it as an ideal way of nurturing scholarly endeavour. Valued as an intellectual training, individualised tutorial instruction eventually became the norm at Oxford—and to this day this ideal sets it and Cambridge apart from the rest of the educational world.[21]

---

[18] 'Letter from a Tutor [of Oriel] at Oxford, to his Friend in the Country', *The Undergraduate* 6 (20 March 1819), p. 50.

[19] Newman's diary, 14 May 1829, *LD* ii, p. 143.

[20] *Apologia*, p. 40.

[21] The modern tutorial system only emerged fully after major reforms. For an account of the way this came about at Oxford see A. J. Engel, *From Clergyman to Don: the Rise of the Academic Profession in Nineteenth-century Oxford* (1983).

The Tutorial System in Dublin

Given the centrality of the tutorial system in Newman's educational thinking, it comes as no surprise to learn that he was determined to incorporate it into the structure of the Catholic University in Dublin. The obstacles were considerable, but that did not deter him. Catholics in Ireland had little idea of what a university education amounted to, except for the privileged few who had attended Trinity College Dublin, the Protestant foundation which regarded itself as a younger sister of Oxford and Cambridge. There was no university tradition among Irish Catholics and certainly no appreciation of the benefits that a tutorial system might confer. For Newman to establish such a system, he therefore had to 'import' into Ireland those familiar with it and capable of working it. And who better than the converts to Catholicism who had been educated at Oxford and Cambridge? Newman was ideally placed to tap into this pool of talent, but there was a problem: the majority were English and this would not please the nationalist element among the Irish episcopate, who had collected the funds for the university and invited Newman to establish it. Then, of course, there was the expense of such a labour-intensive system for a country that was recovering from four years of famine—the Great Famine—which had ravaged Ireland and seen more than a quarter of the population starve to death or forced to emigrate.

In dealing with Paul Cullen, Archbishop of Dublin and cofounder of the Catholic University, Newman realised there would have to be some give and take in deciding between them on the mode of setting up the new university. Nevertheless, he insisted that, as rector, he should have the power of choosing his associates, especially the tutors—at least at the outset; and he warned Cullen to brace himself for an English convert element among the teaching staff.[22] The organising sub-committee, to which Newman belonged, recommended the appointment of a

---

[22]   Newman to Cullen, 11 October 1851, *LD* xiv, pp. 382–3.

small number of professors and lecturers, who between them might teach the main subjects, while also acting as tutors. In the postscript to their main report, Newman dwelt at length on the role of the tutor.

His proposal was to blend the 'Professorial and Tutorial systems' by arranging for the same people to undertake both teaching functions in order that students would benefit from both systems. As with his reforms at Oriel, the question of which system to employ depended on the subject matter being taught. There was no need for Newman to explain why lectures were needed, but he did think it worthwhile to point out that they had their shortcomings: 'the work of a Professor is not sufficient by itself to form the pupil. The catechetical form of instruction and the closeness of work in a small class are needed besides.' Newman explained that, even if the professor was a man of genius, what was gained from his lectures would often be very superficial. Undoubtedly, students who were academically self-motivated would be able to profit from them; but in general, if the reliance was solely on lectures, 'the result will be undisciplined and unexercised minds, with a few notions, on which they are able to show off, but without any judgment or any solid powers'.[23] Arguing in this fashion, Newman arrived at his working rule: 'that the principal making of men must be by the Tutorial system'. In this way the professor, acting as a tutor,

> on a smaller number at a time, and by the catechetical method, will be able to exert those personal influences, which are of the highest importance in the formation and tone of character among the set of students, as well as to provide that the student shall actually prepare the subject for himself, and not be a mere listener at a lecture.[24]

---

[23] Newman develops his thinking on lectures and how to profit from them in his public lecture 'Discipline of Mind' (*Idea*, pp. 480–504).

[24] 'Report on the Organization of the Catholic University of Ireland', *Campaign*, pp. 84–5.

As at Oriel, the tutors were to select the lectures for their students; they were to prepare them by ensuring that they had an elementary knowledge of the subject concerned; they were to question them about their content afterwards; and they were to help them prepare for the university exams. The tutors would be young men who had only recently taken their degrees, though Newman realised that initially he had no alternative but to rely on older men, the Oxbridge converts. It should be noted that Newman also sought to imitate the *collegiate* system of Oxford, grafting it onto the university structure which he copied from the Catholic University of Louvain (founded by the bishops in Belgium in 1834), which Rome had proposed as a blueprint. In this way he would 'combine the distinctive features and strengths of both', that is, of Louvain and Oxford.[25] His choice had nothing to do with a conjectured 'emotional attachment' to Oxford; nor can it be argued that he lacked knowledge of other university systems. Rather, both his choice of university system and the way he implemented it are illustrative of his pastoral vision of education. For Newman, 'It would seem as if a University seated and living in Colleges, would be a perfect institution, as possessing excellences of opposite kinds.'[26]

It was the same conclusion that the royal commissioners reached after investigating Oxford in 1850–52. They thought that by combining the two systems, the professorial system could become 'the crown and completion of the Tutorial': it would answer the need for lecturers in the new academic disciplines, and would encourage tutors to stay on by providing a goal for them. Unlike the universities abroad, where the professorial system had been adopted not from choice but from necessity,

---

[25] I. Ker, 'Newman the Teacher', *Newman and Education*, ed. M. Davies (Rugeley: Spode House, 1980), p. 38. See also Ker, 'Newman's *Idea of a University*, A Guide for the Contemporary University?', *The Idea of a University*, ed. D. Smith & A. K. Langslow (London: Jessica Kingsley, 1999), pp. 15–16.

[26] *HS* iii, p. 229.

Oxford's wealth gave it 'the means of combining the two, and of carrying out the spirit of each more perfectly.'[27]

Newman's scheme involved a system of collegiate or lodging houses—mini-colleges in effect—which would hold up to twenty students, each presided over by a dean, with its own private chapel and chaplain, and resident tutors. Newman expected much from the influence of the tutors. They would be,

> half companions, half advisers of their pupils, that is, of the students; and while their formal office would be that of preparing them for the Professors' Lectures, and the Examinations [...], they would be thrown together with them in their amusements and recreations; and, gaining their confidence from their almost parity of age, and their having so lately been what the others are still, they may be expected to exercise a salutary influence over them, and will often know more about them than anyone else.[28]

Newman explained to an Oxford friend that the tutor's work,

> is more of influence than of instruction. But at the same time influence is gained *through* the reputation of scholarship etc, and the very duty which comes on a Tutor is to do that which the pupil cannot do for himself, e.g. to explain difficulties in the works read in lecture, and to give aid in the higher classics, or to cram for examinations.[29]

That Newman lavished great care on his choice of tutors in the months leading up to the opening of the University—illustrated by his correspondence—indicates that he considered their selection to be of vital importance to the whole enterprise. Though the university needed an 'external manifestation' of lecturers and professors to satisfy, *inter alia*, public expectations, for its inner

---

[27] *Report of Her Majesty's Commissioners Appointed to Inquire into the State, Discipline, Studies and Revenues of the University and Colleges of Oxford: Together with the Evidence*, British Parliamentary Papers, 1852 xxii, pp. 95–6, 99–100.

[28] Report for the Year 1854–55, *Campaign*, pp. 41–2.

[29] Newman to Allies, 6 November 1857, *LD* xviii, p. 164.

working life it required something less conspicuous—namely tutors. For 'the beginning of an inward and real *formation*', the University needed,

> a few persons who thoroughly understand each other, and whom I entirely know; who can quickly and without show be bringing into shape the students who come to us. [...] We must *feel our* way—and get over a mass of prejudice and opposition. *No rules* can do this—but the zeal, energy and prudence of the individuals employed in the work.[30]

The general public needed to be informed about tutorial arrangements, not least because parents of potential students, benefactors and other well-wishers were anxious to know what academic system Newman was intending to adopt. In an article in the *Catholic University Gazette* entitled 'Professorial and Tutorial systems' Newman describes the benefits of both. After explaining what he meant by collegiate living, Newman emphasizes that the student gains still more by receiving tutorial supervision since it complements the education imparted at lectures. While the college was the main setting for general discipline (in the wider sense of 'training'), the college tutorial was the ideal vehicle for the student's *intellectual* discipline:

> his diligence will be steadily stimulated; he will be kept up to his aim; his progress will be ascertained, and his week's work, like a labourer's, measured. It is not easy for a young man to determine for himself whether he has mastered what he has been taught; a careful catechetical training, and a jealous scrutiny into his power of expressing himself and of turning his knowledge to account, will be necessary, if he is really to profit from the able Professors whom he is attending; and all this he will gain from the College Tutor.[31]

After the university had been running for two years Newman composed a digest of the tutorial system for the Scheme of Rules

---

[30] Newman to Wiseman, 23 January 1854, *LD* xvi, pp. 27–8.
[31] *HS* iii, p. 190.

and Regulations. There Newman explains that the duty of a tutor, as an assistant to the dean of a collegiate house, was 'certainly the moral, but more directly the intellectual care of his pupils, of which he relieves the Head'.[32] Turning to the heart of the tutor's task, Newman explains his hope that the tutor would adjust himself to the needs of each student and cater not just for those who were able and studious, but also for those who showed little love of learning, or had not developed study habits, or were backward. The tutor would oversee the reading of the more promising students by starting them off with advice, explaining the difficult passages of texts, testing them now and again, bringing to their attention points they might have overlooked, helping them with summaries, and generally keeping an eye on them. Different tactics were required for the backward, who would need support to remedy their shortcomings and make the most of their lectures, and for the idle, who would need to be kept on their toes and confronted with their lack of diligence in the run-up to exams. All this would demand of the tutor 'a sustained solicitude, and a mind devoted to his charge'.[33]

Newman enlarged on the possibilities of the tutor's role by suggesting that the way to a young man's heart lay through his studies, particularly in the case of the more able. Feeling grateful to the person who takes an interest in the things which are at that moment nearest to his heart, the student opens up to his tutor and from the books before them the two are

> led into conversation, speculation, discussion: there is the intercourse of mind with mind, with an intimacy and sincerity which can only be when none others are present. Obscurities of thought, difficulties in philosophy, perplexities of faith, are confidentially brought out, sifted, and solved; and a pagan poet or theorist may thus become the occasion of Christian advancement.[34]

---

[32]   *Campaign*, p. 117.
[33]   *Campaign*, p. 119.
[34]   *Campaign*, p. 119.

In this way the tutor forms the pupil's opinions and becomes the friend, perhaps the guide, of his life after university. Newman's lofty conception of the 'serious importance' and 'really interesting nature' of the tutor's office for the well-being of the university are captured in the following words:

> In this idea of a College Tutor, we see that union of intellectual and moral influence, the separation of which is the evil of the age. Men are accustomed to go to the Church for religious training, but to the world for the cultivation both of their hard reason and their susceptible imagination. A Catholic University will but half remedy this evil, if it aims only at professorial, not at private teaching. Where is the private teaching, there will be the real influence.[35]

It might be assumed that the founding rector of the Catholic University would have been too busy to involve himself directly in the pastoral affairs of the nascent institution, but this would be to misjudge Newman. Not only did he take on the role of dean of one of the collegiate houses, St Mary's, but he lent a hand with the tutoring there. It was typical of Newman that he resisted the temptation to hide away in administrative isolation. Writing to defend Newman's reputation as a Latinist after his death, one of the students at St Mary's recalled, 'I learnt more as to the writing of Latin from a few classes given privately to the men of his own house by Newman as its tutor than I did from a longer course' of lectures under the two Professors of Latin and Greek; 'to read the Greek tragedians in the same manner with Newman was, indeed, a classical treat I love to recall'.[36]

As Newman feared, the Irish priests running the other collegiate houses proved incapable of entering into the tutorial system, as their minds were steeped in seminary education, and during the four years of his rectorate, 1854–58, Newman battled in vain

---

[35]   *Campaign*, p. 120.

[36]   Charles de la Pasture to the editor, *The Tablet* 114:3618 (11 September 1909), p. 416.

to establish his system. In part this was because it was difficult to find suitable tutors, but it was also on account of the expense. Inevitably points of contention arose over the dovetailing of the tutorial and professorial systems, as, in practice, the complementary teaching roles of faculty and collegiate house meant that decisions arrived at by one party had to be transmitted to the other via Newman. But none of these problems caused Newman to have doubts about the importance of the tutorial system.

Rediscovering the Tutorial System

What can we learn from Newman and his idea of the tutor? Surely it is that personal influence is what gives any system its dynamism: the action of mind on mind, personality on personality, heart on heart. This is lacking in systems based solely on the lecture, and even more so when reliant on 'distance learning'. (The experience of lockdown and online learning in 2020 and 2021 has taught us this lesson in no uncertain terms, if we did not know it before.) And if, by means of personal influence, acquaintance becomes friendship, so much the better since friendship is the privileged way of doing good to someone; 'it requires one to be intimate with a person, to have a chance of doing him good', Newman once told his sister Jemima.[37] All this makes sense on realising that Newman was intent on giving a deep formation to students, a formation which operates at various levels: the intellectual, the social, the moral, the spiritual. Moreover, it operates on both human and supernatural levels, according to an understanding that has a long tradition.

Newman's insistence on the pastoral dimension of the academy is a lesson for us today. In many ways the Oriel common room of his time is a reflection of contemporary universities, which are populated by managers and administrators who personify an impoverished view of education and are blind to its deficiencies. The provost of Oriel was acting for an entire academic

---

[37]   8 February 1829, *LD* ii, p. 119.

ethos when he disallowed the approach of Newman and his tutorial colleagues. Newman the educator was looking for something that was absent from the Oxford of his day, and this is why his pastoral understanding of the tutorial charge meant so much to him.

Newman's daring designs for Oxford came to fruition some fifty years after he sought to reform the tutorial system in the late 1820s. Looking back from the twenty-first century, it seems overly ambitious to have attempted to introduce a modified version of the tutorial system into Ireland in the 1850s when the resources were pitiful and the demand non-existent. Yet it should be noted that Newman's aim was to replicate Oxbridge arrangements at a time when tutors were generally young academics who had not long graduated.

Today, financial pressures are making it hard for the Oxbridge colleges to maintain the tutorial system; elsewhere this luxury cannot even be contemplated. Everywhere, contact time is squeezed out by administrators looking to cut corners and costs. But if some or most of the lectures were to go—or remain—online, could this not free up time for lecturers to engage in small-group or individual tuition?

Newman's idea of the tutor's role touches on much that makes him special as an educational thinker—and much that is characteristic of him as a person: his love of his fellow human beings; his stress on the formative value of personal influence; his appreciation for the personal element in the process of understanding and embracing knowledge and faith; his patience with human weakness in the fitful process of maturation; his insistence on the practical. In particular, Newman held that moral and religious truths were best communicated and most likely to stir the heart by the power of personal influence, and that tutorials should be conducted on this basis. These views were not the outcome of research or reading, but rather the result of many years in education, during which he had established his own high ideals and sought to live them out.

PART SIX

The Great Battle

17 THE COMBAT OF TRUTH AND ERROR: NEWMAN AND CHESTERTON ON HERESY

STEPHEN MORGAN

O F THE MORE than twenty titles credited to him in his sole name in the catalogue of the British Library, not to mention the similar number of those jointly authored or edited works, two of Ian Ker's books stand as not merely monumental (both in size and significance) but as definitive: his biographies of John Henry Newman and Gilbert Keith Chesterton. These books are not simple biographical accounts of the life and work of the two men, but are, rather, works that combine the biographer's task of recounting the events, the words and the circumstances of their subjects, with an attentive, patient and thoughtful analysis of them seen through the eye of the theologian and literary scholar. Given the unrestricted access to the primary source material that Ian Ker was able to enjoy, aside from the inevitable biases that any author brings to any subject, it is no exaggeration to claim that it will be a generation or more before any such treatment of either man will either be necessary or, indeed, helpful. This is not to say that these works close off any further consideration of Newman and Chesterton but that further attempts at such a wide-ranging and complete account of the lives of these men in the short term risks being otiose or simply eccentric. On the contrary, the opportunities for scholars afforded by the sheer comprehensiveness of Ker's biographies provide an indispensable resource for anyone wanting to write about any particular aspect of either man's thought. What is more, they do so in a unique manner for one who would look at the two men together. They do this by virtue of the fact that the observer of Newman and Chesterton is, in these biographies, the same author, which brings a consistency of approach, a commonality of view which allows the consideration of any topic in the work of both men to be presented against a consistent framework of biographical detail and reflection. It is, of course, Ker's contention that there are many parallels between not simply the content of the work of Newman and Chesterton but also the circumstances of their creation, such that the one should be seen as 'the obvious successor' to the other.[1]

Newman and Chesterton could both be called 'occasional writers'. That is not to say that either man wrote only infrequently but that rather than being engaged in an over-arching systematic project, such as an academic theologian with time and the appropriate research funding might attempt over an extended period, they both wrote as the occasion demanded and most often in response to and with a spirit to engage in controversy.[2] When we come to the subject matter of theology, it is as well to remember that despite both having written deeply theological work, neither man understood himself to be a theologian in the professional, academic sense. Newman was primarily a priest whose pastoral and educational concerns predominated, and Chesterton understood himself to be a journalist and writer. Yet despite—or perhaps because of—these self-conceptions, across a wide range of genres the priest and the journalist were able to treat theological topics with a sophisticated subtlety—or, if they saw the occasion demand it, a direct robustness—worthy of the most dedicated theologian.

---

[1]   *Chesterton: Biography*, p. viii.

[2]   Newman himself observed that he had 'nearly always had to write by the piece and to order', (Newman to Malcolm MacColl, 1 February 1867, *LD* xxiii, p. 46) and that 'I write better when I am led to write by what comes in my way' (Newman to Lord Edward Howard, 1 August 1864, *LD* xxi, p. 178). As a journalist the impetus for much of Chesterton's writing was by definition the demands of the occasion. Ker recognises the parallel in the preface to the Chesterton biography.

Others have written thematic accounts of the thinking of Newman and Chesterton in particular areas, although comparative studies are rare enough.[3] As far as the author can establish, however, their approaches to the subject of heresy have not received significant comparative treatment. In a work of the present nature, any such comparative consideration can be but brief. Nonetheless, that does not mean that it cannot be valuable and reveals surprising similarities alongside very distinct takes on the question of what causes heresy, or, perhaps more accurately, what impels heretics. Given these constraints of space, this chapter will confine itself to looking at three aspects of how Newman and Chesterton treated the subject. The first aspect to be considered is methodological, the second is concerned with the subject matter of heresy, and the third with the sometimes trenchant views both men had of the character of heretics, and particularly of heresiarchs.

Write it Historically

Newman's approach to theology was marked by an overwhelming historical consciousness. It was not, as Cardinal Manning was to observe somewhat acidly, simply 'the old Anglican, patristic, literary, Oxford tone transplanted into the Church'.[4] Even before Newman's conversion in 1845, his approach had a subtle and sophisticated awareness of the processes of history that differed markedly from the donnish approach of a kind of theological antiquarianism—itself a caricature revealing more about the 'convertitis' that Manning was never quite able to shake off, than about Newman or anyone else.[5] The approach was, in fact, one

---

[3] For example, see S. Hanson, 'Thinking Chesterton Thinking Newman: English Catholic Revival and the Perambula Fidei', *Faith and Reason* 31:4 (2006), pp. 435–76; D. P. Deavel, 'An Odd Couple? A First Glance at Chesterton and Newman', *Logos: A Journal of Catholic Thought and Culture* 10:1 (2007), pp. 116–35.

[4] E. S. Purcell, *Life of Cardinal Manning, Archbishop of Westminster*, vol. ii (London: Macmillan, 1895), p. 322.

which neglected none of the dogmatic certainty concerning the articles of faith that comprise the *depositum fidei*, but sought to understand its origins, the context of its development and definition, in order to arrive at a deeper understanding, a real assent—to borrow a term from the *Grammar of Assent*. It was an approach which took seriously the circumstances and processes by which the Church came to understand the inexhaustible mysteries of God's definitive revelation of Himself, and to do so the better to understand the *nexus mysteriorum inter se*, something that the evangelicalism and latitudinarianism of his Anglican years and the ultramontanism and catechetical positivism of his Catholic years were manifestly ill-equipped to do. This approach *ad fontes*, this *ressourcement*, can, of course, have its drawbacks in relativising dogma and, in fact, denying the legitimacy of later developments that do not seem obvious in earlier teaching, as any observer of both the narrowly theological and wider ecclesial landscape of the last sixty years cannot fail to see. In *Newman on Vatican II*, Ker more than adequately demonstrates that this is neither inevitable nor, if Newman's ethos is adopted, is it even the natural outcome.[6]

Contemporary considerations of Newman's approach are, nevertheless, as likely to criticise Newman for subordinating history to dogma, rather than the other way around.[7] Indeed, Newman appear to agree. He asserts that, 'I know that the

---

[5]   The term 'convertitis' is of uncertain origin that describes the prickly hostility towards their former confession, that afflicts some religious converts. It is particularly noticeable in Anglican converts to Catholicism but it is by no means restricted to them. In the author's current position, he encounters almost daily converts to Catholicism from Confucianism, Buddhism, Daoism and Chinese folk religion who display the same tendency.

[6]   Ker, *Newman on Vatican II* (Oxford: Oxford University Press, 2014).

[7]   For example, this appears to be Rowan Williams's objection in R. Williams, 'Newman's "Arians" and the Question of Method in Doctrinal History', *Newman After a Hundred Years*, ed. I. T. Ker & A. G. Hill (Oxford: Clarendon Press, 1990), pp. 263–85.

evidences in the history of the divinity of Christianity and the Church are not overpowering—yet I consider them (of course) to be sufficient when men are anxious to acquit themselves to their maker and judge—Christianity is a great and imposing fact.'[8]

The central importance of heresy (and indeed heretics) in Newman's understanding of the development of Christian doctrine has received not inconsiderable scholarly consideration. Stephen Thomas's *Newman and Heresy* is a notable, though flawed, example.[9] Few authors have, it would seem, take sufficient account of the cause in which Newman deployed his approach during his Anglican years, the period when he gives most written attention to heresy. That is not to say that he ignored the subject during his Catholic years, but what he has to say is largely confined to brief mentions in letters and the occasional note in a sermon. In part it may be that this can be accounted for in his remark in the *Apologia* that,

> From the time that I became a Catholic, of course I have no further history of my religious opinions to narrate. In saying this, I do not mean to say that my mind has been idle, or that I have given up thinking on theological subjects; but that I have had no variations to record, and have had no anxiety of heart whatever. I have been in perfect peace and contentment; I never have had one doubt. I was not conscious to myself, on my conversion, of any change, intellectual or moral, wrought in my mind. I was not conscious of firmer faith in the fundamental truths of

---

[8]   Newman to William Dunn Gainsford, 27 August 1870, *LD* xxv, p. 197.

[9]   S. Thomas, *Newman and Heresy: The Anglican Years* (Cambridge: Cambridge University Press, 1991). Curiously given his main thesis, Thomas's major shortcoming is his failure to take his sources sufficiently seriously to try to accommodate even those that do not support his narrative and, too often to ignore, to construct complex, far from obvious explanations for events when simpler, more obvious ones exist and were apparent at the time.

Revelation, or of more self-command; I had not more fervour; but it was like coming into port after a rough sea; and my happiness on that score remains to this day without interruption.[10]

That is to say that there was simply no longer an personally existential dimension impelling him to deal with the matter. He is explicit enough on the subject when he sees the prospect of it rearing its head during the First Vatican Council's consideration of the definition of the dogma of Papal Infallibility:

What have we done to be treated as the Faithful never were treated before? When has definition of doctrine *de fide* been a luxury of devotion and not a stern painful necessity? Why should an aggressive and insolent faction be allowed to make the hearts of the just to mourn whom the Lord hath not made sorrowful? Why can't we be let alone when we have pursued peace and thought no evil?[11]

After the Council, when he was, at last, prevailed upon to write in defence of the definition that he had so regretted in anticipation, in his *Letter to the Duke of Norfolk*, Newman once again adopts the same methodology of historical parallelism that he had first deployed forty years previously and to exactly the same end.[12]

Newman's methodology enabled him the better to situate and explain the developments in Christian doctrine in the early Church—to give, in Rowan Williams's words, 'a *Verfallstheorie* of dogmatic language, the notion of formulation itself being a kind of betrayal of some richer truth [...] a necessary fall, a *felix culpa*, given that the Church lives in a history of change, contingency, and human sinfulness, and that the Gospel must be preached in a variety of contexts'.[13] It is not, however, the whole

---

[10]   *Apologia*, p. 238.
[11]   Newman to Ullathorne, 28 January 1870, *LD* xxv, pp. 18–19.
[12]   Newman, 'A Letter to the Duke of Norfolk', *Difficulties* ii, pp. 179–378.
[13]   Williams, *op. cit.*, p. 270.

truth and, indeed, overlooks Newman's apologetic purpose: the refutation of error in his own time. That this was his explicit purpose from the outset is made clear in a letter to his friend from his undergraduate days, Simeon Lloyd Pope, written as he was working on what was to become *The Arians of the Fourth Century*. He asked Pope for his 'good wishes and prayers [...] especially considering, as I do, that I am resisting the innovations of the day, and attempting to defend the work of men indefinitely above me (the Primitive Fathers) which is now assailed'.[14] Newman was not interested in the question of heresy in the Patristic period primarily for its own sake but in order to refute the heresy that he saw in the Church of England of his own time. For this he would adopt—in some respect it is possible to say develop—the methodology of the principle of historical parallel, which characterised so much of his theological approach and which gives the lie to Manning's accusation. In a licentiate dissertation at the Lateran University, Seán McLaughlin examined both the origin and structure of this methodology and the use to which Newman put it.[15] For the present purposes it will suffice to briefly summarise and adopt McLaughlin's argument.

Newman's treatment of heresy in the age of the Fathers was not to give either an historical or dogmatic account of the heresies themselves, or even to assert the Trinitarian and Christological truths from which they resiled. His purpose was current. In his first book, *The Arians of the Fourth Century* (1833) he makes it clear that he looked to the past to counter present danger, to the Church of the fourth century for the remedy to the ills of the Church of England in the nineteenth. His words, given their

---

[14]   Newman to Simeon Lloyd Pope, 9 April 1832, *LD* iii, p. 43.

[15]   S. McLaughlin, 'John Henry Newman's Challenge to Antioch: the Application of Primitive Christological Heresies to Theological Heterodoxy in Anglican England from 1833–1845' (unpublished STL, Pontificia Universitas Lateranensis, 2010). Ian Ker subsequently supervised McLaughlin's doctoral thesis, S. McLaughlin, 'Consumed yet Quickened by the Glance of God: John Henry Newman's Theology of Purgatory' (DPhil, University of Oxford, 2015).

foundational significance for an approach he would take to the relationship between history and Christianity thereafter, bear quoting *in extenso*:

> And so of the present perils, with which our branch of the Church is beset, as they bear a marked resemblance to those of the fourth century, so are the lessons, which we gain from that ancient time, especially cheering and edifying to Christians of the present day. Then as now, there was the prospect, and partly the presence in the Church, of an Heretical Power enthralling it, exerting a varied influence and a usurped claim in the appointment of her functionaries, and interfering with the management of her internal affairs. Now as then, 'whosoever shall fall upon this stone shall be broken, but on whomsoever it shall fall, it will grind him to powder'. Meanwhile, we may take comfort in reflecting, that, though the present tyranny has more of insult, it has hitherto had less of scandal, than attended the ascendancy of Arianism; we may rejoice in the piety, prudence, and varied graces of our Spiritual Rulers; and may rest in the confidence, that, should the hand of Satan press us sore, our Athanasius and Basil will be given us in their destined season, to break the bonds of the Oppressor, and let the captives go free.[16]

Newman's approach was, of course, to develop, mature and be used in furtherance of other objects than simply countering Christological heresies. He was too subtle and reflective a thinker for the approach to remain identical in all respects to that he took when first he embarked on the *Arians*. For example, in the last work of his period as an Anglican, *An Essay on the Development of Christian Doctrine*, Newman uses the historical parallelism not now to counter heresy, but rather in the search of the principle

---

[16] *Arians*, pp. 393–4.

of ecclesial authority which had, by then come to assume over-whelming personal importance for him. The fundamental meth-odology of historic parallelism remained. Newman was, as his first entry in the 1844 notebook he used when working on the *Essay on Development*, ever committed to '[w]rite it historically.'[17]

Chesterton offers no such explicit endorsement of any partic-ular historiography or even to the use of historical parallel to speak to the problems of his own day. His *Heretics* (1905), which, from its title, might be expected to at least touch upon the subject of its methodology, is silent on the matter, beyond a few refer-ences, such as to reverting 'to the doctrinal methods of the thirteenth-century'.[18] It took a different approach. Indeed, his adoption of the methods of the thirteenth century is seen only in his persistent questioning of the assumptions behind the opinions of those he examined, requiring answers that made proper distinctions and examining those answers against the measure of common sense and observable reality. He was, after all, in the words of the subtitle of Dale Ahlquist's book, 'the apostle of common sense'.[19] The other more colourful techniques employed in the past were not at his disposal nor was he the kind of man who might have had to resort to them had they been, considering them a product of 'the last decadence of the Middle Ages' and one which 'failed altogether in its object'.[20] Chesterton chose, instead, to proceed by pointing out the internal inconsistencies and the absurdity of the positions taken by his largely contempo-rary heretics, and in so doing demonstrated that they were, in fact, holding to opinions which cannot stand scrutiny when compared with observable reality. He was concerned with his targets in no respect other than as heretics: 'I wish to deal with my most distinguished contemporaries [...] in relation to the real

---

[17] 7 March 1844, 'Copybook on Development', BOA, B.2.8.
[18] G. K. Chesterton, *Heretics* (1905): *The Collected Works of G. K. Chesterton*, vol. i, ed. D. Dooley (San Francisco: Ignatius Press, 1986), p. 46.
[19] D. Ahlquist, *G. K. Chesterton. The Apostle of Common Sense* (2003).
[20] Chesterton, *Heretics*, pp. 39–40.

body of doctrine which they teach. I am concerned with [them as Heretics].' Rudyard Kipling was 'a vivid artist' and 'a vigourous personality' but he was still 'a Heretic—that is to say, a man whose view of things has the hardihood to differ from mine'. George Bernard Shaw was 'one of the most brilliant and one of the most honest men alive', yet Chesterton considered him a '[h]eretic— that is to say, a man whose philosophy is quite solid, quite coherent, and quite wrong.'[21]

In fact, he went further. Those who would reject the notion of religious dogma were, he argued, themselves guilty of a doctrinaire attachment to the rejection of dogmatic truth that is itself nothing more than dogma. That dogma was to be found in the rejection of the idea that 'cosmic truth was so important that every one ought to bear independent testimony'. Instead, it appeared that '[t]he modern idea is that cosmic truth is so unimportant that it cannot matter what any one says.'[22] As he memorably put it, 'And so underlying all the contemporary heresies was the heresy that "Everything matters—except everything."'[23] The parallels with Pope Benedict XVI's expression, from the homily he preached as Dean of the College of Cardinals before the conclave that elected him, 'the dictatorship of relativism which does not recognise anything as definitive',[24] are impossible to overlook. This doctrinaire attachment to an 'anti-dogmatic principle', as Newman had called it, becomes the firmest held dogma. As if to close the *chiasmus* with his earlier remark, towards the end of *Heretics* Chesterton puts it in these words, 'Everything will be denied. Everything will become a creed.'[25]

---

[21]   *Ibid.*, p. 46.

[22]   *Ibid.*, p. 41.

[23]   *Ibid.*, p. 40.

[24]   J. Ratzinger, Homily at Mass *Pro Eligendo Romano Pontifice*, 18 April 2005.

[25]   Chesterton, *Heretics*, p. 207.

Sundry Heresies lately Sprung Up

Given the purpose of his methodology, it was hardly surprising that Newman engaged in a detailed analysis of the nature and causes of the heresies that so beset the Church of the fourth and fifth centuries, nor that he would come to locate the spirit of heresy in the Church at Antioch during that period. Since his target was the contemporary Church of England, where it seemed that no amount of dogmatic heterodoxy would bring effective censure, he needed to demonstrate not only the seriousness with which the early Church took heresy but both the mechanisms it used to determine its developing orthodoxy and—no less importantly—the spirit out of which heresy sprang. The mature fruit of those investigations can be seen in the *Essay on Development*, where fundamentally the question being asked is one of authority: where can the Catholic Church be located in those confused and confusing times? That is, however, to anticipate the outcome of a decade and more of concern.

By the fourth decade of the nineteenth century, what Newman was later to call the 'spirit of liberalism'[26] had achieved an entrenched position in the Church of England. Its appeal to intellectual excellence had even seduced Newman for a while. The descent into Unitarianism of his friend Blanco White shocked him, as did that of his brother Francis in later life. What is more, despite an evangelical revival, of sorts, this spirit of liberalism was such that the denial of settled Trinitarian and Christological doctrine was seen as no bar to preferment in the Church by law established. Further proof of this for Newman, who was heavily involved in opposing the nomination, was the election to the Regius Chair of Divinity at Oxford of Renn Hampden, whose views were adjacent to if not entirely identical with Sabellianism and Socinianism. Hampden was later elevated to the bench of bishops.[27] Even his early mentor at Oriel, Richard

---

[26] 'Biglietto Speech', *Campaign*, p. 513.

[27] Renn Dickson Hampden was Regius Professor of Divinity from 1836 to

Whately was, Newman thought 'verging then towards Sabellianism',[28] and yet this was seemingly no obstacle to his being made
Archbishop of Dublin. Once shaken from his own '[a]rianizing',[29]
Newman came to see that the attachment to orthodox dogmas
in the Church of England was not as secure as once he had
thought and that this was not merely a matter to which he could
remain indifferent. Indeed, he saw that exactly the Arianism to
which Whately himself had accused him of inclining had been
present in the Church of England from it's earliest days.[30] Whilst
Paul Avis's opinion that 'Newman saw heresy everywhere'[31] is, to
say the least, an exaggeration of hyperbolic proportions, it is true
to say that between 1827 and 1833, Newman became acutely
sensitive to the heterodoxy that had, he now came to see, been
more or less unchallenged in the Church of England since its
inception. What he came but slowly to realise was the issue was
not so much one of the heresies themselves *per se*, or even the
role that heresy had played in the forgeing of orthodoxy, but
rather a question of how it was possible, through the contingen-

---

1847, and thereafter Bishop of Hereford from 1847 until his death in 1868.

[28]   *AW*, p. 211. Whately was to come to 'adhere to an explicitly anti-patristic,
exclusively economic understanding on the Trinity' (G. Zuijdwegt,
'Richard Whately', *The Oxford Handbook of John Henry Newman*, ed. F.
D. Aquino & B. J. King (Oxford: Oxford University Press, 2018), p. 206).

[29]   *Apologia*, p. 13.

[30]   As McLaughlin notes, as early as 1552 – the year of Cranmer's Articles of
Religion – 'a commision was directed to the Archbishop of Canterbury,
the Bishop of London, and other worshipful persons in Kent to make
inquiry after sundry heresies lately sprung up [...] chiefly, as it would seem,
if not entirely, those of the [Anabaptists] and Arians' (McLaughlin,
'Challenge to Antioch', p. 17). See J. Strype, *Ecclesiastical Memorials:
Relating Chiefly to Religion, and Its Reformation Under the Reigns of King
Henry VIII, King Edward VI, and Queen Mary the First With the Appen-
dixes Containing the Original Papers, Records. Containing the Continuation and Conclusion of the Reign of King Edward the Sixth*, vol. iii (London:
Samuel Bagster, 1816), p. 189.

[31]   P. D. L. Avis, *Anglicanism and the Christian Church: Theological Resources
in Historical Perspective* (Edinburgh: T & T Clark, 1989), p. 247.

cies of history, to establish how doctrines adopted and defined in later centuries could be seen to cohere with the original *depositum fidei*, with 'the faith once delivered unto the Saints' (Jude 3). It was no less than a search for the authority that he came to see Anglicanism lacked: it was a search for the Church.[32]

Recollecting these years from the tranquility of forty years distance and against the background of the papal confirmation of his own unimpeachable orthodoxy that his elevation to the College of Cardinals by Pope Leo XIII in 1878 represented, Newman could point to the precise problem against which he had expended so much energy, then and across his whole subsequent life:

> I rejoice to say, to one great mischief I have from the first opposed myself. For thirty, forty, fifty years I have resisted to the best of my powers the spirit of liberalism in religion [...] the doctrine that there is no positive truth in religion, but that one creed is as good as another, and this is the teaching which is gaining substance and force daily. It is inconsistent with any recognition of any religion, as *true*. It teaches that all are to be tolerated, for all are matters of opinion. Revealed religion is not a truth, but a sentiment and a taste; not an objective fact, not miraculous; and it is the right of each individual to make it say just what strikes his fancy.[33]

Given the *chiasmus* in *Heretics* referred to above, it is hardly surprising that Chesterton could describe its author as 'the flashing arrow that was Newman'.[34] Chesterton similarly saw that heresy lay in precisely the fancy Newman had identified.

---

[32] For a detailed examination of this process and its eventual resolution, see S. D. Morgan, *John Henry Newman and the Development of Doctrine: Encountering Change, Looking for Continuity* (Washington, DC: Catholic University of America Press, 2021).

[33] 'Biglietto Speech', *Campaign*, p. 513.

[34] Chesterton, *The Victorian Age in Literature* (1912): *Collected Works of G. K. Chesterton* xv, ed. A. S. Dale (1989), p. 438, cited in Ker, *Chesterton: A Biography*, p. 328, n. 21.

As Ker points out, Chesterton had a conception of heresy that saw it not as a liberating thing. His *Orthodoxy*, which was intended to clarify that what he had described negatively in *Heretics* could be presented positively and to clarify, in response to critics of the earlier work, that he wanted to present the case for Christian orthodoxy,[35] makes that abundantly clear, albeit implicitly. It was a much later work, however, in which Chesterton expresses this explicitly. In his 1923 biography of St Francis of Assisi he notes the restricting nature of heresy, noting that it has always been 'an effort to narrow the Church',[36] by conforming it to the limitations imposed upon the truth by the choices of the heresiarch. The specific heresies that he attacks in *Heretics* can all be seen to conform to this pattern. Kipling narrows love of country to admiration of national strength; George Bernard Shaw withers humanity because he sees not its wonder but its limitations; H. G. Wells 'is not quite clear enough of the narrower scientific outlook to see that there are somethings which actually ought not to be scientific'.[37] The list goes on and Chesterton ranges widely in search of targets—the Yellow Press, the Smart Set, Slum Novelists and even Celts (the present author is a proud Welshman) and Celtophiles find themselves in the crosshairs of sights—but all share in what amounts to a lack of a broad-minded vision, a failure to see the bigger picture. In a collection of essays published late in his life, in fact the year before he died, and here using the historical parallel of the heresies of Luther and Henry VIII to make a point about the character of all heresies, Chesterton defined it thus: 'A heresy is' the attachment to 'a truth which hides other truths'.[38]

---

[35]   Chesterton, *Orthodoxy* (1908): *Collected Works of G. K. Chesterton* i, p. 215.

[36]   G. K. Chesterton, *St Francis of Assisi* (1923): *Collected Works of G. K. Chesterton* ii, ed. R. Azar & G. Marlin (1986), p. 128, cited in Ker, *Chesterton: Biography*, p. 505.

[37]   Chesterton, *Heretics*, pp. 59, 70 & 77.

[38]   Chesterton, *The Well and the Shallows* (1935): *Collected Works of G. K. Chesterton* iii, ed. by J. J. Thompson (1990), p. 505.

A Man of Singularly Small Views

It is impossible to read Newman's *Arians* without coming away with the impression that Newman thought Arius to be a thoroughgoing scoundrel. He approvingly quoted Alexander of Alexandria writing to Alexander of Constantinople as writing that 'Our present heretics have drunk up the dregs of the impiety of these men, and are their secret offspring; Arius and Achillas, and their party of evil-doers.'[39] He went on to accuse the heresiarch of being '[t]urbulent by character', of displaying 'artifice', 'impiety', and of being 'presumptuous'.[40] Strict biographical accuracy was not Newman's concern here, any more than it was when he later treated of Paul of Samosata, Eusebius, Sabellius, Eutyches, Apollinaris or Nestorius. What concerned him, if not quite as much as the particular doctrinal errors involved in their eponymous heresies, was the connection between the ethos of heresy and the moral character of the heresiarch. As Stephen Thomas observes, 'Prominent [in Newman's thinking] is the view that heresy springs from worldliness', from 'the tragic failure of the inner man'.[41] This worldliness is a product of luxury for Newman, who concluded that 'coldness in faith is the sure consequence of relaxation of morals'.[42] Of course much of Newman's writing here conformed to his apologetic purpose and, one might say, had been more polemic than was strictly necessary to make his point—certainly enough to justify his ambition to be thought of as a 'hot headed man' in this controversy.[43] It was, nonetheless, a central part of his argument that heresy was as much a moral issue as one of dogmatic definition, that doctrinal error and bad character are never far away from one another.

---

[39] Newman, *Arians*, p. 24.
[40] Newman, *Arians*, pp. 23, 114, 232 & 270.
[41] Thomas, *op. cit.*, p. 43.
[42] Newman, *Arians*, p. 9.
[43] Newman to his sister Harriet, 16 October 1831, *LD* ii, p. 367.

Chesterton might be thought to have taken a more generous attitude to his heretics, if the praise he heaped upon their characters in *Heretics* is to be taken at face value. Heretics were wrong, certainly, but were they bad? When he describes the common characteristics of all heretics in *The Thing: why I am Catholic* (1930), there appears to be no hint of moral censure:

> Every great heretic [...] always exhibited three remarkable characteristics in combination. First, he picked out some mystical idea from the Church's bundle or balance of mystical ideas. Second, he used that one mystical idea against all the other mystical ideas. Third (and most singular), he seems generally to have had no notion that his own mystical idea was a mystical idea, at least in the sense of a mysterious or dubious or dogmatic idea.[44]

In that 'having no notion', he appears to be acquitting heretics of the charge of being culpably bad. This, however, would be to mistake a rhetorical device for his real opinion. Chesterton praises the moral character of his chosen targets precisely to deflect the accusation of holding a personal *animus noxialis* against each of them and to ensure that his readers focus on the precise heresy he attributes to them, and on that alone. It is true, as David Dooley puts it in the introduction to the first volume of the Ignatius Press collected works (37 vols), that he viewed Robert Blatchford, the editor of *Clarion* and the man with whom Chesterton had been engaged in a lengthy argument for nearly two years, between 1903 and 1904, which was to be the spur to the writing of *Heretics*, as 'not an enemy but a genial adversary'.[45] Chesterton praised his interlocutor's large-heartedness in generous terms in the first of the papers in the exchange edited and published by George Haw in 1904: 'Mr Blatchford's magnanimity, like all magnanimity, is

---

[44] Chesterton, *The Thing: Why I Am a Catholic* (1930): *Collected Works of G. K. Chesterton* iii, p. 152.

[45] D. Dooley, 'Introduction', *Collected Works of G. K. Chesterton* i, p. 11.

profoundly philosophical and wise.'[46] Despite these laudatory remarks, it is clear from the three articles and from the remarks in *Heretics* that Chesterton did not view Blatchford—or any of his other targets—with an entirely benign gaze. At best they were, for him, ignorant of the damage their heresies caused, but their choice to privilege one aspect of the truth to the prejudice of the whole made them all the more complicit in the evil that ensued. Kipling's idolising of national strength, which manifests itself in an aggressive militarism, is prone to 'shrill irritation' when speaking of races he looks down upon and in the consequences of his heresy '[h]e is the philanderer of nations'.[47] Indeed Chesterton compares him to Cecil Rhodes, who was a bad man 'with singularly small views'.[48] Here again he returned to his conception of heresy as a narrowing, as he did, perhaps rather surprisingly, when writing of Nietzsche in *Orthodoxy*, as 'truly a very timid thinker'.[49] Shaw fares no better: for all his honesty, justice and greatness, he is a man unable see 'things as they really are',[50] with the result that he is, in fact, a misanthrope. H. G. Wells is, because of his 'splendid mental equipment', all the more culpable for his 'immoral hero-worship'.[51] In the end, for Chesterton, men (and no doubt women, but those in his sights are almost entirely men) are morally responsible for their heresies and the wickednesses that follow in their wake, all the more so because of the immorality of the choices they make, whether they are ignorant of their absurdity or not.

---

[46] Chesterton, 'Christianity and Rationalism', *The Religious Doubts of Democracy*, ed. George Haw (1904): *Collected Works of G. K. Chesterton* i, p. 373.

[47] Chesterton, *Heretics*, p. 59.

[48] *Ibid.*, p. 61.

[49] Chesterton, *Orthodoxy*, p. 309.

[50] Chesterton, *Heretics*, p. 67.

[51] Chesterton, *Heretics*, pp. 77 & 82.

Conclusion

In this brief chapter, it has been possible only to provide the briefest of sketches of how Newman and Chesterton approached the question of heresy. Both men, in their differing styles, were much concerned with the question of truth and of religious truth in particular. It mattered to them greatly because to be indifferent to it or, worse still, to be mistaken about it had (and has) consequences. Both men rejected entirely the proposition 'No theological doctrine is any thing more than an opinion which happens to be held by bodies of men. Therefore, e.g. no creed, as such, is necessary for salvation.'[52] Consequently, for neither man could the question of heresy be avoided, and they dealt with it in their respective characteristic styles. Both were talented polemicists, both unafraid of coming at what might have seemed familiar subjects from new and unexpected directions.

Newman's development of the use of historical parallel allowed him to show (often painstakingly) that the problems faced in the Church of his own time could usefully be illuminated by understanding problems in the distant past. Whilst Antioch in the fourth and fifth centuries was not a perfect analogue for the Church of England in the nineteenth—after all, no analogy walks on four legs—the parallels were sufficiently close to enable a workable diagnosis of the problem as a necessary antecedent step to finding the remedy. Chesterton approached the subject of heresy with a different methodology. He looked directly at the errors being proposed and showed that they had about them the absurdity of too narrow a view: 'what [can they] know of England who know only England'.[53]

Whilst the heresies (and heretics) with which Newman and Chesterton varied—and the latter dealt with heresies which were arguably the inevitable working out of the widespread adoption of the anti-dogmatic principle opposed by the former with such

---

[52]   Newman, *Apologia*, p. 294.
[53]   Chesterton, *Heretics*, p. 59.

consistent and life-long vigour—they all shared a common origin in the asserting of the veracity of a part of the truth to the prejudice of the whole. A concentration on one detail, one aspect of the conspectus of truth, of reality, so distorted the heretic's view of the entire picture as to bring not only error but clear and present danger.

Finally, both men understood, almost instinctively, that heresies carried within them a moral guilt imputable to the heresiarch (if not always to the heretic) that cannot be entirely excused by invincible ignorance. What begins in what Newman might have called a deficient ethos ends in what Chesterton called 'war in the night'.[54]

There is one other similarity between Newman and Chesterton of which mention must be made and which is not confined to their concern with heresy. They are both masters of the memorable written expression; they are both unsurpassably quotable. In part that is the reason that this chapter contains so many quotations from their own words and relatively few references to the extensive secondary literature. It is simply too challenging to render in words other than each man's own both the content and flavour of their distinctive expressions of the essential truths they seek to convey. It is, therefore, fitting to end this consideration in honour of the biographer of the two men's respective battle with heresy, that 'combat of truth and error',[55] with the words excised in the earlier quotation from Newman's great Biglietto Speech: 'Never did Holy Church need champions against [heresy] more sorely than now, when, alas! it is an error overspreading, as a snare, the whole earth.'[56] In Newman and Chesterton she has them.

---

[54] *Ibid.*, p. 46.

[55] The expression 'combat of truth and error' was first used by Newman in *Anglican Difficulties* i, p. 387. There he writes: 'The drama of religion and the combat of truth and error were ever one and the same.' He repeats the expression, with minor changes in the punctuation in *Apologia* p. 215.

[56] 'Biglietto Speech', *Campaign*, p. 513.

18 DE-CHRISTIANISING ENGLAND: NEWMAN, MILL AND THE STATIONARY STATE

Fr Dermot Fenlon

Deism is not a new creation of the Enlightenment: it is merely the return of the Deus, otiosus of the mythical religions.

Cardinal Joseph Ratzinger[1]

I ever tell friends that they must look among Catholics, not for natural excellence, but supernatural. But many Catholics do not like to allow this.

Newman to J. Spencer Northcote, 18 June 1862[2]

I T IS WELL to remember that the mythical religions of antiquity subserved a purpose of social control. The same is true of the mythology of secularism in the contemporary world. The wars of the Reformation frightened men of property. In England, Deism after 1660 mounted, in the name of reason, science and history, an assault on the sacramental principle embedded in the Anglican liturgy. A brand of Latitudinarian Christianity, minimising doctrine, established the preponderant tone of Anglican Christianity. The proposed emasculation of Christianity, the project of Hume and Gibbon was, however, postponed by the triumph of Wesley and the Evangelical Revival. The political requisite of a Christian Crusade against Napoleon

---

[1]   J. Ratzinger, *The Feast of Faith* (San Francisco: Ignatius Press, 1986), p. 22.

[2]   *LD* xx, p. 210.

ensured that it was only after 1815 that the attack on Christianity in the English-speaking world was renewed and 'became routine'. The role of John Stuart Mill in that enterprise, the hidden, tactical character of his prose, and especially the importance of his private correspondence, was first identified by Philip Hughes in 1950, and then by Maurice Cowling, in a work which became the prelude to a remarkably penetrating study of the assault on Christianity in England, *Religion and Public Doctrine in Modern England* (3 vols, 1980–2001).[3]

Cowling's achievement was to identify Mill as the father and teacher of a new clerical estate, 'the clerisy' (Coleridge's description adopted by Mill). Newman, Pusey, Keble and Hurrell Froude called it the 'Aristocracy of Talent'. Each of the parties understood the process as a replacement for the clergy by a secular administration deferring to the supposedly empirical criteria deriving from the university intelligentsia. Within the clerisy, by the close of the nineteenth century, Mill came to exercise what John Morley, secretary to the Liberal Party, described as 'pontifical authority'.[4] His function was to supply a doctrine—that of zero population growth—and a rhetorical strategy, applicable through Common Law institutions, to Africa, India and the Colonial World, based on a norm of 'scientific' conduct replacing the imperatives of traditional religion. After World War II that

---

[3] See vol. 2 (Cambridge: Cambridge University Press, 1985), pp. 104–8 for the 'routine' character of the nineteenth century attack. The author's *earlier Mill and Liberalism* (1963) was republished in a second edition in 1990, with a political preface which may be thought unhelpful. See also my essay 'The "Aristocracy of Talent" and the "Mystery" of Newman', *Louvain Studies* 15 (1990), pp. 203–25. For the Enlightenment in England, see J. G. A. Pocock, *Barbarism and Religion* (2 vols, 1999). For Philip Hughes see the reference in footnote 23 below.

[4] Morley, *Recollections*, vol. i (New York: Macmillan, 1917), p. 55. The expression is quoted in Janice Carlisle, *John Stuart Mill on the Writing of Character* (1991), p. 324. The death of Gladstone in 1896 may be regarded as the moment of Mill's posthumous triumph and the final displacement of Christianity as the doctrine of the state.

became the objective of American foreign policy, pursued through the United Nations and World Health Organisation. Reproductive medicine became the key to command of resources through control of population. The strategy was Anglo-American. Mill held an important place in the origination of that policy.

In this paper I wish to explore the role of Mill, especially as we see it reflected in his correspondence with Harriet Taylor. For it was through Harriet that Mill, the 'saint' of nineteenth-century rationalism, became the 'pontifical authority' constantly invoked in legislation which throughout the twentieth century advanced the secularisation of the reproductive act. The emptying out of religious meaning from the encounter between man and woman entailed an increasing tendency to regard the human child as a threat, a burden, or a designer product, in which the designer was no longer God. The child became a utilitarian possession. It was through Mill and Harriet Taylor that the difference between the sexes increasingly came to be considered a matter of social construction, and therefore of potential reconstruction, rather than more fundamentally, and biologically, 'given'. The loss of that 'giveness' is at the root of the confusion of identity which is the hallmark of contemporary sexuality and human culture. It is the final *Entzauberung*, the loss of meaning surrounding the reproductive act and invading the whole human life. Already, Mill, who himself felt bitterly the taunt of being a 'manufactured man', a 'mere reasoning machine', sought to redress his dilemma by looking to Harriet Taylor for conversion to a credo of feelings, which in turn supplied the criterion of 'harm' proposed by Mill as the basis of moral legislation—'harm', that is to say, which by the late twentieth century had come to mean, especially, to others' 'feelings'.[5]

---

[5] Roger Scruton's *Sexual Desire* (1986) and *An Intelligent Person's Guide to Modern Culture* (1998) identify the 'disenchantment of the sexual act' as constituting the essence of modern secularism. So, in a different way, does Alastair Macintyre's *After Virtue* (1981). The 'emptying out' of the sacramental presence of God finds its completion, therefore, in the destruction of matrimony. Scruton, though not Cowling, identifies the aesthetics of 'right feeling' as the only available substitute for faith—

It is no coincidence that Mill should have been invoked with canonical regularity in the legislation of the later twentieth century: in the discussion surrounding the Wolfenden Report on homosexuality in 1959; in the Abortion Law Reform Association's account of its victory in 1967; in Baroness Warnock's appeal to the *Uses of Philosophy*, where Mill is enlisted to sustain the recommended view of the Warnock Report on Human Fertilisation and Embryology, that 'In real life morality [...] there is no single "correct" view'.[6] Finally, and most interestingly, in Conrad Lord Russell's recent *Guide to Liberalism*, the views of Mill on liberty have become 'for the first time', so we are told, 'part of the essence of the Liberal creed'. That creed, he informs us, has gained its 'extra boost' from the contraceptive pill and the sexual revolution, which ensure that 'there will never again be a single agreed standard of sexual morals'. In such a world we must 'whether we like it or not' adopt Mill's concept of individuality.[7]

---

thereby adopting the aesthetic–moral criterion proposed in Mill's *Essay on Bentham and Coleridge* (1840) which, taken up by Matthew Arnold, and developed by F. R. Leavis, has remained the 'substitution for Christianity' proposed by English culture since the nineteenth century. I wish to acknowledge Professor Robert George's helpful identification of an 'ethos' of 'good feeling' as the proposed substitute for the Ten Commandments in contemporary Liberalism (viva voce contribution to the discussion following the first version of this paper at Cambridge University in July 2000). For Mill's sensitivity to the taunt of being 'a manufactured man', see his *Autobiography*, ed. Jack Stillinger (Oxford: Oxford University Press, 1969), p. 93. The standard edition of Mill's output is the *Collected Works* published by the University of Toronto Press. I have used whatever editions have come to hand.

6   Mary Warnock, *A Question of Life. The Warnock Report on Human Fertilisation and Embryology* (Oxford: Basil Blackwell, 1985), p. x. For Warnock's appeal to Mill as the authority for a utilitarian jurisprudence linked with an irreducible moral pluralism, see Mary Warnock, *The Uses of Philosophy* (1992), ch. 6, 'Towards a Moral Consensus', pp. 84–101. See also Keith Hindell & Madeleine Simms, *Abortion Law Reformed: With a Foreword by David Steel*, MP (1971), with a preliminary citation of Mill's *Essay on Liberty*.

7   *An Intelligent Person's Guide to Liberalism* (London: Duckworth, 1999), p. 90.

What Lord Russell understands by that is illustrated by his recollection of 'an elderly Oxford Fellow' complaining in 1969 'that undergraduates were no longer content to be able to have their girlfriends in all night: they were demanding a *right* to do so'. From that, Lord Russell concludes, the sexual revolution, as a matter of right, ensures that 'the moral basis of authority has been changed'. Given that change, he tells us, we are to call on Mill. What for? For the defence of liberty—the individual's 'right' to 'choose'.[8]

This is Mill's language alright. Is it also what he means? In what follows I wish to raise the question whether it is not merely an accurate, but a sufficient account of what Mill intended, and to examine Mill in the light of what his contemporary, John Henry Newman, thought about the issues he raised. For Mill and Newman stand to each other and to us as the very type of secularism and its opposite—Mill the rationalist, Newman the shepherd of souls, uttering the response of the Church, in the mind of Christ, to the crisis of humanity at the end of a millennium which has seen the progressive de-Christianisation of the industrial West.

To begin with Mill. Mill is modern. He was born and grew up without baptism 'in London', he tells us, 'on 20th May 1806 [...] the eldest son of James Mill, the author of the *History of British India*'. British India hung over Mill as a destiny from birth. His father worked for the East India Company. As a boy, the young Mill helped his father to correct the proofs of his *magnum opus*. As a man he rose to be 'chief conductor of correspondence with the Native States of India'. Father and son: Mill was a child of the eighteenth century; he became preceptor of the twentieth. His influence, more than that of Marx, was decisive for the contemporary world order.

Mill was educated to reform humanity. His father, the son of an Angus farmer, lost his Christian faith as a student for the Scottish Church. He embraced the faith of the Scottish Enlightenment, and imported it to London. 'My father', wrote Mill,

---

8   *Ibid.*

'impressed upon me from the first [...] that the question "Who made me?" cannot be answered.' At the same time 'he taught me to take the strongest interest in the Reformation, as the great and decisive contest against priestly tyranny for liberty of thought'.[9] What Mill understood by that was to become clear in his account, given in 1848, of the imminent replacement of Christianity by the principles of 'political economy':

> The principles of the Reformation have reached as low
> down in society as reading and writing, and the poor will
> not much longer accept morals and religion of other
> people's prescribing.[10]

Instead, the poor were to accept the morals prescribed by Mill's 'principles' disseminated through the schools, the press, and the institutions of the state. Among these, the central principle was the education of the people in the prevention of birth. That was not an easy undertaking in the Christian climate of Victorian England. Indeed, it would only become, what Mill wanted it to become, a 'duty', in the following century. With the arrival of the concept of contraceptive 'duty', Christianity ceased to be the shaping influence in English life and culture.

Meanwhile, 'liberty of thought' meant for Mill's own early education at home, Greek at the age of three, the histories of Gibbon and Robertson between the ages of four and seven, logic, leading on to Hobbes by the age of twelve, all preparing the young Mill to bring to completion the Scottish Enlightenment and to domesticate England in the principles of the French Revolution, not with the weaponry of steel but through a civil service grounded in the logic of Mill's *Principles of Political Economy*.

Mill's hero, he tells us, was Condorcet. In Bentham he found what he called his 'unifying conception [...] a creed, a doctrine, a philosophy, in one among the best senses of the word, a

---

9   Mill, *Autobiography*, p. 27.
10   *Principles of Political Economy*, ed. Jonathan Riley (Oxford: Oxford University Press, 1994), p. 135.

religion'. Through Auguste Comte he learned to call it the religion of humanity. It was to be propounded by the educational methods of von Humboldt with the consent and indeed co-operation of Christians. 'From the winter of 1821, when I first read Bentham'—Mill was fifteen years old—'I had what might be called an object in life; to be a reformer of the world.' Not just England, mind you, but the world; India, in the wake of the Napoleonic Wars, was secure, and India *meant* the world. It has become more so. Through its economy, and through its participation in British common law, India has become central to the mind of the twenty-first century.

In 1823 Mill followed his father into the East India Company. By the close of the decade he was proposing, through the pages of the *Westminster Review*, a change of public opinion on the fundamentals of moral conduct. Among Mill's youthful acquaintances 'Malthus's population principle was a banner, and point of union.' This 'great doctrine', he says, we took up 'in the contrary sense' to that intended by Malthus. To improve mankind, the first step was to reduce it.

Malthus, a clergyman of the Church of England, had intended a warning against faith in the perfectibility of man through science and economics alone; in later life, he urged a limitation of population growth by self-restraint. The younger Mill and his associates now turned Malthus on his head. The indefinite improvement of humanity must be secured precisely by population restriction. Mill called it 'the sole means' of human improvement. The poor must be educated accordingly.[11]

Mill belonged to what may be called the 'Malthusian turning point'. The new Poor Law Act of 1834 made the children of the poor the target of the municipal ratepayer. The middle classes were resolved that the poor should no longer be what hitherto they had always been, their Christian responsibility. The Marriage Registry Act of 1835 and the Municipal Corporation Act of 1836 replaced

---

[11]   *Ibid.*, p. 64. See Adrian Desmond & James Moore, *Darwin* (1991), pp. 153–4 for Harriet Martineau and the 'gangrene of the State'.

the Christian idea of charity with a purely secular regulation of human relations. When Darwin, on board the Beagle, in 1834, received a packet of booklets advocating sexual restraint as a way of escaping starvation, he distributed the booklets to the men on board. They were the 'political-economical tales' of delayed marriages and couples rescued from the poor house, written by the government-sponsored novelist Harriet Martineau. In these booklets she described the poor as 'the gangrene of the State'. It was thus that Darwin in due course arrived at the metaphors of natural selection and the survival of the fittest. The doctrine of zero population growth as the basis of sustainable development, at once economic and biological, contraceptive and educational, the doctrine, in short, of the Reith Lectures and of the World Health Organisation as we know it today, was born of the Malthusian moment. Mill was among the earliest promoters of the creed. He was the philosopher who supplied the requisite mental equipment for the replacement of Christianity.

In the autumn of 1826, he experienced his first great crisis of faith:

> I was in a dull state of nerves, such as everyone is liable to; unsusceptible to enjoyment or pleasurable excitement; one of those moods when what is pleasure at other times becomes insipid or indifferent; the state, I should think, in which converts to Methodism usually are, when smitten by their first 'conviction of sin'. In this frame of mind it occurred to put the question direct to myself: 'suppose that all your objects in life were realised; that all the changes in institutions and opinions which you are looking forward to, could be completely effected at this very instant: would this be a great joy and happiness to you?' And an irrepressible self-consciousness distinctly answered No! At this my heart sank within me: the whole foundation on which my life was constructed fell down. All my happiness was to have been found in the continual pursuit of this end. The end had ceased to charm, and how could there ever again

be any interest in the means? I seemed to have nothing left
to live for.[12]

In this condition he read Wordsworth and discovered Coleridge.
The Romantic revolt of the nineteenth century against the
eighteenth—a world of inner feeling—seized him. In 1830, at the
age of twenty-four, he met Harriet Taylor. She was twenty-three.
She was married with young children. Mill's views on women's
suffrage impressed her.

By the end of 1832 'she to whom my life is devoted', wrote Mill,
had sought from him a memorandum, 'a written exposition of
my opinions' on divorce.[13] There was no liaison between them.
Harriet insisted on Mill making this known when they eventually
married in a registry office after her husband's death in 1851. But
the twenty-year friendship caused scandal, and accounts for
much of Mill's alienation from and inner hatred of English
society. That was the driving force behind his *Essay on Liberty*:
his chosen target, Christian, and specifically English Protestant
public opinion. Indeed, if we would understand the motivations
of published works, we must take full account of the inner life
disclosed in the letters and papers of Mill and Harriet Taylor.

In his response to Harriet's appeal for a memorandum in
1832–33, Mill considered that first choice in matrimony should
'very generally (be) persevered in [...] repeated trials for happiness
have the most mischievous effects on all minds'; children would
be 'better cared for if their parents remain together.' The family
remained, for Mill, the cradle of humanity.

Chastity before marriage was, however, an 'arbitrary ceremo-
nial'. Affection was the sufficient criterion of conjugality.[14]

---

[12]   Mill, *Autobiography*, pp. 80–1.
[13]   *Sexual Equality. Writings by John Stuart Mill, Harriet Taylor Mill, and
       Helen Taylor*, ed. Ann P. Robson & John M. Robson (Toronto: University
       of Toronto Press, 1994), p. 3.
[14]   Mill borrowed here from Robert Owen, just, as from Coleridge he
       borrowed the idea of the 'clerisy'. See *ibid.*, p. 16, for the reference to Owen.

Harriet's memorandum of the same date strikes a different note. She is imbued with the vision of a brave new world:

> If I could be Providence to the world for a time, for the express purpose of raising the condition of women, I should come to you to know the *means*—the *purpose* would be to remove all interference with affection [...] I have no doubt that when the whole community is really educated, tho' the present laws of marriage were to continue they would be perfectly disregarded, because no one would marry.

And again:

> on this plan, it would be in the woman's interest not to have children.[15]

In such a world, libido 'educated' in 'affection' would be its own objective. The 'condition of women' would be 'raised' by the replacement of Christian maternity. The ideal of the female eunuch would substitute for providence a new world order. It would provide for a 'really' educated rearrangement of the world's population and resources. It would be left to Mill strategically to advance the project through the education of public opinion.

By 1854, after more than twenty years of friendship, and three of civil marriage, Mill was prepared to express in his diary, for Harriet's eyes only, a regret that the marriage vow should legally oblige; by 1855, he was communicating the same view privately in his correspondence with others:

> Nothing ought to be ultimately rested in, short of entire freedom on both sides to dissolve this like any other partnership. The only thing requiring legal regulation would be the maintenance of the children when the parents could not manage it amicably—and in that I do not see any considerable difficulty.[16]

---

15   *Ibid.*, p. 3.
16   *Ibid.*, p. 49.

Partners may part and call it freedom. Children must be expected not to mind.

Harriet had gained over Mill's earlier, more cautious self. By 1854 she and Mill were planning a series of essays on questions of the day. She wrote to him:

> About the Essays, dear, would not religion, the utility of Religion, be one of the subjects you would have most to say on [...] to account for the existence nearly universal of some religion (superstition) by the instincts of fear, hope, and mystery etc., and throwing over all doctrines and theories, called religion as devices for power [...] to show how religion and poetry fill the same want, the craving after higher objects, the consolation of suffering, the hope of heaven for the selfish, love of God for the tender and grateful—how all this must be superseded by morality deriving its power from sympathies and benevolence and its reward from the approbation of those we respect. There, what a long sentence.[17]

One has the impression here of listening to a conversation, in which Mill has 'most to say' on 'the utility of Religion', and on 'fear, hope and mystery, the hope of heaven (and) love of God'—a conversation in which Mill and Harriet discussed how best to replace these with a morality based on 'sympathies, benevolence and. approbation'. Harriet's plea was for an open assault on Christianity. But Mill did not oblige. He hung on to the 'utility' of religion.

When his *Essay on Liberty* appeared in 1859, one year after Harriet's sudden death, he said: 'None of my writings have been either so carefully composed, or so sedulously corrected as this.'[18]

---

[17] Cowling cited this as the frontispiece to his *Mill and Liberalism*. He followed the citation with one from W. Somerset Maugham: 'Phillip thought this over for a moment. Then he said: "I don't see why things we believe absolutely now shouldn't be just as wrong as what they believed in the past." "Neither do I." "Then how can you believe anything at all?" "I don't know."' (*Of Human Bondage*, (1915), p. 121).

[18] Mill, *Autobiography*, p. 144.

He consecrated it to Harriet's memory. To her he attributed its authorship. The text was, so to speak, her 'room', everything in place just as she had left it. But it had been tidied by Mill. His emphatic attribution of the authorship to Harriet only underlines the absence, from the text itself, of any plea for the liquidation of the marriage vow. What there is in the text that bears on Christianity touches only on the Protestant Sunday—a plea for the pubs to be open for the sake of non-believers—and a striking passage arguing against 'misapplied notions of liberty' enabling parents to regard children 'as their peculiar property not thinking what a danger they might constitute to the State by their ignorance and poverty'. Mill was throwing on the state the primary responsibility for the education of the children. Compulsory education at school would compensate for 'ignorance' and 'poverty'. It would alter the condition in which 'children. are a real obstacle to the fulfilment by the State of its duties'. Here we are tacitly in the presence of Mill's doctrine of the 'stationary state', a world of zero population growth with an adequate supply of public parks and national reserves to protect the planet for the middle classes.[19] As we have seen, Mill had arrived at that before Harriet recognised its potential for 'raising the condition of

---

[19]   *Essay on Liberty*, ed. S. Collini (Cambridge: Cambridge University Press, 1989), pp. 105–9. What Mill meant by the stationary state is explained in his *Principles of Political Economy*, p. 128: 'There is room in the world, no doubt, and even in old countries, for a great increase of population, supposing the arts of life to go on improving, and capital to increase. But even if innocuous, I confess I see very little reason for desiring it.' He considered it 'scarcely necessary to remark that a stationary condition of capital and population implies no stationary state of human improvement.' He expressed a 'hope, for the sake of posterity, that they will be content to be stationary, long before necessity compels them to it.' (*Ibid.*, p. 129). Cowling considered that there was a hidden coercive agenda in Mill's strategy for mankind. Janice Carlisle in a subtle analysis of the *People's Edition of the Principles* (1865) confirms Cowling's view. Her work tends to remove any ground for Conrad Russell's confidence that Mill can be unambiguously claimed as a champion of the sexual revolution. (Carlisle, *Mill*, p. 155).

women' so that she (through Mill) could thereby be 'Providence to the world'.

The stationary state, as Mill was to argue in the *Principles of Political Economy*, would repose on full employment, attained by family limitation; the poor would be educated to comply, and Mill would educate the educators. 'Read Mill' was Leslie Stephens' account of the advice given by Oxford and Cambridge tutors to their charges, in the second half of the nineteenth century, in the years following the dissemination of Mill's *Logic*, which made its first appearance in 1843. It was an injunction more extensive than the book's title might lead us to imagine. Had the title accurately described its purpose, it would have sunk stone dead into the dustbin of history. But the real purpose of Mill's *Logic* was fully described in Leslie Stephens' words as 'a Sacred Scripture for Liberal Intellectuals [...] a logical armoury for all assailants of established Dogmatism'.[20] Established dogmatism included traditional beliefs about matrimony and the procreation of children. Among Mill's disciples it became an axiom that 'obedience to Malthus makes prosperous the French peasant, disobedience, the pauperised English labourer.[21] That became the doctrine of the new caste of professional administrators, professionally examined—teachers, architects, doctors, lawyers, engineers and not least civil servants—the makers of the Empire—issuing from the universities and conjoined by the work of 'the theological learned'. These were to be taken as 'essential to the scheme', not as 'priests whose office was to conciliate the invisible powers, and to superintend the interests that survive the grave'.[22] Rather, the task of theology must be to promote the interests of humanity, to become an instrument of civilisation.

---

[20]   Quoted by Basil Willey, *Nineteenth Century Studies* (London: Penguin,1964), p. 161.

[21]   *Ibid.*, p. 172.

[22]   Cowling, *Mill and Liberalism*, p. 16, quoting from Mill's *Three Essays on Religion* (1874), p. 82.

We should note that the clergy were to be regarded as 'essential to the scheme'. The sacerdotal idea was to be relegated and the clergy re-educated to subserve the 'principles' of Mill's 'political economy'. The stationary state was to be advanced with the complicity of the clergy.

To Auguste Comte, Mill wrote in 1844:

> The time has not yet arrived when, without compromising our cause, we can in England direct open attacks upon Christian theology. We can only by-pass it, peacefully eliminating it from all philosophical and social discussions, and ignoring all questions proper to it as irrelevant to daily life.[23]

Here we see Mill as the master of the media, and the re-educator of the Church. Theology would be enlisted to promote the contraceptive state and the universities would be transformed into purely secular academies of human development. Thus:

> The very first step should be to unsectarianise them [...] by putting an end to sectarian teaching altogether. The principle itself of dogmatic religion, dogmatic morality, dogmatic philosophy, is what requires to be rooted out; not any particular manifestation of that principle.[24]

We may suppose that this essay of 1836 was well known to Newman. It throws clear light on what he was to write in his *Apologia pro Vita Sua* in 1864, describing his life-long commitment to revealed truth enshrined in Christian Doctrine:

> First was the principle of dogma: my battle was with liberalism; by liberalism I mean the anti-dogmatic principle and its developments.[25]

---

[23]   Quoted by Philip Hughes in *The English Catholics 1850–1950: Essays to Commemorate the Centenary of the Restoration of the Hierarchy of England and Wales*, ed. G. A. Beck (London: Burns & Oates, 1950), p. 5, n. 3.

[24]   Cowling, *Mill and Liberalism*, p. 20, quoting form Mill's 'Civilisation' (1836) in *Dissertations and Discussions*, vol. i (1859), pp. 200–1.

[25]   *Apologia*, p. 48.

In fighting the 'anti-dogmatic principle' in religion Newman was fighting Mill, and through Mill, the ethos of the stationary state. He was fighting the recruitment of the clergy to that enterprise. He was reaffirming the divine constitution of the Church, her apostolic vocation and her mission, in the face of a Christianity eviscerated from within, relativised, and serenely allocated a civilising role among the historical sciences. The clergy were to promote the creed of secularism. Thus Mill, in 1869, urged the students of St Andrews destined for holy orders to 'use your influence to make the doctrines [regarded as essential to remaining in orders] as few as possible'.[26] This was Mill speaking to the clergy and through the clergy. It clearly illuminates his strategy: convert the clergy and complete the indoctrination of humanity in the principles of the stationary state.

As a matter of fact, it was precisely this kind of influence, which Mill had already found serviceable in the theologians of Oriel College, Oxford, as early as 1830. What Oriel promoted was a rejection of the appeal to authority in theology, falling back on logic to decide the application of Christianity to the now political economy. In that year Mill told a French correspondent, Gustave d'Eichtal, that if he wanted to promote his ideas in England, he should establish contact with two of the Oriel theologians, Blanco White and Richard Whately: 'Any impression made upon these two men', he wrote, 'will spread far and wide.'[27] Through such influences the poor would be encourage by the clergy to follow the logic of the new Poor Law. The effect would be to discourage the poor from breeding. Fear of the workhouse would do by supposedly 'Christian' persuasion what Mill would elsewhere propose in his *Principles of Political Economy*.

Oriel was Newman's College. Whately was Newman's preceptor in logic.

---

[26] Cowling, *Mill and Liberalism*, p. 114.

[27] Quoted in Martin Murphy, *Blanco White: Self-banished Spaniard* (London: Yale University Press, 1989), pp. 153–4.

By 1831 Newman's tutorship at Oriel had come to an end. He was deprived of students because he took his office as involving something more than a means merely of securing high examination results for his students. He took it as a pastoral office, involving the cure of minds as well as souls, a view now anathema to the university authorities and to the state which stood behind the new professional administrators. It is often said that Newman lacked a doctrine of state. That was far from being true. It was in opposition to the secularised political economy as promoted through the universities that Newman saw and viewed his vocation as an affirmation of the Church's teaching office to proclaim the Christian meaning of holy matrimony and love of the poor in the face of the subtraction of Christianity from marriage, education and what would come to be called 'welfare'. Thus, in later life he wrote, looking back on a century of de-Christianisation:

> For the last fifty years, since 1827, there has been a formidable movement among us towards assigning in the national life political or civil motives for social and personal duties, and thereby withdrawing matters of conduct from the jurisdiction of religion. Men are to be made virtuous, and to do good works, to become good members of society, good husbands and fathers, on purely secular motives. We are having a wedge thrust into us, which tends to the destruction of religion altogether; and this is our misery that there is no definite point at which we can logically take our stand, and resist encroachment on principle. Such is the workhouse system, such was the civil marriage act.[28]

Not long after the termination of his tutorship, Newman left Oxford. He fell ill in Sicily. He returned to England in 1833. His prophetic ministry of the word from the pulpit of St Mary the Virgin, all that became the Oxford Movement, dates from that

---

[28]   Newman to Thomas Longman, 28 May 1878, *LD* xxviii, pp. 363–4.

moment, and should be seen in response to the unfolding of the utilitarian state.

Towards the end of his life, in 1879, on the occasion of his cardinalate, Newman made a speech recalling the course of his Christian life and ministry:

> For thirty, forty, fifty years I have resisted to the best of my powers the spirit of liberalism in religion. Never did Holy Church need champions against it more sorely than now.[29]

He then explained his meaning:

> Liberalism in religion is the doctrine that there is no positive truth in religion [...] It is inconsistent with any recognition of any religion, as *true*. Revealed Religion is not a truth, but a sentiment and a taste [...] Devotion is not necessarily founded on faith.[30]

Was he thinking about Comte? Was he thinking about Mill? The world 'positive' in the above passage might lead us to think so—logic, yielding positivism, the conviction that for 'proof positive' you needed the relegation of all dogma, and the elevation of the experimental principle as the only principle in life. Auguste Comte's 'religion of humanity', promulgated through the academy and promoting the apotheosis of humanity, anglicised by Mill, shorn of its prescriptive character, transformed into an educational imperative—that was what Newman was talking about, and he knew it first as the doctrine of Oriel College, of Whately, Thomas Arnold and Rugby School—a broad, comprehensive, nationally-based, useful religion, with few doctrines—yielding by 1859 to the attenuated Christianity of *Essays and Reviews*, introduced by the chaplain of Rugby School, urging a religion which would go beyond that of the Apostles, to construct a future for humanity based on truly scientific credentials of historicity and progress. That was where the good and Christian intentions of Whately and Thomas Arnold had ended up by

---

[29] 'Biglietto Speech', *Campaign*, p. 513.
[30] *Ibid.*

1859—in Rugby Chapel, whence Matthew Arnold would shortly mourn the demise of Christianity, in 'Dover Beach', 'Where ignorant armies meet and clash by night.'

The loss of Christianity in England: Newman knew that loss in his lifetime and in his own family. He knew it in his elder brother, Charles. He knew it in his younger brother, Francis, who helped to found the Secular Society. He knew it as a personal temptation while at Oriel College 'to prefer intellectual to moral excellence'.[31] He knew it as a temptation of the mind, and a great temptation, to decide the content of Christian teaching according to the logic of personal investigation, social policy and ecclesiastical promotion. From that logic he was rescued by grief. The death of his sister, Mary, in 1828 taught Newman the truths which he was to communicate to a generation intent on substituting political welfare for eternal welfare. He knew the temptation as the cancer tearing out the life of Christianity in England. He knew it in the Froude family, especially in William who married Catherine Holdsworth and became agnostic on the principle that he, as a naval engineer and scientist, could not but 'doubt', could never embrace 'dogma' or 'creed', while Catherine, his wife, and children followed Newman into the Catholic Church, after 1857.[32]

Newman's *Apologia* in 1864 gave expression to his view of the present age:

> And in these latter days [...] outside the Catholic Church things are tending—with far greater rapidity [...] to atheism in one shape or another. What a scene, what a prospect, does the whole of Europe present at this day! And not only Europe, but every government and every civilisation through the world, which is under the influence of the European mind! Especially [...] how sorrowful, in

---

[31]   *Apologia*, p. 14.

[32]   Joyce Sugg, *Ever Yours Affly: John Henry Newman and his Female Circle* (Leominster: Gracewing, 1996), pp. 103–7, carries a fine account of William and Catherine Froude and their family.

the view of religion, is the spectacle presented to us by the educated intellect of England, France, and Germany![33]

And then an extraordinary passage:

> Lovers of their country and of their race, religious men, external to the Catholic Church, have attempted various expedients to arrest fierce wilful human nature in its onward course, and to bring it to subjection. The necessity of some form of religion for the interests of humanity, has been generally acknowledged: but where was the concrete representative of things invisible, which would have the force and the toughness necessary to be a breakwater against the deluge?[34]

Who did Newman refer to as the 'lovers of their country and of their race, religious men, external to the Catholic Church'? Was Newman thinking about Whately and Thomas Arnold? No, I think we can detect a reference here to his closest friends in the Oxford Movement, Pusey and Keble. To Henry James Coleridge he wrote, immediately following the completion of the *Apologia* in 1864 (Fr Coleridge had questioned him concerning Keble's views on certitude of faith):

> I believe I must say that I allude to Keble's conversation more than to anything he wrote [...] He considered that religious truth came to us as from the mouth of Our Lord—and what would be called doubt was an imperfect hearing as if one heard from a distance. And, as we were at this time of the world at a distance from Him, of course we heard indistinctly and faith was not a clear and confident knowledge or certainty, but a sort of loving guess.[35]

But 'indistinct hearing' and 'a sort of loving guess' would not do, to meet the challenge to Christianity in the coming age. Nothing would suffice except a certitude of faith:

---

[33] *Apologia*, pp. 243–4.

[34] *Apologia*, p. 244.

[35] Newman to Henry James Coleridge, 24 June 1864, *LD* xxi, p. 129.

the very claim of the Catholic Church [...] a provision adapted, by the mercy of the Creator, to preserve religion in the world, and to restrain that freedom of thought, which of course in itself is one of our greatest natural gifts, and to rescue it from its own suicidal excesses.[36]

The word 'suicidal' carries a distinct resonance in a culture which has wanted to 'choose' death. That choice, the creation of a culture of death, would be attained by habituation. 'I have often thought' wrote Newman in 1873:

how soon I might get over the sense that murder, as such, is a sin [...] after I have killed half a dozen persons. I suppose some nurses [...] have not any great horror at the idea of killing children. And thus the idea of a God may go.[37]

Against the suicidal freedoms of the modern age there must be no half measures:

The initial doctrine of the infallible teacher must be an emphatic protest against the existing state of mankind. Man had rebelled against his Maker. The Church must denounce rebellion as of all possible evils the greatest. She must have no terms with it; if she would be true to her Master, she must ban and anathematise it [...] But in the next place she knows and she preaches that such a restoration, as she aims at effecting in it, must be brought about, not simply through outward provisions of preaching and teaching, even though they be her own, but from an inward spiritual power or grace imparted directly from above, and of which she is the channel. She has it in charge to rescue human nature from its misery, not simply by restoring it to its own level, but by lifting it up to a higher level than its own. She recognises in it real moral excellence though degraded, but she cannot set it free from earth except by exalting it towards heaven. It was for this end that a renovating grace was put into her hands and therefore [...]

---

[36] *Apologia,* p. 245.
[37] Newman to H. P. Liddon, 2 March 1873, *LD* xxvi, p. 268.

> she goes on [...] to insist, that all true conversion must
> begin with the first springs of thought [...][38]

And again:

> Such truths as these she vigorously reiterates, and pertina-
> ciously inflicts upon mankind; as to such she observes no
> half-measures, no economical reserve [...] 'Ye must be
> born again' is the simple, direct form of words which she
> uses after her Divine Master: 'Your whole nature must be
> reborn; your passions, and your affections, and your aims,
> and your conscience, and your will, must all be bathed in
> a new element, and reconsecrated to your Maker,—and
> the last not the least, your intellect.'[39]

'Not the least'; and we should note also the words 'conscience'
and 'affections'—each standing in need of re-consecration. This
is the difference between Mill, Harriet and Newman—the conviction that 'affections' without re-consecration would simply
destroy the capacity to love.

Newman, on entering the Oratorians, took as his patron St
Philip Neri, who used to tap his brow and point to his intellect,
saying: 'It is here, in the space of three fingers' that we must
mortify ourselves. Newman, the theologian, knew what it was to
suffer for that truth, to suffer in his intellect, from the decree of
silence imposed upon him by the Church in 1859. He also knew
where his Vindicator was to be found, in the Tabernacle. When,
in 1879, he was elevated by Leo XIII to the College of Cardinals,
his one concern was that the Church should identify the crisis
facing her for what it was. Newman did not call it secularisation.
He called it apostasy. 'The general character of this great *aposta-
sia* is one and the same everywhere'.[40]

> If a man puts on a new religion every morning, what is that
> to you? It is as impertinent to think about a man's religion

---

[38]   *Apologia*, pp. 246–8.
[39]   *Apologia*, p. 248.
[40]   'Biglietto Speech', *Campaign*, p. 515.

as about his sources of income or his management of his
family. Religion is in no sense the bond of society.[41]

The question whether human wilfulness, human nature, intellectual pride, selfishness, could in fact generate the 'benevolence'
and 'sympathies' creative of a 'new' morality, also occurred to
Mill. What Newman condemned, Mill had laboured lifelong to
achieve. 'You know', he told his daughter-in-law, Helen Taylor,
on his deathbed in 1873, 'You know that I have done my work.'[42]
Yet as the end approached it seems possible that Mill may have
entertained a doubt. What would replace Christianity as the bond
of society? Benevolence? Education?

Externally, Mill continued to sustain his creed and confidence
to the end. Internally, a doubt, a caution, a voice, the same
perhaps that spoke to him in 1826, may seem to have continued
to put the question—happiness?

Humanity, he wrote, in the *Utility of Religion*, composed
between 1850 and 1858—we seem to hear the other side, Mill's
side, of his conversation with Harriet—humanity may find
religion, without its dogmas, 'morally useful without being
intellectually sustainable', but when mankind no longer needs it,
'a future existence as a consolation', it will and can, even in the
present 'perfectly well do without the belief in heaven'.[43] Indeed,
in a better condition of human life 'not annihilation but immor-
tality may be the burdensome idea'. Yet Mill did not publish these
reflections. Then between 1868 and 1870, he wrote on theism,
and concluded, against the creed of his childhood, that a creator
there might be, after all. Mill's creator was not, however, benevolent. He was not the creator of Judaeo–Christian theism. Yet
Mill, passing on to the person of Christ, could write:

---

[41]   *Ibid.*, p. 514.

[42]   Carlisle, *Mill*, p. 229.

[43]   Quoted in Willey, *Nineteenth Century Studies*, p. 193, from Mill, *Three
       Essays in Religion* (1873), p. 109.

> And whatever else may be taken away from us by rational
> criticism, Christ is still left, a unique figure [...]

Mill then allowed himself to reflect on the 'unique figure':

> as the ideal representative and guide of humanity [...]
> When to this we add [...] a possibility that Christ actually
> was what he supposed himself to be—not God [...] but a
> man charged with a special express and unique commis-
> sion from God to lead mankind to truth and virtue [...][44]

Here the creator emerges as benevolent. Mill's Christ is not the
Redeemer, the Son of God, the sacramental Christ. It is the ethical
Christ of the Victorian agnostics. But it does seem to be a
distinctly personal Christ; and that, in Mill, is surely remarkable.

All his life, Mill had worked to deprive Christianity of its
revealed and sacerdotal character, to deprive its clergy of authority, to replace its authority by a professional civil administration.
But he had never attacked Christ. And at the end of his life it
seems that he may have begun to revere Him.

Something in Newman seemed to sense as much. He always
held back from attacking Mill. In 1859, when Mill published his
Essay on Liberty, the moment seemed opportune for a Catholic
reply in *The Rambler*. Newman considered giving the review to
Richard Simpson, an able controversialist. Yet he restrained
himself, remarking how subtle Mill's doctrine was, and how
considerable an opponent: he expressed a reluctance to see Mill
and Simpson fighting 'like two Kilkenny cats' merely contributing
to the ever-growing tide of scepticism.[45] Then in 1876, three years
after Mill's death, Newman wrote to thank his friend Frederic
Rogers, Lord Blachford, for his review of Mill's *Autobiography*,
which had been published posthumously. Newman expressed his
keen appreciation of Blachford's account of the Christian virtues,
in implicit contrast to Mill's unchristian ones. He then added the
remarkable sentence: 'I wonder if I have made a great sbaglio [i.e.

---

[44]   *Ibid.*, quoting *Three Essays*, p. 225.
[45]   Newman to Richard Simpson, 6 July 1859, *LD* xix, p. 169.

mistake] in thus expressing myself' concerning 'the delineation of poor Mill's ethos and history and his gradual shifts to maintain his first views and filial faith.' Newman found Mill's account of his own views 'as powerful as it is painfully interesting'.[46] It is clear that Newman was moved to profound sympathy by the newly disclosed detail of Mill's childhood and upbringing.

To another correspondent Newman recognised in Mill's final reflections on Christianity, a feature of 'modern infidelity'— namely its inability to believe in itself.[47] It may be that he was thinking of Mill, when he remarked in his Biglietto Speech as Cardinal in 1879:

> And thirdly, it must be borne in mind, that there is much in the liberalistic theory which is good and true; for example, not to say more, the precepts of justice, truthfulness, sobriety, self-command, benevolence [...] and the natural laws of society. It is not till we find that this array of principles is intended to supersede, to block out, religion that we pronounce it to be evil. There never was a device of the enemy, so cleverly framed, and with such promise of success. And already it has answered to the expectations which have been formed of it. It is sweeping into its own ranks great numbers of able, earnest virtuous men, elderly men of approved antecedents, young men with a career before them.[48]

But had it, in the end, convinced Mill? Newman was aware of Mill's commitment to 'justice' and 'truthfulness': Mill's courageous interventions in support of a just settlement of the land question in Ireland; his public declaration against brutalism in Jamaica; his concern to protect, by just inheritance laws, widows, and to promote among men, a non-proprietorial attitude to women. This did not amount to Christianity. But it did amount to 'an array of principles' sincerely lived—an expression of real

---

[46] Newman to Lord Blachford, 15 August 1876, *LD* xxviii, p. 102.
[47] Newman to Lady Herbert of Lea, 19 August 1879, *LD* xxix, p. 169.
[48] 'Biglietto Speech', *Campaign*, pp. 515–16.

virtues which, only if intended to 'supersede' and 'block out' religion, could be identified as the form of a cleverly framed evil.

Mill has been hailed in the twentieth century as the patron saint of the emancipation of women. We have seen that it was Harriet who selected him for the task. How does Mill's doctrine compare with Newman's Christian understanding of the vocation of women to and in the Christian family? Clearly, the difference resides in Newman's appreciation of his own vocation to virginity and to fidelity rooted in God's revealed plan for humanity.[49]

Newman's understanding of the priesthood and the religion of the home earned him the lifelong gratitude of a succession of women converts. His appreciation of the vocation to domestic holiness, and the consecrated affections of Christian prayer and piety was something which Mill, through his immensely sad and emotionally deprived childhood, had never experienced. Contrast Newman's letter of thanks to Charlotte (or Chattie) Bowden, aged fifteen, who 'showed her affection to him by baking him some cakes':

> Who is it that moulds and makes
> Round, and crisp, and fragrant cakes?
> [...] One it is, for whom I pray,
> On St Philip's festal day,
> With a loving heart that she
> Perfect as her cakes may be,
> Full and faithful in the round
> Of her duties ever found
> Where a trial comes, between
> Truth and falsehood cutting keen;
> Yet that keenness and completeness Tempering with a winning sweetness.
> Here's a rhyming letter Chat,
> Gift for gift, and tit for tat.[50]

---

[49]   'Love of Relations and Friends', *Parochial and Plain* ii, pp. 51–60.
[50]   W. Ward, *Life of John Henry Cardinal Newman*, vol. ii (London: Longman, Green & Co.,1912), p. 318.

One of William Froude's daughters, Isy, married Baron Anatole von Hugel, the younger brother of Friedrich. She became one of the foundresses of Newnham College, Cambridge. In her later years, she would gather some students at her house, Croft Cottage, and read to them from Newman's works. As Joyce Sugg remarks 'these clever young women, going out to live their lives amongst the uncertainties of the twentieth century, had the privilege and the challenge of a university education',[51] not untouched by the kindly voice of Newman. It is well to remark at this point what Newman stressed to his convert friends about the distinction between natural and supernatural talents:

> Samuel was disappointed when he saw Eliab, that 'the Lord's anointed was not before him.' I ever tell friends that they must look among Catholics, not for natural excellence, but supernatural. *But many Catholics do not like to allow this.*[52]

In those few italicised words, we can see summarised the history of the collapse of the Catholic Church in the twentieth century West. Religion as utility; education as the road to the top, to (in Manning's marvellous phrase) the 'latch-keys to Grosvenor Square';[53] Newman as the patron and exemplar of a worldly eminence: 'they think'—Newman remarked in a sermon at the newly established Catholic University in Dublin—'we mean to spend our devotion upon a human cause, and that we toil for an object of human ambition.'[54]

---

[51]   *Ibid.*, p. 299.

[52]   Newman to J. Spencer Northcote, 18 June 1862, *LD* xx, p. 210.

[53]   'In truth, nobody cared for higher studies. Certain Catholic parents wished to get their sons in to English society, and to have latch-keys to Grosvenor Square', quoted in E. S. Purcell, *Life of Cardinal Manning*, vol. ii (London: Macmillan, 1896), p. 303.

[54]   *Various Occasions*, p. 57. Newman was speaking of those who were outside the Church. But the application can be made to those inside it. Hugh McLeod, remarks: 'As early as the 1890s English political Nonconformity was being crushed by the weight of its own success; by the 1960s the same was true of the political Catholicism of countries like Belgium and the Netherlands. The various forms of discrimination and persecution had

As a graduate of that university, I can verify the truth of Manning's prediction. Newman as the key to Grosvenor Square: the twentieth century seized on him as the promoter of an educated laity. This was Newman circulated to advantage. But Newman as the promoter of a supernatural excellence, rather than a purely natural one, of that, scarcely a word. Newman's vision tended to elude us. Perhaps I should say we eluded him.

That has been the great betrayal of the twentieth century. Its climax came in 1968, with the development of Newman as the supposed promoter of the rights of conscience in the reproductive act against *Humanae Vitae*. With no pretence of sincerity or love of truth, but with every appearance of plausibility, a conspicuously educated phalanx of Catholics made play of Newman's doctrine of conscience to appeal against the Pope. They quoted the famous words of his *Letter to the Duke of Norfolk*:

> Certainly, if I am obliged to bring religion into after-dinner toasts, (which indeed does not seem quite the thing) I shall drink—to the Pope, if you please—still, to conscience first, and to the Pope afterwards.[55]

So disturbing was the construction placed upon these words that the then Archbishop of Birmingham, George Patrick Dwyer, made a personal visit to the Oratory to enquire as to their context. When it was brought home to him that Newman's appeal to conscience, 'the aboriginal Vicar of Christ', was to conscience as confirmed in matters of doubt by the certitude of faith and morals enunciated by Christ's living vicar the Pope, the archbishop was

---

been overcome. Now the ghettos were beginning to feel claustrophobic. The secularising effect of a pluralist society lay primarily in the fact that the religious community was ceasing to be a necessary source of identity and support, and that neighbours who had once been regarded largely in terms of hostile stereotypes could now be seen as offering alternative ways of living.' *Religion and the People of Western Europe, 1789–1989* (Oxford: Oxford University Press, 1981), p. 141.

55   'A Letter to the Duke of Norfolk', *Difficulties* ii, p. 261.

confirmed in his agreement to advance the cause of Newman to the altar.

It was during the 1960s that Newman's cause began to gather pace worldwide, and shortly after the conclusion of the Second Vatican Council that *Humanae Vitae* was published. Now the restoration urged by *Humanae Vitae*, the restoration of the Creator to His creation, to return the sacramentality of the marriage act that, of course, is the only remedy of the sexual revolution. But it is we who have to do it. We have to believe it. We have to teach it, and help people to put God back into the sacrament, not to contracept the sacrament. And when we do that we might then ask the question whether it is fair to the memory of John Stuart Mill to credit him with the patronage of the spiritual disasters of the sexual revolution of the twentieth century.

Yes, if you want to stick to the letter of the words he wrote, a qualified yes. Mill provided the state with the doctrine that it wanted for its new electorate: the doctrine that there are no doctrines, in faith or morals, that can survive Mill's vague criterion of 'harm to others'. It was not just Baroness Warnock and Lord Russell who credited Mill with the patronage of the sexual revolution. Keynes in 1924 attributed to Mill the decisive intellectual influence in removing from the educated mind the claim of theology, and of the clergy, to any authority whatsoever in matters of truth. Whitehead, in 1926, reflecting on the concluding chapter of Mill's *Logic*, saw in Mill what he considered causative in his own generation, the doctrine of necessity in yielding to emotional drives, the inner 'permission' accorded to Victorian and Edwardian England, to follow the compulsions of the libido where they lead.[56]

So there is no failure of logic in Conrad Russell's drawing the conclusion that Mill's understanding of individuality extends to a 'right' to what St Paul understands as fornication, and indeed

---

[56]   J. M. Keynes, *Essays in Biography* (London: Rupert Hart-Davis, 1961), p. 135. A. N. Whitehead, *Science and the Modern World* (Harmondsworth: Penguin, 1926), p. 97.

to unnatural vice. Lord Russell considers that the promotion of homosexuality as morally equivalent to matrimony is something which schoolteachers should adopt as protective of the liberty of minorities.[57]

All this was within the logic of Mill's doctrine of necessity. But I should think it doubtful that he would have been pleased with the consequences of that logic. Mill was not a libertarian.

I think we should regard Harriet Taylor, not Mill, as the patron saint of secular feminism—and Mill as her chosen spokesman, to lend what, by the close of the nineteenth century, had become his 'pontifical authority' to the secularism of a society which had not yet quite decided that Harriet's vision, more than Mill's, was what was wanted. That happened in the wake of two World Wars, and it happened through the propaganda of Marie Stopes, Margaret Sanger and the doomed mentality of the post-Hiroshima, post-Suez, collapse of the Victorian ethos of living 'as if' Christianity were 'socially' true. The sexual revolution could and did adopt Mill as its patron saint. It seems unlikely that Mill would have adopted it.

Was Mill responsible for the holocaust of the unborn? No, if you consult his meaning. What he did was to supply a philosophical framework for a century which wished to promote abortion as the continuation of contraception by other means. That is why the author of the Abortion Law Reform Society's report on its victory of 1967 invoked Mill—to the surprise of the Abortion Act's promoter in Parliament, David Steel. He seems to have believed that he was promoting, not abortion on demand, but 'just a few' abortions.[58]

Was abortion Mill's business? I think not. But the really important thing about the Abortion Law Reform Report is what it revealed about the testing of Catholic opinion in England. The Prime Minister of the day, Harold Wilson, was reluctant to

---

[57]   Letter to *The Times*, 1 June 2000.

[58]   K. Hindell & M. Simms, *Abortion Law Reformed* (1971). See the foreword by David Steel.

introduce abortion because he feared the loss of the Catholic—largely Irish Labour—vote.[59] So a private poll was organised. The poll revealed that there would be no Catholic opposition. The Act went ahead. The poll was verified. Catholic silence was the one thing requisite.

Since then, the real question for the Church has been to name our problem. The problem is what Newman called it—not secularism, but apostasy, our apostasy, the apostasy which has converted the stationary state into the stationary Church, in which parents have put their teenage daughters on the pill thereby effecting the contraception of the Church. This has happened in the silence created by the rejection of *Humanae Vitae*. The question is how should the Church conduct her mission in a time of apostasy? What Professor John Finnis calls 'secularism by default'[60] is a temptation which Newman invites us to address with the assurance that we know how to recognise the voice of Christ teaching, in his aboriginal vicar, the voice of conscience, and in His living, earthly vicar confirming that voice and calling it to consecration.

'If it be inquired', wrote Newman, 'what is the proper conduct of the Church in a time of apostasy?' Let us give the last word to Newman himself:

> Christianity has been too often in what seemed deadly peril that we should fear for it any new trial now. So far is certain; on the other hand, what is uncertain, and in these great contests commonly is uncertain, and what is commonly a great surprise, when it is witnessed, is the particular mode by which, in the event, Providence rescues and saves His elect inheritance. Sometimes our enemy is turned into a friend; sometimes he is despoiled of that special virulence of evil which was so threatening; some-

---

[59]   I am grateful to Dr Thomas Ward for this information which he gleaned from his personal inquiries into the matter.

[60]   This refers to an article 'On the practical meaning of secularism', *Notre Dame Law Review*, 73:3 (1988).

times he does so much as is beneficial, and then is removed. Commonly the Church has nothing more to do than to go on in her own proper duties, in confidence and peace; to stand still and to see the salvation of God.

Mansueti hereditabunt terram,
Et delectabuntur in multitudine pacis.[61]

'To go on in her own proper duties, in confidence and peace': what does that mean for us? It means, I think, that we should not blame Mill (or much less something impersonal called 'secularisation') for the evils of the age; but that we identify apostasy for what it is, and adhere in all confidence to the duty of the Church to preach, to pray, and to provide; such providence, for example, as the Liverpool Life Hospital offers to little children who would otherwise be aborted because born 'defective'. We need to fund such initiatives. We need more such, many more; hospices of hope, for the weak.

We do not have to blame Mill for the failure of Christianity. We have to blame ourselves. We do not have to be beguiled by the desperate attempts of people like Mill who sought to promote a world order which they had inherited as a bequest of the eighteenth century, without having any basis in reality, in human nature, or in the interior life of the soul—Mill's soul, as we have seen, rebelled against what he had received from the secular tradition. He was wounded by the taunt that he was 'a manufactured man', a 'mere reasoning machine'.[62] How many other 'manufactured' children have suffered likewise? Are they to be treated as 'enemies' of Christ? Mill looked for feeling, and Harriet supplied his need—on her own terms. But Mill's need was for Christian feeling. His tragedy was that first his father, and then Harriet, constructed and re-constructed his 'mission' and his 'feeling'. It was Harriet who reconstructed in Mill the mission

---

[61]   'Biglietto Speech', *Campaign*, p. 517. 'The meek shall inherit the earth, and shall delight in abundance of peace.'

[62]   Mill, *Autobiography*, pp. 66, 93.

and the feeling that there was nothing more to life, to marriage, to human relations, than feelings. Change the feelings, substitute feeling for religion, and happiness is all.

But something in Mill was unconvinced, unconvinced by his father's refusal of the question 'Who made me?' and unconvinced by Harriet's confidence in the 'provision' of happiness by 'benevolence' and 'education' in contraceptive 'affections'. Something in Mill spoke of the 'unique figure': Christ. And that unique figure, speaking in the soul, has commanded us to preach the Gospel to souls like Mill. How? By preaching it—first among our own congregations.

Might it not be possible, four times a year, to preach the Gospel of Life from the encyclicals *Humanae Vitae* and *Evangelium Vitae*, and from the apostolic exhortation *Familiaris Consortio*? To urge the simplicity of morning and night prayer, of Grace before and after meals, of regular sacramental confession—of *Evangelium Vitae* as matter of confession?

Mill's *Essay on Liberty* rested on a single criterion that actions which do not harm others are to be permitted. But the criterion of 'harm' was ill-defined. It came in the end to signify the 'duty' not to 'harm' other people's feelings. That is what we have today: and *that* is what is so harmful, so destructive socially, spiritually, morally, of human happiness. But it is only harmful because we surrender to it.

So if we ask the promoters of the permissive society who invoke Mill, whether they have not merely a literal, but a sufficient account of Mill, the answer is 'No', in my opinion. It is insufficient to human need. Mill's own inner voice, the voice of Christ within, needed the outer echo of the Gospel preached. So does the society which hails him as its authority on life and death.

Mill's *Essay on Liberty* proposed and successfully transmitted a doctrine that there can be no doctrines and, hence, no moral consensus. But that was a rhetorical strategy concealing the imperative of the stationary state. That is the imperative today, all-pervasive in our legislatures. Today the doctrine *proposes*, as

Mill did not, a 'right' to fornication, to abortion, and an 'equivalence' between matrimonial bonding and homosexual 'affectivity'. That is what Mill's individualism is now taken to mean.

Mill was concerned to adapt into English the perspective of Tocqueville on the possible corruption of democracy. He was aware of the real danger of democracy imposing majority tenets on minority consciences. On that basis, of course, once you go behind Mill to Tocqueville, you arrive at John Paul II—the doctrine of *Evangelium Vitae*, which warns against the strong imposing their tyranny of power over the weak, the unborn and the defenceless.

To conclude, Who's to blame? Not Mill. The problem is much deeper. The issue is the Catholic Church. Everybody knows it. The issue is our fidelity to the sacramental meaning of matrimony, and our willingness to teach it to our own congregations and in seminaries. If we are faithful to the gift of God, He will do everything else. But if we are not, we are guilty of contracepting God.[63]

---

[63] My thanks are particularly due to Gerard Tracey for his generous help in enabling me to investigate the question of Newman's attitude to Mill. I also wish to thank David Allen, Luke Gormally, Philip Trower and Tom Ward for help in various phases of this paper. An earlier version of this paper was published in *Culture of Life—Culture of Death: Proceedings of an International Conference on The Great Jubilee and the Culture of Life*, ed. Luke Gormally (London: Linacre Centre, 2002), pp. 27–48.

ABOUT THE CONTRIBUTORS

Fr Keith Beaumont was born in Melbourne, Australia. He obtained a PhD from the University of Warwick and taught French literature at Leicester University between 1970 and 1991, when he entered the French Oratory. He was ordained a priest in 1996. He has since taught at various Catholic universities and preached numerous retreats in France. He has published a dozen books and numerous articles on Newman, including anthologies and critical editions, mostly in French, amongst them a collection of Newman's writings on St Philip Neri preceded by a lengthy introduction.

Bishop James Conley has been serving as bishop of the Diocese of Lincoln in Nebraska since 2012. Previously he served as an auxiliary bishop in the Archdiocese of Denver. He was raised in a Presbyterian family and became a Catholic while studying at the University of Kansas. After his ordination to the priesthood, besides parish work, he has served as an official of the Congregation for Bishops in the Roman Curia, a lecturer in theology, and as a university chaplain.

Sr Kathleen Dietz is a member of the Spiritual Family The Work and has worked in the chancery of the Diocese of Erie for the past nine years. She gained her doctorate on Newman's ecclesiology at the Angelicum in Rome and, along with Sr Mary-Birgit Dechant FSO, has co-edited *Blessed John Henry Newman: A Richly Illustrated Portrait*. She has written a number of articles and given numerous talks on Newman, including 'Newman and the Call to Holiness' at the Newman symposium that took place in the Vatican on 12 October 2019, the day before he was canonised.

Fr Dermot Fenlon read history at the National University of Ireland before undertaking postgraduate studies at Peterhouse, Cambridge. He was a Fellow and Tutor in history at Gonville and Caius College, Cambridge, before studying for the priesthood at the English College, Rome. While a priest for the diocese of East Anglia he lectured in history at Oscott College. Besides writing various articles on early modern history and, since 1990 when he joined the Birmingham Oratory, on Newman, he has published *Heresy and Obedience in Tridentine Italy: Cardinal Pole and the Counter Reformation*. He is currently a residential chaplain to a Benedictine convent in County Cork, Ireland.

Fr Hermann Geissler gained his doctorate on 'Conscience and Truth in John Henry Newman'. A member of the Spiritual Family The Work, he was ordained a priest in 1991. From 1993 to 2019 he worked at the Congregation for the Doctrine of the Faith in Rome. He directs the International Centre of Newman Friends in Rome and teaches theology in Italy and Austria. He has published numerous articles on Newman's life and work.

Serenhedd James teaches ecclesiastical history at St Stephen's House, Oxford; he is also a writer, a schoolmaster, and a member of the *Catholic Herald* editorial team. His first book, *George Errington and Roman Catholic Identity in Nineteenth-Century England* was based on doctoral research supervised by Fr Ian Ker.

Fr Carlton Jones is a member of the Dominican Province of St Joseph in the United States, where he has served mainly as a parish priest. His Angelicum dissertation, 'Three Latin Papers of John Henry Newman: A Translation and Commentary', argues for the compatibility of Newman's writings on reason and faith and doctrinal development with the Roman School of theology that prevailed at the time of his conversion.

Andrew Meszaros is a lecturer in systematic theology at St Patrick's Pontifical University, Maynooth, Ireland. He studied at Boston College, the University of Oxford, and Louvain (KU Leuven). He is the author of numerous articles on Newman and Catholic theology, as well as the monograph, *The Prophetic Church: History and Doctrinal Development in John Henry Newman and Yves Congar*, and is editor of *The Center is Jesus Christ Himself: Essays on Revelation, Salvation, and Evangelization in Honor of Robert P. Imbelli*.

Stephen Morgan is Rector of the University of Saint Joseph, Macao, the only Catholic university in the People's Republic of China. Fr Ian Ker chaired the examination of his DPhil thesis and wrote the foreword to his book *John Henry Newman and the Development of Doctrine: Encountering Change, Looking for Continuity*. Originally from Wales, he is a Permanent Deacon of the Diocese of Portsmouth, England.

Cardinal Gerhard Ludwig Müller was Prefect for the Congregation for the Doctrine of the Faith from 2012 to 2017. He was born in Mainz, Germany, and studied philosophy and theology in Mainz, Munich and Freiburg, then gained two doctorates, one on the Protestant theologian Dietrich Bonhoeffer and another on the theology of the Communion of Saints. After his ordination to the priesthood he served as a pastor of three parishes before being appointed to the chair of dogmatic theology at the Ludwig Maximilian University, Munich.

Andrew Nash read English at Trinity College, Cambridge, and spent his career in Catholic education, including many years as Head of English and a Housemaster at the Oratory School founded by Newman. Later he was Headmaster of St Edward's School, Cheltenham. He has published critical editions of Newman's *Lectures on the Present Position of Catholics in England* and his *Essays Critical and Historical*, Volume I. He is Associate Editor of Gracewing's ongoing Millennium Edition of the works of Newman.

Cardinal Marc Ouellet has been the Prefect of the Congregation for Bishops and President of the Pontifical Commission for Latin America since 2010. He was born in La Motte, Quebec, studied at the Major Seminary of Montreal, and after his ordination to the priesthood worked as a theologian, seminary teacher and administrator in Canada, Colombia, and Rome. He gained his doctorate at the Lateran University with a thesis on Hans Urs von Balthasar. He was Archbishop of Quebec and Primate of Canada from 2003 to 2010.

Cardinal George Pell was born in the State of Victoria, and played professional Australian Rules football before entering the seminary; after ordination in Rome, he gained a DPhil in early Church history in Oxford. During his time as Archbishop, first of Melbourne (1996–2001) and then of Sydney (2001–14), he maintained a high public profile with statements on moral issues. He was named a member of the Pope's Council of Cardinal Advisers (2013–18) and the inaugural Prefect of the Secretariat for the Economy (2014–19). Accused of crimes of abuse in 2017, he spent over a year in prison before being unanimously acquitted on appeal in 2020. He was made a Companion of the Order of Australia in 2005.

Fr James Reidy is retired Associate Professor of English at the University of St Thomas, Minnesota, where he taught from 1958 to 1996.

John Roe is a professor in Renaissance literature at York University and a member of the Centre for Renaissance and Early Modern Studies. He read English literature at the University of Cambridge and gained his PhD in Comparative literature at Harvard University. Comparative literature, mainly English and Italian, has remained a keen interest, which shows principally in his monograph *Shakespeare and Machiavelli*.

Edward Short is the author of *Newman and his Contemporaries, Newman and his Family*, and *Newman and History*. He has also published a critical edition of *Difficulties of Anglicans*, Volume I. His most recent books, published by Gracewing, are *What the Bells Sang: Essays and Reviews* and *The St Mary's Book of Christian Verse*, which he has chosen and introduced. He lives in New York with his wife and children.

Paul Shrimpton is a graduate of Balliol College, Oxford and teaches at Magdalen College School, Oxford. He has published *A Catholic Eton? Newman's Oratory School* and *The 'Making of Men': the* Idea *and Reality of Newman's University in Oxford and Dublin*, as well as critical editions of Newman's *My Campaign in Ireland, Part I* and *Part II*. He has also written *Conscience before Conformity: Hans and Sophie Scholl and the White Rose Resistance in Nazi Germany*.

IAN KER: A SELECT BIBLIOGRAPHY

Biography

John Henry Newman: A Biography (Oxford: Oxford University Press, 1988; 1990; rev. ed. 2009)

G. K. Chesterton: A Biography (Oxford: Oxford University Press, 2012)

Monographs

The Achievement of John Henry Newman (Indiana: University of Notre Dame Press, 1990)

Newman on Being a Christian (Indiana, University of Notre Dame Press, 1990)

Newman and the Fullness of Christianity (Edinburgh: T&T Clark, 1993)

Healing the Wound of Humanity: The Spirituality of John Henry Newman (London: Darton, Longman & Todd, 1993)

Newman on Vatican II (Oxford: Oxford University Press, 2014)

Criticism

The Catholic Revival in English Literature 1845–1961 (Indiana/Leominster: University of Notre Dame Press/Gracewing, 2003)

Apologetics

Mere Catholicism (Steubenville, Ohio: Emmaus Road, 2007)

Scholarly Editions

J. H. Newman, *The Idea of a University* (Oxford: Clarendon Press, 1976)

J. H. Newman, *An Essay in Aid of a Grammar of Assent* (Oxford: Clarendon Press, 1985)

The Letters and Diaries of John Henry Newman, ed. I. Ker & T. Gornall, vols 1–4 (Oxford: Oxford University Press, 1978–80)

Other Editions

The Genius of John Henry Newman: Selections from his Writings (Oxford: Oxford University Press, 1989)

J. H. Newman, *An Essay on the Development of Christian Doctrine* ed. I. Ker (Indiana: University of Notre Dame Press, 1989)

Newman the Theologian: A Reader, ed. I. Ker (Indiana: University of Notre Dame Press, 1990)

Selected Sermons of John Henry Newman, ed. I. Ker (New York: Paulist Press, 1993)

J. H. Newman, *Apologia pro Vita Sua*, ed. I. Ker (Harmondsworth, Middlesex: Penguin, 1994)

J. H. Newman, *Meditations and Devotions*, ed. I. Ker (London: Darton Longman & Todd, 2010)

The Everyman Chesterton, ed. I. Ker (New York: Knopf, 2012)

Essay Collections

Newman After a Hundred Years, ed. I. Ker (Oxford: Oxford University Press, 1990)

Newman and Conversion, ed. I. Ker (Indiana: University of Notre Dame Press, 1997)

Newman and the Word, ed. I. Ker & T. Merrigan (Louvain: Peeters, 2000)

Newman and Faith, ed. I. Ker & T. Merrigan (Louvain: Peeters, 2001)

John Paul the Great: Maker of the Post-Conciliar Church, ed. I. Ker & W. Oddie (San Francisco: Ignatius Press, 2005)

Newman and Truth, ed. I. Ker & T. Merrigan (Louvain: Peeters, 2008)

Cambridge Companion to John Henry Newman, ed. I. Ker & T. Merrigan (Cambridge: Cambridge University Press, 2009)

Pamphlets

John Henry Newman: His Life and Legacy (London: Catholic Truth Society, 2017)

INDEX

CPSIA information can be obtained
at www.ICGtesting.com
Printed in the USA
LVHW111211191122
733278LV00026B/1436